SOCIAL TEXTS AND CONTEXT
LITERATURE AND SOCIAL PSYCHOLOGY

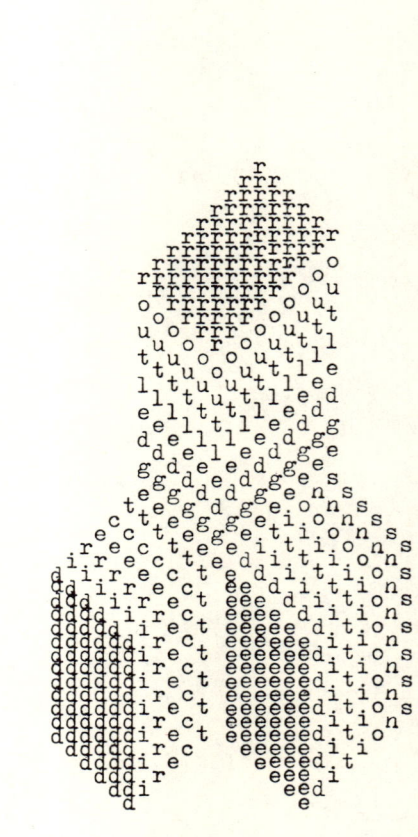

SOCIAL TEXTS AND CONTEXT
Literature and social psychology

Jonathan Potter
Peter Stringer
Margaret Wetherell

DIRECT EDITION

ROUTLEDGE & KEGAN PAUL
London, Boston, Melbourne and Henley

First published in 1984
by Routledge & Kegan Paul plc
39 Store Street, London WC1E 7DD, England
9 Park Street, Boston, Mass. 02108, USA
464 St Kilda Road, Melbourne,
Victoria 3004, Australia and
Broadway House, Newtown Road,
Henley-on-Thames, Oxon RG9 1EN, England
Printed in Great Britain
by Hartnoll Print Ltd, Bodmin, Cornwall
© Jonathan Potter, Peter Stringer and Margaret Wetherell 1984
No part of this book may be reproduced in
any form without permission from the publisher,
except for the quotation of brief passages
in criticism

Library of Congress Cataloging in Publication Data

Potter, Jonathan, 1956–
   Social Texts and Context.

   Bibliography: p.
   Includes indexes.
   1. English fiction – psychological aspects –
Addresses, essays, lectures. 2. English fiction –
social aspects – Addresses, essays, lectures. 3.
Social psychology and literature – addresses, essays,
lectures. I. Stringer, Peter. II. Wetherell,
Margaret, 1954– . III. Title.
PR830.P75P67 1984 801'.92 83-21303
ISBN 0-7100-9553-8 (pbk.)

CONTENTS

Acknowledgments vi

Introduction 1

Part 1

1 Writing Gender 9
2 Character and Environment 30

Part 2

3 Some Unsatisfactory Positions 51
4 From Action to Discourse 65
5 Dissecting Factual Texts 84
6 Victim of Realread 100

Part 3

7 Elites and Stereotypes 119
8 The Discursive Self 139

Notes 161

Bibliography 175

Author Index 185

Subject Index 188

ACKNOWLEDGMENTS

The authors and publishers are grateful to the following for permission to quote from copyright material: Simon & Schuster and Michael Joseph Ltd for material from The Golden Notebook, © 1962 by Doris Lessing; Simon & Schuster and Granada Publishing Ltd for material from The Martha Quest and The Ripple from the Storm, © 1953, 1958 by Doris Lessing; A.A. Knopf Inc. and Secker & Warburg Ltd for material from The Man Without Qualities by Robert Musil, translated by Eithne Wilkins and Ernst Kaiser.

INTRODUCTION

This book contains an integrated collection of eight essays on certain aspects of the relation between social psychology and literature. We hope that the reader will not find that either social psychology or literature have been privileged in our treatment. The aim is to demonstrate in a concrete fashion the basis, rather, for their mutual interaction. We shall argue that literature and social psychology are not the exclusive categories which they may appear to be. In certain important respects they share their concerns, methods and theoretical perspectives. An appropriate metaphor for expressing their inter-relationship, as we see it, is the mathematical concept of 'over-lapping fuzzy sets'; although a space of many dimensions might possibly be more evocative of the way in which the two disciplines should interpenetrate and fold in upon one another. In doubting the separate identities of social psychological and literary activities, our intention is to encourage the reader simultaneously to re-examine the definition and subject-matter of each. Through the challenge to inter-disciplinary boundaries a new research perspective will, we hope, emerge in both fields.

On what basis do we claim this mutuality of concerns? Social psychology, literary theory, literary criticism and the objects of that criticism are all involved with 'sense-making'. This similarity provides the connection. Social psychology, as the science of the individual in a social context, is in part concerned with the structure and organisation of people's everyday interpretations of their social worlds. Under this heading we include the structure of justifications, understanding appropriate norms for action, collectively-shared representations of important institutions (e.g. medicine, education, finance, sexuality), the generalised images (or stereotypes) held of one's own and other groups, and so on. In describing and explaining the ways in which people make sense of their social worlds, social psychological theory also becomes, reflexively, a kind of making sense itself, with its own routinised patterns of interpreting and accounting.

Sense-making is a constructive activity. Neither the external social world nor the literary object which the critic analyses is an inevitable entity imposing itself upon the subject. Many different interpretations of phenomena can be put forward, provided that they can be successfully negotiated back into the literary or social world. One can identify a shifting currency of more or less acceptable and understandable systems of interpretation which are open to exchange. We have come to see that a crucial task for both the social psychologist and the literary critic is to describe the mechanisms of circulation of this currency; to analyse the accounting systems which a person or novelist uses to make sense of social life and to convey their impressions to others.

For the social psychologist and the literary critic following this line of thought the interest lies in 'texts' - though obviously the concept of 'text' has to be highly generalised to apply within social psychology. It must cover, for example, quite informal conversations which may be loaded with essential paralinguistic and non-verbal features. This emphasis on the study of discourse in all its forms is an unusual one for the social psychologist; but, as we hope to demonstrate, a fully justified one. Texts - as various as novels, conversations, accounts of activities, descriptions of a reasoning process, news broadcasts - typically present themselves as unproblematic. Inevitably they work to naturalise their subject-matter. They have us believe that matters are the way in which they are presented. Even if the text is difficult to make sense of, the conventional way to unravel it is to search for what the author 'must be saying', in the belief that the language in which the message is expressed merely acts as a convenient filter between the reality, the speaker and the audience. Very simple and very complex texts are equally seductive: the former because of their apparently undeniable nature, the latter because of the investment put into unravelling them. The realist or expressive view of text analysis is not, we shall argue the best way to proceed. We hope to work towards a new and more coherent approach.

In the chapters which follow we hope to demonstrate how some of the familiar concepts of social life (femininity, the environment, groups, the self - the substance equally of novels and social psychology) are constructed textually. Familiar meanings and frames of reference will be viewed as effects of language, as discursive productions. This stress on linguistic construction, rather than on the simple transmission through language of an underlying reality, does not, of course, deny the very real constraints on production. Instead it emphasises the collectively-produced limits on individual thinking. In looking at how femininity, for instance, is represented in modern socio-psychological theory (which relies for its definition on contemporary culture) and in literary works such as the novels of Barbara Cartland and Doris Lessing, we are approaching the regularly patterned frames which organise everyday thought and talk. This perspective on the connections between social psychology and literature will seem an unusual one to most psychologists; although it should be more familiar to the literary critic or theorist who is versed in current critical debates over the role of interpretation and reading.

Introduction

Social psychology has traditionally been an experimental laboratory science, ill-used to handling qualitative textual material and having few conceptual tools for the task. Because of this shortcoming Chapters 3,4 and 5, which comprise the 'theoretical' core of the book, describe recent programmatic attempts to develop appropriate methods, such as Harré's ethogenics. Through a demonstration of problems associated with those attempts, we outline how our own perspective on textual data combines certain insights from literary theorists with the practical knowledge of the social scientist.

To most social psychologists, particularly those with a humanistic inclination, the most obvious way of treating literary material would be to see great art as a source of insights into social life and human psychology; perhaps also as a repository of data. Many literary critics would once have been happy to encourage this belief, because it reflected their own opinion on the relationship between literature and life. Indeed, we ourselves initially conceived the interaction in a similar way, before we began active work on this book. But we soon discovered, for reasons which are discussed in several of the following chapters, that analytically this is one of the least interesting routes.

In general, the relationship between social psychology as an academic discipline and the events of everyday experience is one which is weakly articulated. Students of the discipline often express their concern that the search for the clear operationalisation of variables of theoretical interest, the insistence on controlled observation, and a monolithic emphasis on the college student as experimental subject takes place at the expense of human interest and relevance. Literature often seems to offer a more subjectively and experientially valid picture of the movements of the psyche. However, in our view, injections of 'high art' are not the means to achieving a more relevant, applicable social psychology.

This book does not wish to treat social psychology as parasitic upon literature. Not only is that an unnecessarily demeaning status, but it gives just that privileged position to literature, to certain kinds of texts, which we have come to distrust. We see no reason why we should not be equally critical of features of literature, as well as of social psychology. Admittedly, many novelists do seem to give unique insights into the human condition; but this appearance of insight needs to be questioned and its mechanisms analysed. Privileging literature, by making it a special resource for the social scientist, gives it undue significance as a very different and quite distinct form of life. We have concluded that this special quality is illusory. There is a need for a fuller interdisciplinary work, which foregrounds neither discipline, but which works in their interstices to reveal what is missing.

The reader will not find that novels are treated as Zola hoped they might be - as experimental laboratories where characters are set in motion to work through a set of psychological events, while the astute social scientist reader makes notes on the theoretical wisdom and inductive descriptive power of the novelist. The issue of 'subjectivity' and 'objectivity', or the epistemological status of literary and scientific material which is central to the resource approach, is peripheral to our main concerns.

For similar reasons psychology will not be put to the service of literature. One might expect psychological interpretations of plot, episode, and character; and of the life and motivations of the author. Psychoanalytic theory has been most commonly used to these ends. But, again, these objectives play no part in this book. Because we feel that it may be possible to read parts of our argument as though these were our aims, the reader should be most strenuously disabused of any expectations of this kind. We can only insist that if we appear to be talking about, say, the motivations or intentions of authors or characters we want to be taken as referring to no more than the text which presupposes them. The first of the more theoretical chapters, Chapter 3, discusses our reasons for rejecting various uses of psychology and literature, and includes a review of the 'influence' model which we also want to dismiss. This model focuses on literature as a medium of communication and tries to ascertain to what extent and how authors manage to convey their message to readers; and how readers comprehend and evaluate that message.

We see this book as an introductory text suited to students and researchers of both literature and social psychology. It is intended to stimulate further thought rather than mark out a definitive position. In part it covers ground one might expect to find in the sociology of literature. But, by contrast with that discipline, our process is more interactive, with literary theory and material being used to suggest changes to the face of social psychology. A full interaction also 'unfreezes' literary studies, demonstrating the social and political context of what seem at times the most arcane objects one could study.

The structure of the book may be deceptive. As we noted earlier, the more theoretical chapters have been placed at the centre of the book (Chapters 3, 4 and 5) rather than at the beginning or the end. Chapter 6, which considers the work of the group dynamics theorist, Irving Janis, is included in this section because its detailed analysis of the interpenetration of social psychology and 'documentary' accounts of 'groupthink' follows naturally from other examples in the theoretical chapters. The first two chapters, one on the concept of femininity and the other on the concept of place in the novels of Thomas Hardy and in environmental social psychology, are intended to serve as a gentle point of entry into the theoretical chapters. The last two chapters, 7 and 8, are a further substantiation of our theoretical position. Chapter 7 discusses the work of C.P. Snow and the social psychology of groups; while Chapter 8 adopts a more synoptic view of the way in which different notions of self have underpinned literary and psychological discourse.

The topics considered here - femininity, place, groups, the self - have been selected both for their current interest and their appositeness to our general objectives. The choice of literary authors may be somewhat idiosyncratic. We have concentrated on authors who particularly interest us. We expect that this introductory text will be superseded, not only by the application of our ideas to a more variegated range of authors, but also by more detailed studies of the particular topics and works which we have chosen. We have also placed some stress on ordinary utterances and everyday concepts, again in the hope that subsequent explorations will complement this emphasis, by including and comparing research on other sorts of discourse (conversations, scientific talk, official documents, and so on) and on other sorts of media (film, television).

We are aware that our greater knowledge of social psychology may at times have sabotaged the attempt to treat both disciplines equally. Perhaps this book will stimulate some readers to improve on this general objective from the standpoint of their own discipline.

PART 1

1 WRITING GENDER

One of the main functions of the modern novel is, undeniably, self-revelation and self-discovery. Modern readers are expected to gain insight and sometimes even concrete knowledge about the effects of past and present social, economic and political conditions. The confessional genre, in particular, dominates the market. This revelatory function novels offer is especially salient at the moment for the woman reader. As Rosalind Coward has pointed out, a spate of novels have recently been published which claim to analyse the situation of the modern woman, and which even threaten to 'change women's lives' through their insights. (1) Books like Erica Jong's Fear of Flying, Marilyn French's The Women's Room and Doris Lessing's The Golden Notebook (to name but a few representatives) are consistently attributed the explicit purpose of portraying what it means to be feminine and oppressed in Western society. These works are marketed with their self-discovery tags prominently displayed and their discourse is clearly labelled as a collective women's discourse. They are seen as a source of self-knowledge for all women, everywhere.

In this sense, these novels can be said to compete with psychology. It is the psychologist who is 'officially' supposed to give people knowledge about themselves. The social psychology of sexual identity, for example, is supposed to chart out female and male experience, identifying the different realms of subjectivity which accrue to gender. On a superficial level, therefore, it seems there could be a competition between the novelist and the social psychologist. Their goals are, at least, remarkably similar, encouraging cross-fertilisation between the two.

Social psychology is generally regarded as facing a crisis at the moment. (2) In part, this crisis concerns its apparent failure in areas where the novel clearly excels. Very few people, it seems, turn to social psychology for a satisfactory, non-trivial understanding of their subjective experience. It is often felt that social psychology should become relevant and 'real' in the way that certain kinds of novels appear profound, critical and insightful.

10 Chapter 1

In light of these criticisms, the suggestion that the psychological insights contained within literature could become a resource of new material for the social psychologist is particularly appealing. An appropriately flexible new social psychology might be able to incorporate literary knowledge. If novels do provide a guide to feminine psychology, and we have merely sketched out their claim to do so, then surely the social psychologist should be interested. Here are a number of descriptions and theories about the nature of femininity in modern society which might be included in the discipline. The relationship between literature and social psychology could become, in other words, more symbiotic, with the novel harnessed and put into service, to improve social science.

This chapter discusses this proposal. It seems straightforward. Indeed, the concept of literature as a resource for social science is probably one of the first that occurs when thinking about the connections between the two areas of study. It certainly provided much of the initial stimulus for this book. However, when we start to consider this project certain basic problems become apparent. This chapter thus also records these problems, eventually concluding that the notion of literature as a resource is unworkable, as is the conception of literature it implies.

We start by taking up two strands which should fit together if the model of literature as a resource was to apply. First we flesh out the view that 'women's novels' could be used as a psychological guide, considering the school of literary criticism which allows for this possibility, and, then, we describe the social psychology of sexual identity, the area where this literature could make its most obvious contribution. The discussion of the reasons why these two do not fit together should lead us to reassess affect not only the model of literature endorsed but, we hope, the way issues such as sexual identity are raised in social psychology. First, however, literature is considered as a guide to a woman's self.

SELF-KNOWLEDGE THROUGH LITERATURE

> If she had longed for nothing else steadily all these years it was for a close complete intimacy with a man [...]
> There is a type of woman who can never be, as they are likely to put it 'themselves', with anyone but the man to whom they have permanently or not given their hearts. If the man goes away there is left an empty space filled with shadows.. she mourns him who brought her 'self' to life. She lives with the empty space at her side, peopled with the images of her own potentialities until the next man walks into the space, absorbs the shadows into himself, creating her, allowing her to be her 'self' - but a new self, since it is his conception which forms her.
>
> [Martha's] 'self' with William was something she had never seen

before. [...] Already Martha was impatient to be rid of that
image of herself, so much less than she was capable of being.
But who, next, would walk into that empty space? She knew of
no one: not one of the men about her now fed her imagination,
or at least, not more than for a few moments of fantasy. (3)

In this extract, Martha, the chief protagonist of Doris Lessing's
novel series <u>The Children of Violence</u>, sums up for herself the conclusions experience forces upon her. Her explanation of her own
reaction is, however, also couched in broader terms, as a general
truth for a certain type of woman. It is the kind of 'truth' one
might expect to find in the feminist classics, in Simone de
Beauvoir's <u>The Second Sex</u>, for instance, or in similar investigations of the female psyche. Simone de Beauvoir similarly argues
that women seek self-definition through their relationships with
men. In this respect, Martha's insight is hardly unique.

All the same, this quotation helps demonstrate why certain critics
might want to treat literature as a source of knowledge about the
self. More personal and intimate than even the psychologist,
Lessing seems to be recording the subtle fluctuations of female subjectivity which cruder measuring instruments obscure. The subject-
matter of her novels and of the whole genre of 'woman's novels'
typically concerns women characters who can be described as 'half-
emancipated'. Socialised into the usual dominant/submissive sex-
roles, these characters' emotions and expectations are discordant
with the lives they lead. These literary works appear to be a
record of this contradiction. (4)

What might a woman reader gain from reading these novels? According
to some early feminist literary critics the benefits can be easily
specified. This school of thought would argue that through reading
Lessing, Sylvia Plath or Margaret Drabble, a woman can discover the
measure of herself. (5) Writers in this league, they claim, offer
a veridical and psychologically penetrating description of feminine
experience. Experiences which the woman reader may be unable to
make sense of, the woman writer can articulate in bold and masterly
form. Shaping, defining and accounting for feminine reality, the
novelist offers self-understanding. The heroines can, in their
view, in some way, explain and contextualise through their own history. From Sylvia Plath, for example, one critic learns that:

> No longer was I alone or wholly responsible for my ambivalent and
> sometimes seemingly hypocritical feelings. I, like Esther
> Greenwood, was a victim of a socialization of dancing classes,
> Girl Scouts, junior proms and motherly advice. (6)

This kind of self-definition and self-knowledge are not the only
benefits, other advantages are also claimed. This type of recognition of oneself in an external text can produce a sense of identification with other women; it also generates, perhaps for the
first time in literature for women, a feeling of being understood.

There may be a cathartic release or sense of vindication and finally, these critics maintain, the reader can learn for the future, distilling guidelines for action while refusing to repeat the dysfunctional patterns played out by the heroines.

The attitude of this school of thought is not completely reverential, perils are identified as well; however, it is generally assumed that a certain class of novels fit readily into general 'consciousness-raising' programmes and form part of broader social and political movements. The brand of early feminist literary criticism which makes these claims emerged in opposition to the predominant formalist tradition - 'that great block of aesthetic ice' with its 'cold fantasy of "pure" and isolated cerebration'. (7) It stresses, in contrast, the socio-historical context in which literary works are produced, seeking not only to interpret modern works by women but also to recover a feminine literary tradition, unearth distorted 'phallic' criticism and provide a distinctive, feminist, theory of literary production as well as the context of this production. (8) Literary interpretation becomes seen as a personal and progressive as well as a scholastic art from this perspective, as each woman critic discovers more about her own oppression through studying the images in texts and the general constraints on female writers. 'Feminist criticism leads the literary scholar through the history of the novel, poem and play into the healing waters of her innermost being.' (9)

It is in this context that works by Lessing and others take their place as starting points for 'voyages of self-discovery'. If we take the frame of reference of early feminist criticism, then literature becomes an integral part of self-development and part of wider social struggles. But what kind of assumptions need to be made about the relationship between literature, life and experience?

These early feminist critics take what can be called a 'truth and insight' model of literature. This model which also seems to underpin commonsense views of how literature works, has been stoutly defended by literary critics of many different persuasions and interests. The argument, however, is a very simple one, dependent on the concepts of mimesis, or literal description, and realism. It is considered that particularly acute and perspicacious novelists offer truth and insight into the human condition; in fact, this is the basis of their talent and reputation. Bad art, according to Iris Murdoch, 'is a lie about the world'; while good art is 'in some important evident sense seen as ipso facto true and as expressive of reality'. (10)

Novels are, of course, fictions yet, although the events and characters may be mythical conveniences, great authors also:

> search for and find logical relationships between a perception of life and the composition of aesthetic forms. Original works

have a revelatory function as regards the hidden, inadmissible aspects of what we call social, economic or psychological life: they are both the search for and the expression of their sense, or, rather, of their essence. (11)

Novels, in other words, tell us about life. Their very form and methods of construction help in this revelation. Their accounts are in some sense literal and real.

It is within this general framework, that feminist literary critics turn to the new genre of books written by women writers for women readers and recognise their value as a source of self-knowledge. Literature, they maintain, reflects life; women writers' psychological models and sociological critiques of patriarchal society offer concrete knowledge and information on time present and on past generations of women. Reality depicted through fictional means is still reality they would argue and, furthermore, it is a reality which tends to powerfully resonate with the female reader.

LITERATURE AND THE SOCIAL PSYCHOLOGY OF SEXUAL IDENTITY

We have already noted the feeling that social psychology for a variety of reasons to do with its traditional methods and history, fails to capture the immediacy of subjective experience in the way that a novelist or other commentator can. Take, for instance, Nigel Armistead's confession that 'for me, Doris Lessing's novels have more to say about women and men than any social psychology I have read'. (12) If this is generally correct, and we accept the 'truth and insight' premise that self-knowledge and social insight flow from great literature, then an obvious conclusion, as noted in the introduction, is to incorporate literature within new approaches to social psychology. Perhaps certain novelists' work should be treated as especially discerning participant accounts? Lessing's writings and the work of similar authors could be seen as a testament or a document of a woman's self. They could provide a source of vividly enacted theories and detailed naturalistic descriptions which could be subsumed into socio-psychological thinking. (13)

Novelists working in traditional humanistic modes generally work off the premise that characters have fixed identities dependent upon their sex. No one would ever confuse Lessing's heroines Martha, Anna or Ella with their counterparts Douglas, Thomas, Michael and Paul or Tess of the d'Urbervilles, for example, with Angel Clare. The details of personality, activity and individual style seem to flow naturally from sexual essence. What better way, then, to find out the nature of this sexual essence? Even if we would want to see these psychological forms as encumbrances to be eventually shrugged off by modern women and men.

Let us turn now to our second strand and outline in some detail the socio-psychological study of sexual identity with which this literature competes. Scientific research on the general topic of male and female differences can fortunately be roughly divided into three areas in line with three different, although intertwined, concepts: sex-role, sexual identity and sex-stereotype.

The study of the first of these, sex-roles, is usually carried out under the aegis of the sociologist or social anthropologist. It involves investigating the activities of women and men at different times, ages and in different cultures. (14) Here what is the case, the actual pattern of tasks, needs to be carefully distinguished from what people believe should be the case, although the sociologist of sex-roles is also interested in the way norms and rules regulate the typical interactions between the sexes.

The second concept, sexual identity or gender, is more familiar to the psychologist and, we shall argue defines the area where the new genre of women's literature might be thought to have the most impact. It can be understood, in part, as the sexual self-concept - as the psychological dimension which results from the parcelling out of different activities and roles to the sexes. How do men and women differ psychologically: in terms of their abilities, traits and subjective experiences? It is assumed that women and men develop different representations of themselves and different actual character traits, in line with their roles. The socio-psychological study of these is the study of gender or sexual identity. (15)

The study of stereotypes, the third main research area, is related to sexual identity in the sense that stereotypes or consensual images will probably constitute part of a man or woman's self-image. They will provide some of the raw materials for a masculine or feminine self-concept. None the less the study of stereotypes, it is generally agreed, unlike the study of real psychological differences, moves into the realm of ideology, myth and fantasy. The study of character and personality sex-stereotypes concerns, for instance, the effects and functions of the widely held beliefs that women are, inter alia, illogical, submissive, dependent, narcissistic and overly emotional or the belief that men are aggressive, independent, blunt, insensitive, decisive and objective. (16) The point of research on sex-stereotypes such as these is not to find the kernel of truth about real-life sex differences in personality but to accurately map people's beliefs at any given time.

Social psychologists usually combine the study of roles, gender-experience and stereotypes with a theory which firmly locates the cause of any differences between the sexes in society rather than in biology, although sometimes a complex interaction between the two is advocated. It is generally understood that as societies and cultures change so do the stereotypes of women and men, their roles and their psychologies even though biological sex remains immutable. It is assumed, therefore, that becoming masculine or feminine involves internalising the current, culturally constructed, symbolic order. Malleable and psychologically neutral biological boys and girls are moulded, it is argued, in line with societal expectations in the guise of parent, peer and teacher role-models. Much of the empirical research is aimed at demonstrating how these mechanisms of learning and socialisation might work in practice. (17)

The most murky area in this field is the study of gender difference or sexual identity. The two sexes have different roles to play in society, they are consensually stereotyped in different ways, but how do they really differ in their thinking, personalities and experiences? If literature can offer psychological insight this is one of the domains in which it could perhaps contribute most.

The main difficulty experienced here concerns the scientific establishment of difference. Maccoby and Jacklin, after a close examination of the research in this area, concluded that few differences can be guaranteed. (18) It appears that men are more aggressive than women, women have a slight edge on verbal skills while men are better at visual-spatial tasks. But these highly disputed differences are hardly sufficient to form the basis for two categorically separate genders. What about all the other subjective and behavioural qualities that would be needed to mark out two different and separate domains of masculinity and femininity?

Despite the empirical failure (and new efforts are being initiated all the time to obtain more and more subtle parameters), the assumption of gender difference is still commonly taken to be a reasonable one. (19) Indeed it is ingrained in all our thinking. It seems eminently sensible to assume that different socialisation histories and different roles as well as different biologies, will lead to contrasting psychologies and sets of experiences. The experience and character of a woman should be affected by her position in a social and natural order.

Novelists like Doris Lessing, Simone de Beauvoir and many others certainly assume that it is so affected and their literary works repeatedly draw upon the notion of subjective differences. They concentrate particularly on woman's role as Other or object rather than subject and actor and the emotions, expectations and reactions that go along with that identity. It is at this level then, that humanistic social psychologists and critics such as Armistead might prefer the psychological penetration of a particularly talented writer to the empirical studies of a social psychology which, necessarily, focus on the outward, less subtle, manifestations of inward differences. Certainly it is an area where literary anecdotes abound, they are constantly used as examples, and if the resource model was taken more seriously we might have seen attempts to use literature more systematically as, indeed, Ann Oakley, one of the best known sociological investigators in this field, has recently tried to do. (20)

We have now sketched out in more detail, for one particular area, the proposal that social psychology might be 'humanised' through literature. The kind of model of literature which fits with this hypothesis, the 'truth and insight' model, has also been presented. This notion of literature as a viable resource seems quite plausible. And, even though the psychologist reader can probably think of a score of practical and validational problems, it is in accord with most psychologists' belief that great novels are able to describe things as they really are. We have come to the conclusion that this model is inadequate, however. To see why, let us look more closely at the kind of 'knowledge' literature appears to be offering in this area. It should become clear that literature is not as straightforward a category as it seems and its complexity raises some important issues for the way social psychologists conceptualise their own subject-matter.

VERSIONS OF FEMALE EXPERIENCE: CARTLAND, COOPER AND LESSING

To begin with, let us take two other authors, Barbara Cartland and Jilly Cooper and compare their descriptions of the 'woman in love' with Lessing's more cynical and critical view.

> Rory suddenly saw a taxi and flagged it down. We kissed all the way home.
> God - I was enjoying myself. I'd never felt a millionth of that raging, abandoned glory the whole time I'd known Cedric, but it was all tearing along much too fast [...]
> 'I'll make some coffee,' I muttered. 'Really, I am engaged to Cedric and he wouldn't approve at all.'
> 'Shut up,' he said gently. This time he moved in slowly and deliberately. I had plenty of time to move away, but instead I found myself leaning forward. With his free hand he began to stroke my face, then my neck. No, wait! Stop! I said to myself, but I couldn't move.
> 'Oh baby,' he said huskily. 'We're going to be so good together.' The last thing I remember thinking was that Cedric's photograph should certainly have been turned to the wall. (21)

> Adolph swung his legs up so that he lay parallel, and began to make love to her, using the forms of sensitive experience, so that she was partly reassured and partly chilled, while she arranged the facts of what was occurring to fit an imaginative demand already framed in her mind. Nor was she disappointed. For if the act fell short of her demand, that ideal, the-thing-in-itself, that mirage, remained untouched, quivering exquisitely in front of her. Martha, final heir to the long romantic tradition of love, demanded nothing less than that the quintessence of all experience, all love, all beauty, should explode suddenly in a drenching, saturating moment of illumination. And since this was what she demanded, the man himself seemed positively irrelevant - this was at the bottom of her attitude, though she did not know it. (22)

> 'I am .. happy,' Simonetta managed to stammer. 'I am .. happy, Pierre .. but I thought it would be .. impossible for me to .. m.marry you.'
> 'You will be my wife,' he said, 'and I will never allow you to cry like this again.'

> He turned her face up to his. Then he was kissing away the tears from her eyes, her cheeks and lastly her mouth.
> At the touch of his lips Simonetta felt thrill after thrill flash through her and it was like coming back to life from the dead.
> Once again he was carrying her up into the sky and there was the rapture and wonder of being close to him, of belonging to him.
> 'I .. love .. you .. I love you .. I love .. you,' her heart was saying. (23)

The insipid Simonetta (with the fetching speech impediment) and 'madcap' Emily (Rory's friend) contrast oddly in these quotations with Lessing's heroine, Martha. The reader can tell that Martha differs from Simonetta and Emily: she will eventually work through the Mills and Boon fantasy which provides the playground for Emily's stylish antics and Simonetta's moment of glory. Martha will lose her faith in 'real men' while Simonetta's faith will never waver for a second. Emily seems to work off the principle that the more unpleasant and domineering the man the better and she appreciates that, these days, rugged Rorys are over-satiated with sweet young things, but she still resembles Simonetta more than Martha.

These three quotations, placed together, unavoidably raise the question of versions. All three of these extracts comment on the supposed experience of the woman in love. Which version, however, is to be taken seriously? For a literary critic committed to the truth and insight model, a discussion of genres, conventions and the mimesis formula would clarify this particular conundrum. Cartland and Cooper novels belong to a very clearly delineated genre, romantic fiction, and their plots, characters and descriptions of subjective experience are governed closely by the conventions of this genre. The critical consensus would be against Cartland and Cooper. Their art is considered demonstrably frivolous; it is manipulative, merely a packaged product for a mass-market, satisfying demands for vicarious fantasy. In socio-psychological terms romantic fiction is analogous to the stereotypes of masculinity and femininity. Stereotypes like romantic fiction distort life as opposed to enhancing it.

This type of discussion of genres thus goes hand in hand with the mimetic or realist argument noted earlier which assumes that there is a more or less unproblematic relationship between reality and the literary or linguistic representation of that reality. Either novels are realistic, they give a lucid picture, or they are flawed and distorted. They can be placed on a continuum which will establish their accuracy and inaccuracy. In the case of a particularly famous artist like Doris Lessing, the relationship with real experience is probably seen as one to one or virtually so; critics in fact often remark on her sociological style, she is seen as a journalist rather than a novelist, a fact-recorder rather than a story-teller. (24) Cartland and Cooper's renditions are generally seen as much further down the accuracy continuum: as flawed and perhaps even perniciously inaccurate representations of actual female experience.

This question of the relative status of different kinds of accounts (which is crucial also to socio-psychological investigation) is not so easily solved, however. Perhaps, Lessing's text is no less conventional than Cartland or Cooper's? It could be that the conventions she uses work towards the impression of realism and create the sense that here is an almost sociological record of subjective experience. Or it could be that Lessing's supporters are overrepresented in the highbrow literary community with respect to Cartland's. If this is so, then the mimesis argument for 'good art' simply and effectively works to obscure the conventions that Lessing might be using, by minimising the artifice in her work and overlooking her constructive skills.

In the introduction to The Golden Notebook, Lessing claims that her aim is to transmit experience rather than transmute it. (25) The form of the novel is deliberately anarchic, she says, to convey the formless, disordered, chaotic nature of 'true experience'. The type of rationale Lessing presents for her work thus matches the appearance the texts give of uncovering and reproducing psychological and social basics. But does Lessing have any greater access to 'reality' than Cartland and Cooper? We should at least consider the possibility that her novels are organised in such a way that they can more easily be read as realistic. We should examine whether the codes and conventions she uses stimulate the reading of her material as vividly 'right' or 'true', just as one would want to examine the ways in which Barbara Cartland, for instance, makes use of conventional stereotypes.

THE MANUFACTURE OF FEMININE EXPERIENCE IN DORIS LESSING'S TEXTS

Let us take another extract to put with the Martha and Adolph scene quoted in the last section.

> Carrie Jones, seated beside Tommy, regarded her ten red fingernails which were spread out on her knee. She wore a yellow linen dress as smooth as butter, and her face had the smooth prepared surface of a very pretty girl who feels men's eyes play over her like sunlight. Martha thought: She's what I used to be: she looks at herself in the looking-glass, and she sees how her face and body form a sort of painted shell, and she adores herself, but she is waiting for a pair of eyes to melt the paint and shoot through into the dark inside - well, she'll have to wait! (26)

These two quotations typify a kind of textual construction or accounting device used repeatedly in the early novels of Lessing's Children of Violence or Martha Quest novel series. In particular, these texts set up two contradictory 'voices' or accounting systems and work in terms of the tension between them. One of these voices could be taken directly from a Cartland or Cooper novel. It is the voice of melodramatic experience, the discourse of 'very pretty girls', tall, dark, strangers, intense men whose glance is sufficient to melt a woman, and burning sexual encounters which are exquisitely mystical and meaningful. Carrie Jones 'is waiting for a pair of eyes to melt the paint and shoot into the dark inside', while Martha with Adolph expects the sexual act to become the 'ideal, the thing-in-itself' which will be the 'quintessence of all experience, all love, all beauty' exploding suddenly in a 'drenching, saturating moment of illumination'. Remove the commentary which frames this talk and the skeleton of a Cartland novel can be detected.

The essential difference is, of course, that a Cartland novel, with some slips and elisions, adheres relentlessly to the romantic discourse while Lessing's text depends on the development of an ironical commenting discourse or meta-language. In the Martha and Adolph quotation in the previous section, a 'truth-telling' narrative voice tells us things that Martha herself is not aware of - the real nature of her demands and the fact that many other women have gone before her in this 'romantic tradition of love' only to be disillusioned. The romantic discourse is thus revealed as a myth or fantasy, its claim to reality is sabotaged.

In the second extract, the truth-telling voice becomes Martha's own commentary; wise after the event, she now detects, with the benevolent approval of the text, these unrealistic beliefs in other women. Carrie is like Martha used to be and like Martha 'she'll have to wait!' for the tall dark handsome stranger who will give meaning to her life, presumably for ever.

This second commenting voice appears, therefore, as the discourse of common-sense and rational criticism. It unmasks the Cartland/ Cooper type of discourse depicted in all its fine array and assiduously demonstrates its fraudulent basis. It is this process of critical unmasking and the incessant tension between the two voices which displays Lessing's text as feminist, making it appear to consist of sociologically orientated statements rather than outright fiction.

Ironically, the textual re-evaluation of the romantic discourse which establishes it as an ideological illusion is the very thing which guarantees the authority and seeming veracity of the second, commenting, meta-language. By revealing that supposed truths about women's experience are only reactionary talk, the critical-evaluative voice protects itself from being similarly undermined. We can easily fail to see that this voice might also support an ideological position or identity (the world-weary Anna, the naive, rebellious Martha who knows that something is wrong but is not quite sure what); the text gives the appearance of revealing an immutable truth, not a flawed and contingent accounting system, as it provides for the characters Carrie Jones and Martha in the extracts just discussed. By these means the text can readily seduce the reader into accepting the evaluative-revelatory pose, and ultimately the many implicit claims of the meta-language.

Let us take this way of analysing seemingly 'feminist' literary texts and apply it to another example from Lessing's work.

> What is terrible is that after every one of the phases of my life is finished, I am left with no more than some banal commonplace that everyone knows: in this case, that women's emotions are all still fitted for a kind of society that no longer exists. My deep emotions, my real ones, are to do with my relationship with a man. One man. But I don't live that kind of life, and I know few women who do. So what I feel is irrelevant and silly ... I am always coming to the conclusion that my real emotions are foolish, I am always having, as it were, to cancel myself out. I ought to be like a man, caring more for my work than for people; I ought to put my work first, and take men as they come, or find an ordinary comfortable man for bread and butter reasons - but I won't do it, I can't be like that... (27)
>
> I lay on the bed, happy. Being happy, the joy that filled me then was stronger than all the misery and madness in the world, or so I felt it. But then happiness began to leak away, and I lay and I thought: What is this thing that we need so much? (By we, meaning women). And what is it worth? I had it with Michael, but it meant nothing to him, for if it did, he wouldn't have left me. And now I have it with Saul, grabbing at it as if it were a glass of water and I were thirsty. But think about it and it vanishes. I did not want to think about it [...]
>
> I lay on the bed in the dark, listening to Saul crashing and banging over my head, and I was already betrayed. Because Saul had forgotten the 'happiness'. By the act of going upstairs, he had put a gulf between himself and happiness.
> But I saw this not merely as denying Anna, but as denying life itself. I thought that somewhere here is a fearful trap for women, but I don't yet understand what it is. For there is no doubt of the new note that women strike, the note of being betrayed. It's in the books they write, in how they speak, everywhere, all the time. It is a solemn, self-pitying organ note. It is in me, Anna betrayed, Anna unloved, Anna whose happiness is denied, and who says, not: Why do you deny me, but why do you deny life? (28)

In these last two extracts, the style changes matching the change from the early novels of the Martha Quest series to the <u>Four-Gated City</u> and to Lessing's most famous work, <u>The Golden Notebook</u>. Throughout, however, textual devices structurally similar to the ones discussed above, continue to be used to establish the authority of the definitions of female experience being proposed. Again, one can identify two voices but this time the two voices are internalised within the same character, different aspects of the one self, rather than being split between younger or older versions of a character or between a narrator and a character. The substance of the voices also changes. The Cartland/Cooper romantic discourse is replaced with a more subtle and complex discourse concerning women's emotions or the sense of betrayal, which are seen as constitutive parts of the women characters: essential, intimate and everyday aspects of the self, rather than as external projections which characters like Martha and Carrie accept for a while and then reject.

In the first extract, a contradiction is generated between two parts of the self. One part experiences the emotions considered typically feminine - 'my deep emotions, my real ones, are to do with my relationship with a man. One man.', while another part of the self rejects this emotive caring facet as 'silly' and inappropriate. The emotive self is perceived as almost out of control, the narrative, evaluative voice is not really responsible for this self-discourse which seems to arise merely because the character is a woman living in a certain kind of society.

The second extract concerning the sense of betrayal sets up the same kind of opposition. One part of the self experiences a strong emotional reaction, betrayal, simultaneously a critical thinking voice separates itself from this emotional experience and examines it. Again, as in the Carrie Jones and Martha/Adolph extracts, this latter voice is depicted as veridical; its description is contrasted with the socially induced distortions of the first voice. In this case the aura of 'truthfulness' is protected not only by the establishment of a tension and contradiction between two discourses but also because cultural conventions respect the 'rock-bottom' honesty of confessional comments from this kind of 'divided self'.

The division of the self into two components, a contemplating I and a me which is the object of that contemplation, is a standard literary and social scientific practice. (This particular representation of self-experience is discussed in greater detail in Chapter 8.) The structure of our language and the organisation of personal pronouns ensure the familiarity of a doubled-self reading of Lessing's texts. (29) It is commonplace to see one part of the self as made up of any number of psychological traits, emotional reactions, social roles, socialisation patterns, habits and so on. This part of the self is the part which is dramatised and put into action, it reacts as the situation demands according to its own limits, history and constraints. However, the whole person is also more than this 'me', there is also the surveying I which can observe the me's performance with regret, compassion, anger or criticism.

Lessing's text continually exploits this fundamental but unexplicated device for representing ourselves. The main characters in The Golden Notebook are continually fragmented into the I and me aspects which supposedly constitute their selves. Through fitting the two discourses, the women's discourse of emotions and betrayal and the narrative commenting discourse into the same person in this way, the text both draws upon and reproduces the everyday assumption that the 'I part' of the self knows and speaks the truth. The me, the discourse of emotions, the social reservoir of habits and roles, is represented as confused and reactionary, destructive rather than progressive. Yet the core of the self, the rock-bottom basis of personality (the furtherest you can go in self-analysis) is not deceived. The I, the critical, thinking, commenting, internal voice, is presented as telling you all it knows, its discourse is not contingent, not dependent upon passing feelings and oppressive socialisation experiences, but is considered to be detached and above these things, and therefore able to provide the acute insights into subjectivity which are then seen as significant for psychology. By identifying the meta-commentary with the I part of the character's self, Lessing's text thus enhances its own impression of realism.

The impact of Lessing's analysis of female subjectivity is not only enhanced by these subtle 'reality-construction' devices it is also increased through the presentation of these extracts as though they were talking for all women. It is not simply Martha or Anna, the heroine of <u>The Golden Notebook</u>, who are discovering their essential nature, the lessons apply more generally. The additional techniques used to generate this impression are straightforward. The text continually genderises and universalises.

The beginning point is always the two natural categories, women and men. Sets of experiences are then constructed and marked off for one sex only. Certain types of reactions, for instance, are, for good or for bad, seen as belonging solely to a woman's domain. Femininity is stamped all over them: 'women's emotions', 'by we, meaning women', 'the new note women strike' and so on. While masculinity consists in 'caring more for (one's) work than for people', not being caught in 'fearful traps'. At the same time as the experiences are genderised, they are also generalised: for all women and all men. On this point, Lessing's text shares many of the assumptions of the social psychologist. Descriptions of basic experiences 'out there' are evoked and then inextricably tied to one or other natural category of people who tend to be seen as homogeneous integrated wholes rather than heterogeneous entities who are continually 'reconstructed' and represented in language.

LANGUAGE, EXPERIENCE AND IMAGINARY IDENTITIES

We started out by considering the claim that novelists of the stature of Doris Lessing offer a particularly penetrating and honest account of feminine subjectivity. What conclusions can now be reached about this claim in the light of our, albeit tentative, comparative analysis of the writings of Lessing, Cartland and Cooper?

It is apparent that it is becoming more and more difficult to sustain the 'truth and insight' model of literature. (30) Bad art, according to this model, is a lie about the world and Cartland and Cooper fit into this category because of the particular genre they represent. Their use of its conventions, it is claimed, ensures that their descriptions of reality are distorted. Lessing's texts, on the other hand, are seen, in terms of this model, as realistic and acutely literal to the extent that certain critics recommend her work as a psychological guide for the woman reader.

Our analysis, limited and preliminary through it is, starts to illustrate the way in which Lessing's texts are based on conventional forms of sense-making and therefore are clearly no less constructed and no more innocently literal than Cartland or Cooper's. At least in the cases we have examined the appearance of unproblematic description, the impression that this is a literal representation of reality rather than a contingent version of it, is carefully manufactured and dependent on the use of a number of routine textual devices. The aura of facticity is partly a product of the contrast between the calm, truth-telling voice and the 'blatant lies' fostered by romantic novelists. Moreover, an extra sense of realism is gained when the truth-telling voice is attributed not to a narrator or to a character but to some basic, essentially disinterested, part of the self. Self-revelation hence comes to combine with quasi-feminist factual statement.

It thus becomes clear that the polarity implied in the truth and insight model between literally descriptive and false or stereotyped texts is analytically unhelpful. It is not that one set of texts 'expresses reality' and the other does not; rather each draws upon different textual devices in the construction of alternative versions of 'feminine experience'. Lessing's version is avowedly 'realistic'; yet it is an analytic confusion (based on a too simple notion of the way texts function) to see this as implying veridical representation. Put another way, if we assume that certain types of literature are realistic in their portrayal of experience, then literary discourse must be seen as a blank space in which messages about an independent world can be neutrally inscribed. In this view, the language from which Lessing's texts are crafted is seen as connecting two realms of experience, the reader's and the writer's.

But is this the case? Does literary discourse act in this kind of neutral, merely reproductive, way? We have seen with respect to Lessing's texts some of the ways in which its meaning is constructed. Literary discourse in this instance is not functioning as a transparent medium for the transmission of the author's insights and intentions; rather it is organised to actively produce particular kinds of discursive effects. The picture, then, we gain from a text is not determined so much by some underlying experience of the author but by the arrangement and structure of the words in the text and their place in general cultural systems of meaning.

A further difficulty with the truth and insight model and the related notion of literature as a resource for social science concerns its failure to take a properly social perspective on literary discourse. When literature is treated as a neutral medium of communication between two individuals, the author and the reader, its fundamental dependence on social resources and shared systems of sense-making is ignored. The cameos Lessing presents are not immutable psychological truths, they are fragments of discourse which, because of their organisation and place in a cultural repertoire of accounting systems appear vividly 'right' and 'true'. (31)

As we begin to see literary accounts of female subjectivity as contingent versions rather than as literal descriptions, we can begin to speculate about the social and ideological function of this type of self-revelatory statement. We can begin to treat them less reverentially and more critically. Early feminist criticism wanted to place literature in its socio-historical context but, as we have seen, this school adopted a set of assumptions which privileged certain texts viewing them as realistic and thereby removing them from the sphere of social influence. This procedure is surely not commensurate with a comprehensive social analysis of all kinds of literature. Literature needs ultimately to be seen as an '*institution,* caught up in certain relations of social power, rather than as a set of isolated "works".' (32)

If Lessing's extracts are no longer seen as informative, literal representations of experience then how should we categorise them? One potential solution is to see them as presenting a gallery of 'imaginary identities'. This concept comes from the literary critic Terry Eagleton (who is, in turn, paraphrasing the French psychoanalyst, Lacan). For Eagleton, imaginary refers to that 'consoling state in which our egos are confirmed by an image in which we can find ourselves securely reflected [...]' Dominant ideologies, he argues, 'exploit "imaginary" devices in order to keep us in place, bolster(ing) up relatively fixed identities; and certain literary texts - "realism" in particular - collude in this process by making of language a mere transparent window through which we find a securely familiar world reflected back to us.' (33) The pieces of discourse or voices that Lessing's text presents can, therefore, now be seen as social constructions or as social representations and powerful constructions at that.

Imaginary identities of this kind can liberate since their novelty for one reader may allow the conception that an expansion of understanding has taken place. This seems to be one effect of Lessing's set. These identities can also constrict as they become tied to a role (the lover, the wife, the career woman) and must be 'dealt with' by the person who accepts that role. Eventually for particular groups of people at different times, over-exposure may turn what was once a powerful and apparently sophisticated self-characterisation into a subjective stereotype or undeniable cliché, as may have happened with the images of romantic fiction. The recognition that these identities are clichés may lead, however, to a new kind of liberation and so on.

Apart from the impact of these images on the reader, we need, as modern feminist literary criticism appreciates, to examine in detail their specific ideological functions. The construction of images of women needs to be examined in all kinds of works especially in the recent genre of 'women's novels' represented by Lessing, Margaret Drabble, Marilyn French, etc. where these effects are perhaps least understood. We need to understand how these images work, how they are transmitted, under what conditions they appear most evocative and whether these identities are ultimately oppressive. (34) It is in terms of this enterprise that the social psychologist and the literary critic may be able to most profitably work together. We turn now to the implications of these arguments for the social psychology of gender.

THE SEXUAL IDENTITY THESIS REVISITED

At the beginning of this chapter an apparently straightforward, credible model of literature and its potential significance for psychology was introduced. Exploration of this model has suggested, however, that literature cannot be used as an analytic resource in the way the model suggests. It is not possible to treat literary accounts as unproblematic, veridical descriptions. When we examine these texts closely, as we have done with Lessing, Cartland and Cooper and will do with others in the course of this book, their conventional character and complex organisation becomes apparent.

In our view, this more skeptical approach to literature should also affect the way social psychologists think about gender and the psychology of sexual difference. We noted in a previous section the kind of assumptions made in this research area. (35) Principally, it is taken for granted, despite the lack of empirical evidence, that the different roles and biologies of the two sexes produce different psychologies, sets of experiences and self-concepts. This assumption is, in fact, strikingly similar to the one presupposed in Lessing's text. Indeed, the general points made about her work and the truth and insight model apply equally well to social psychology.

Both social psychology and Lessing's text assume that experience and the meaning accorded to that experience are tied to certain types or groups of people. The extracts from Lessing continually universalised and genderised experience so that, as we saw, experiences were associated with all women, the whole group, or all men. Social psychology, we shall argue, similarly homogenises and reifies sexual categories, lumping all women together, and smoothing over the plurality of individual difference.

We noted that the truth and insight model evoked experiences 'out there' or rather 'in the head', as does Lessing's text, thereby downplaying the part that language plays in the definition and identification of experience. Again, the social psychology of gender tends towards a similar practice, since it is concerned to specify behaviours or personality traits seen as concrete experiential entities rather than looking at how sexual difference is produced through language and everyday talk.

Finally, we argued that Lessing's text constructs imaginary identities and a truth and insight model of literature, mistaking these identities for 'real subjective experiences', fails to properly investigate their social and ideological function. Social psychology also, in asking, for instance, questions about the 'real' nature of psychological gender or masculinity and femininity, has similarly tended to set up imaginary identities and has ignored the ideological implications of the particular identities it chooses to endorse.

Let us now look at these points more closely. How does social psychology reify sex as a psychological determinant and how does it create imaginary identities? Many examples of this process could be given but one should suffice - Sandra Bem's Sex Role Inventory. (36)

Bem, accepting the sexual identity thesis, assumed that one could specify meaningful categories of masculinity, femininity or androgyny. That is, people could psychologically identify with masculinity or femininity or they could be androgynous. These self-concepts and types of experience need not, she argued, be tied to biological men and women, but, they were, none the less, important psychological entities. Bem's goal was to measure these attributes, through an inventory, so that people could discover which psychological type they were.

Presumably, because of the absence of any detailed empirical knowledge about the characteristics which differentiate the psychologically feminine from the psychologically masculine or androgynous, Bem asked student judges to decide on the characteristic attributes of men and women. She collected together 400 personality characteristics (affectionate, soft-spoken, self-reliant, competitive, etc.) and asked the students to rate each characteristic in terms of its desirability for a woman or a man. It is important to note that the judges were not to think in terms of their own criteria for desirability but were to intuit the kinds of criteria 'American society' would use.

As a result of this process, 20 highly desirable masculine characteristics and 20 highly desirable feminine characteristics were identified and collected together along with some filler items into an inventory. Thus, if a person wished to find out which gender they identified with then, according to Bem, all that is required is to sit down with the personality inventory, read each characteristic, and decide how accurate it is on a numerical scale as a description of oneself. A few calculations later, the person can be given their femininity score, their masculinity score and their androgyny score (computed from the relationship between the masculinity and femininity score). They might discover, for example, that they are highly masculine with very few feminine or androgynous traits or that they are equally masculine and feminine and hence highly androgynous.

Bem's work is typical of the kind of perspective adopted by those interested in the social psychology of sexual identity or gender. Her work differs in that she separates psychological identity from biological sex and adds a third possibility the 'liberated' androgynous individual. Unfortunately, the concept of androgyny alone cannot rescue Bem's theory, it still suffers from the same problems as the general sexual identity thesis.

In seeking to define sexual identity or psychological gender for each individual Bem has taken the stereotypes student judges can generate for the majority of Americans and elevated them to the status of universal truths about the nature of masculinity and femininity. Her work is linked to common sense models of sexual difference in an unacceptable way. Unable to find and defend many empirical and substantive differences in character traits between the sexes, the sexual identity thesis appears here to resort to stereotyping to pad out its supposition that if two biological sexes exist then different feminine or masculine realms of experience must exist as well. Bem takes everyday stereotypes of men and women and encourages those who fill in the inventory to believe that conformity to these stereotypes means being 'truly' feminine or masculine.

It should be clear how this type of approach reifies sex as a determinant of behaviour, and homogenises people, maximising inter-sex differences and intra-sex similarities. Just as Lessing's text sees all women as psychologically interchangeable because subjective experience is continually linked to the natural category, female, so the social psychology of gender separates people into two psychological categories and ignores individual variety. Perhaps men and women are not, after all, psychologically different? We should at least question the main assumption of the sexual identity thesis as opposed to artificially propping it up, through the study of stereotypes disguised as the study of gender.

It should also be clear how Bem's Sex-Role Inventory like Lessing's text constructs imaginary identities. People can recognise themselves in the sex-role inventory just as they can recognise themselves in Lessing's novels. The identities discovered, however, are still imaginary. They are not what they appear. Portrayed in both places as concrete parts of experience, as character traits or, in the case of Lessing, as subjective emotional reactions, these identities are better viewed as social and linguistic constructions. When we read Lessing or fill in a personality inventory we are not so much learning phenomenological or even behavioural truths about ourselves, we are adopting for the meantime the ways of making sense of self presented in the text. And, we are even more likely to accept the version of self offered to us if it is couched in the conventions of realism.

The reification evident in Bem's work is only a small part of the general reification of the biological categories, women and men, and the psychological categories masculine and feminine, throughout social psychology. This process has been particularly evident for the categories woman and feminine.

A woman's biological sex has traditionally marked her difference in social psychology and has indicated the need for special, sexually-contingent, essentialist, theories. As we have noted throughout, women, like blacks, children, the working class, etc. have generally been treated as a 'group', requiring a special research perspective and even their own chapters in textbooks. Admittedly there is a great deal of point to this separation. However, it has had the important but unintended consequence of marking off the category human or mankind (sic) from the category female. (37) Two areas of research have emerged: one investigates general human processes, the other investigates women as a special group. As Black and Coward have pointed out, men consequently become desexed; as representatives par excellence of the category human, their biology does not usually generate a demand for special theories. (38)

In line with this emphasis, the main questions asked have resembled Freud's classic 'what do women really want?' Or now, more reflexively, women researchers have been asking 'what it means to a woman to be a woman'. (39) The effect of these types of question along with the general sexual identity thesis has, unfortunately, often only served to establish even more firmly the marginal position of women which was the subject of investigation in the first place. This result appears to be an inevitable consequence of the assumption that experience or psychology is intrinsically connected to types of people rather than constructed more generally through language.

John Shotter has argued that social psychology has a quasi-moral or political responsibility towards the people it studies. (40) Unlike other sciences, the social sciences are confronting reflexive human agents who will try on the images suggested to them for size and will circulate them further. This argument seems particularly applicable to the imaginary identities articulated by gender research. Everyone 'knows' that women need assertiveness training, lack confidence, are people-centred rather than task-centred, partly because these images are reinforced by the psychology of sexual difference and some sociology of sex-roles. (41) It is in light of these comments that social psychology's failure to investigate the ideological and general social functions of the concepts of gender and the particular identities it recommends becomes especially telling.

Social psychology, says Moscovici, has been engaged in a long interview with society about itself. Psychologists have uncritically adopted contemporary cultural and social values and used them to decide what topics are important and how they should be investigated. (42) This argument is developed further in Chapter 5. The sexual identity thesis in general and Bem's work in particular seem to be good examples of this process. Most of the tenets of this research reflect common sense (not necessarily a bad thing in itself) but very few of them have ever been seriously questioned. It is this process of critical questioning that this chapter recommends; social psychology in our view needs the kind of critical deconstruction which the category literature has recently received.

Finally, perhaps the most startling aspect of Bem's work is her decontextualisation of sex. Gender identities are seen in the inventory in abstract, independently of the kind of situations in which they may seem relevant. Literature also dresses up a cultural repertoire of images as 'real experience'; however, at least there, each image is presented in a context or situation. An urgent task facing the social psychologist, therefore, is not merely the study of sexual talk or everyday discourse about roles, stereotypes and identities but the investigation of how this talk functions in different situations.

In conclusion, then, we can formulate a rather different approach to the social psychology of gender. Instead of treating gender as an inherent property of people, we can start to examine the ways in which people adopt particular 'versions' of sexual identity for characterising their own and others' actions in specific situations. Furthermore, we can direct our attention towards the issue of what is 'achieved' by these different kinds of accounts. We have discussed this question in a preliminary way earlier, when looking at the different uses of the discourse of romantic fulfilment in the texts of Lessing, Cartland and Cooper. The next stage would be to look at the use of these versions in different sorts of everyday discourse. In the chapter which follows we will extend this perspective to the notion of 'place' and look in detail at the way it is used in both literary and ordinary talk.

2 CHARACTER AND ENVIRONMENT

The previous chapter provided a discussion of the ways in which certain categories of feminine experience can be seen to be articulated in literary and socio-psychological discourse. Despite their supposedly different emphases a striking uniformity is revealed in the way in which femininity is reified in the two fields. Even in supposedly critical literary and socio-psychological analyses we find a shared form of sense-making which takes femininity as an enduring aspect of discrete individuals. We suggested that this implicit notion of sex-role can only be transcended by way of a more rigorous analysis of feminine discourse.

The substantive concern in this chapter is with 'place', with the 'sense of place' which can have us attach such deep and important values to our surroundings and to remembered or imagined locales. The concern is widely shared. Like the question of sex-roles, it has acquired considerable significance in contemporary culture - through the environmental movement of the 1960s and 1970s. Psychology was influenced by this movement, to acquire a sub-discipline of environmental psychology. (1) As it developed, and typically pronounced that the 'place-specificity of behaviour is the fundamental fact of environmental psychology' or that place is a 'psychological unit of the geographical environment', hopes were raised that a new understanding of this fundamental construct might be found.

In what follows we shall show how a coincidentally simultaneous reading of a Thomas Hardy novel and an analysis of psychological studies of environmental crowding revealed similarities in one set of structures or 'code' by which we can make sense of 'place' in the two types of discourse, as well as in an example of everyday talk. After brief suggestions about how the concept could be elaborated in Hardy criticism and in environmental psychology, we point to some difficulties which arise from the use of the code. If a dual reading between literature and psychology produces shared forms of sense-making, they are not mutually legitimising so much as indicative of higher-order problems in the analysis of discourse.

31 Chapter 2

ENVIRONMENT AND PSYCHOLOGY

To give an instance, how might our understanding be enriched of this woman's sense of place? What follows is a short extract from her much longer description of the estate on which she lives in the New Town of Milton Keynes. (2) She describes the walk from her home to the local shops.

> In the square on the right side there is a house which the owner has recently painted in yellow and brown, the colours of a Pullman coach, and I really like it. There have been very few houses on the estate painted by their owners.
> The second play area on the right, my daughter is a devil to get past with. There are ramps and steps and also it has some lovely cylinders made out of solid concrete. There is also a little climbing-frame for smaller children. My daughter can just manage it.
> Coming farther down the path, there is a Japanese lady in the end house whom I often help with her English. Arriving at Market Hill - to the right there is that wonderful slide, which is the greatest amenity of the estate as far as the children are concerned. Nearby there is a place to sit. Probably this would be the place where I would most likely sit and talk to people, because the shop is nearby. Here I would watch Abby go round and round the slide, and look at people come and go to and from the shop. There would also be people waiting for the telephone sitting on the bench.

Environmental psychology contains studies of colour aesthetics, the connotative meaning of artefacts, personal control, home ownership, play environments and the spatial world of children, neighbourhoods and mixed communities, and the distribution of facilities. All those topics can be disaggregated from the passage above. And yet it is difficult to reassemble them from the psychological literature into a new Gestalt which provides the insight we long for.

If one examines a volume explicitly devoted to the 'psychology of place', (3) its contents again look as though they should increase our understanding of the experience of a place like the estate where the woman lived. They include studies of cognitive mapping, distance estimation, environmental evaluation, behaviour as appropriate or inappropriate to particular places, role differences in environments, and design decision-making. But however valuable these attempts may be at formally recording and measuring environmental behaviour, they disappoint when one looks to capture an experience of place. The disappointment reflects more than the gulf which has separated behavioural from phenomenological approaches to psychology. It has to do with a whole series of puzzles about the space between different areas of discourse.

One of the most frequently referred to topics of environmental psychological research in the textbooks is 'crowding'. And the origin of the present chapter lies in the coincidence of reading <u>The Mayor of Casterbridge</u> (4) while en route to a conference on 'The human consequences of crowding' in Southern Turkey. In Thomas Hardy's novel there are some striking descriptions of a 'crowded place' - the market-place in Casterbridge. Spatially, and through its association with commerce and work, this place provides a major focus in the novel. Much of my reading of The Mayor on this occasion was done during a protracted stopover in Istanbul. On arrival at the conference in Antalya it was quickly apparent that the academic papers on offer conveyed none of the teeming and uproarious streets of Istanbul. They had little to say about crowding as a personal, social or political phenomenon. Typically the psychological study of crowding has tended to concentrate on its effects on the individual, human organism; and when solutions for its ill-effects have been proposed they have been of a rational, bureaucratic kind.

I had decided beforehand that my contribution at the conference would be to try to uncover something of the unsatisfactory nature of the psychological work on crowding by analysing the assumptions which it made about the nature of Man and his relation to society. (5) In the event this analysis also seemed applicable in a reading of The Mayor of Casterbridge. The contingency of travelling with Hardy to Antalya gave rise to an impetus to read and make sense of, within a common framework, two quite different types of discourse about crowded places. The experience incidentally brought home a realisation of how much space I had allowed to intrude between two long-standing interests, psychology and the novel, even when their substance coincided with a central concern in my own life.

MODELS OF MAN

The common framework which I used for the analysis was provided by the notion of 'models of Man'. Psychologists have a recently renewed realisation that such models incorporate important aspects of the stipulations which lie behind their theories and experiments. (6) A model is usually implicit only, it has strong normative elements and embodies much of the ideology of psychology. A complex classification of alternative types of model might be possible. But we shall simplify the question here by making a crude distinction between three ways of considering Man and society, which will be referred to as 'organismic', 'role' and 'relational' models. (7)

The 'organismic' model is quite well characterised by behaviourism. Man is seen as a passive object; as determined by his basic biological nature; and as an individual, rather than as an essentially social being. There is a mechanical flavour to the model. It deals with the present and future as essentially a replication of the past. Static conditions or equilibrium are assumed to be the appropriate mode. The environment or a 'place' would be defined as a set of stimuli which moves and contains the individual, without regard for his own powers or his relations with others.

The approach through roles, as in 'role theory', has been described in these terms:

Man has certain positions within the social system and related to these positions are normative expectations concerning the individual's behaviour and concerning relevant attributes. Positions are independent of a specific occupant. The same is true of the expectations directed towards a position; they are defined as the role of the incumbent of a position. (8)

Man's definition is in social terms, without reference to his individuality or to his relations as a person with others. A place would be conceived of in predominantly organisational, institutional or categorical terms.

In a relational model, Man is active and acting. He is both a subject and an object, influencing and being influenced by his social environment. He is not conceived of as a bundle of traits or their properties, but as his social relations. Man is the sum of his social interactions. Throughout his constant interaction with others, his self is continuously changing. Interaction is fully reciprocal. Unlike the assumptions of the other two models, relational assumptions give priority neither to the individual nor to social processes. In this case, a place would be seen as an environment which facilitates Man's own attempts to relate to other individuals and to become integrated in a reciprocal relation with social and political institutions.

For the present argument the fact that these models may be neither mutually exclusive nor exhaustive will be ignored. The crucial point is that they have been detected as unwitting assumptions underlying the greater part of social psychology. They have emerged from the discipline of social psychology; they have not been the formal and explicit basis for its organisation. In the particular case of psychological research into crowding, studies can not only be categorised by the assumptions which they make, but the assumptions can also be seen to contain dubious implications for policy which might follow from the research.

To demonstrate the nature of these models and the effective use to which they can be put in narrative, we need only refer to the opening pages of <u>The Mayor of Casterbridge</u>. Considerable critical attention has been paid to the beginnings of Hardy's novels. The remarks made here could be repeated for other instances.

The novel begins with a passage describing the approach of a couple and child to the village of Weydon Priors. There is a clear transition through the three models. The first paragraph contains very slight organismic, then role references: 'were approaching on foot', 'plainly but not ill clad'. The second paragraph reiterates these models at greater length, and the relational model appears in paragraph three. The male character's physique is first described (organismic), followed by details of his clothes and more particularly of the tools of his trade (role). His way of walking is analysed and read as a further indication of his economic status. Then, in the next paragraph, allusions are made to the couple's relationship, from the way in which they walk side-by-side, silently and without contact. Immediately afterwards a new cycle of transitions begins: first with a physical description of the young woman's face; then an inference of the role positions of the three characters (husband, wife and daughter); and finally the supposition that the relationship between husband and wife was one of 'stale familiarity'.

The ease and power with which the reader is drawn into Hardy's novels by the use of structures such as this should prepare us for a more thorough search for their presence at other points of the narratives. The search would be far from disappointing. Their effectiveness, the facility with which they can be read, also suggest that they are not a recent invention of psychology, but a well-established and readily available code.

CASTERBRIDGE MARKET-PLACE

Let us now turn to the market-place in Casterbridge, as it is described in Chapters 9,22,23, and 24 of the novel. Lucetta, with whom Mayor Henchard has some years previously had a love affair, inherits a fortune and travels from Jersey to settle in Casterbridge. She hopes to resume the relationship. In the event she marries Farfrae, the protégé and subsequently the business rival of Henchard. Before that Farfrae had seemed likely to marry Henchard's daughter, Elizabeth-Jane.

On her arrival Lucetta rents a large house in the centre of Casterbridge. High-Place Hall is the scene of some of the most important events in the development of relations between the principal characters. Its position overlooking the market-place is used by Hardy as the mise-en-scène for the realisation of Lucetta's attraction to Farfrae. The progressive descriptions in the novel of the market-place illustrate views of people and places which move from the organismic to the role-based to the relational.

It is in Chapter 9 that the market-place is first described.

> It was about ten o'clock, and market-day, when Elizabeth paced up the High street.... The old-fashioned fronts of these houses, which had older than old-fashioned backs, rose sheer from the pavement, into which the bow-windows protruded like bastions, necessitating a pleasing *chassez-déchassez* movement to the time-pressed pedestrian at every few yards. He was bound also to evolve other Terpsichorean figures in respect of door-steps, scrapers, cellar-hatches, church buttresses, and the overhanging angles of walls which, originally unobtrusive, had become bow-legged and knock-kneed.
> In addition to these fixed obstacles which spoke so cheerfully of individual unrestraint as to boundaries, movables occupied the path and roadway to a perplexing extent. First the vans of the carriers in and out of Casterbridge, who hailed from Mellstock, Weatherbury, The Hintocks, Sherton-Abbas, Kingsbere, Overcombe, and many other towns and villages round. Their owners were nu-

merous enough to be regarded as a tribe.... Their vans had just
arrived, and were drawn up on each side of the street in close
file, so as to form at places a wall between the pavement and the
roadway. Moreover every shop pitched out half its contents upon
trestles and boxes on the kerb, extending the display each week a
little further and further into the roadway, despite the expostu-
lations of the two feeble old constables, until there remained
but a tortuous defile for carriages down the centre of the
street, which afforded fine opportunities for skill with the
reins. (9)

This description coincides with Elizabeth-Jane's first impression of
the market-town as she goes to see Henchard for the first time. It
is the scene as it would appear to a stranger. The account is much
more of a detached, objective record than later descriptions of the
market-place in the novel. People are presented primarily as organ-
isms. There is no particular attention to their roles in society,
other than the fact that they are at market. There are no indications of their relations in the sense intended here. In the immediately following paragraph, which could almost be read as an introduction to the present-day study of non-verbal communication, the
market men are vividly described as isolated individuals signalling
to one another across empty space. The social and relational context is as minimal as in a psychological experiment. (This is not
to say that the language used cannot be read as having social and
relational content; but the passage is not written in such a way
as to draw on that content for the purposes of the story as it is
being currently pursued.) The physical setting, or place, has a
similar significance. The scene is described, for example, in terms
of buildings and other objects as obstacles to free movement. Hardy
is giving a highly literary account of circulation problems. But if
the market-place is very crowded, the crowding is given no particular social or relational significance as it is in later chapters.

When Lucetta moves into High-Place Hall it is described as being:

empty for a year or two, while before that interval its occupancy
had been irregular. The reason for its unpopularity was soon
made manifest. Some of its rooms overlooked the market-place;
and such a prospect from such a house was not considered desirable or seemly by its would-be occupiers. (10)

And we are led to interpret its undesirable location primarily in
terms of the 'organismic' image which we have gained of the market-
place - in psychological jargon, as a place carrying 'high sensory
overload'.

Shortly after Lucetta has taken up residence in the house, she is
found waiting with Elizabeth for a call from Mr Henchard. She
watches him move about in the busy market-place below.

They sat in adjoining windows of the same room in Lucetta's great
stone mansion, netting, and looking out upon the market, which
formed an animated scene.... The farmers as a rule preferred the

36 Chapter 2

> open *carrefour* for their transactions, despite its inconvenient jostlings and the danger from crossing vehicles, to the gloomy sheltered market-room provided for them. Here they surged on this one day of the week, forming a little world of leggings, switches, and sample bags....
> All over-clothes here were worn as if they were an inconvenience, a hampering necessity. Some men were well-dressed; but the majority were careless in that respect, appearing in suits which were historical records of their wearer's deeds, sun-scorchings, and daily struggles for many years past. Yet many carried ruffled cheque-books in their pockets which regulated at the bank hard by a balance of never less than four figures. In fact, what these gibbous human shapes specially represented was ready money - money insistently ready - not ready next year like a nobleman's - often not merely ready at the bank like a professional man's, but ready in their large plump hands.
> It happened that to-day there rose in the midst of them all two or three tall apple-trees standing as if they grew on the spot; till it was perceived that they were held by men from the cider-districts who came here to sell them, bringing the clay of their county on their boots. Elizabeth-Jane, who had often observed them, said, 'I wonder if the same trees come every week?'
> 'What trees?' said Lucetta, absorbed in watching for Henchard. Elizabeth replied vaguely, for an incident checked her. Behind one of the trees stood Farfrae.... Elizabeth-Jane sighed.
> 'Are you particularly interested in anybody out there?' said Lucetta.
> 'O no,' said her companion, a quick red shooting over her face. Luckily Farfrae's figure was immediately covered by the apple-tree.
> Lucetta looked hard at her. 'Quite sure?' she said.
> 'O yes,' said Elizabeth-Jane.
> Again Lucetta looked out. 'They are all farmers, I suppose?' she said.
> 'No. There's Mr Bulge - he's a wine merchant; there's Benjamin Brownlet - a horse dealer; and Kitson, the pig breeder; and Yopper, the auctioneer; besides maltsters, and millers - and so on.' Farfrae stood out quite distinctly now; but she did not mention him. (11)

The first account of the market-place was a relatively objective description, as it might have appeared to Elizabeth-Jane as she moved along the High Street. It was free of any particular significance for the relations of the principal characters in <u>The Mayor of Casterbridge</u>. Now, the view is from above, from a first-floor window, as it appears to the two young women. The significance of the scene for Elizabeth-Jane is in Farfrae's appearance. For Lucetta it is less charged. She is introduced to the roles of people they observe, by way of their occupation, and understands that they are not all farmers, undifferentiated as to role. The greater part of the passage is concerned with observations that bear primarily on the social status of the market-goers.

Place is referred to in social terms: 'mansion', 'open *carrefour* for their transactions', 'sheltered market-room provided'. Clothes, and even more so money, have always been indicators of social position or role. Expectations about people's behaviour and values follow readily on observing what they wear, how much money they have or how they use it. Fashion has been interpreted by social scientists as primarily a device for communicating aspects of the wearer's position in society. For some, money is the entire key to the analysis of social roles.

The market-place is now a 'world of leggings, switches and sample-bags'. Suits tell a man's story. The social worlds of farmer, nobleman and professional are characterised by their dealings with money. The man who sells cider apple-trees advertises himself and his trade by appearing with his trees. This role-prop is used at the critical moment of the passage as far as the developing relations of the characters are concerned. It saves Lucetta from spotting Farfrae and Elizabeth-Jane's interest in him.

Two chapters further on Lucetta's interest has also turned to Farfrae:

> ... in addition to Lucetta's house being a home, that raking view of the market-place which it afforded had as much attraction for her as for Lucetta. The *carrefour* was like the regulation Open Place in spectacular dramas, where the incidents that occur always happen to bear on the lives of the adjoining residents. Farmers, merchants, dairymen, quacks, hawkers, appeared there from week to week, and disappeared as the afternoon wasted away. It was the node of all orbits.
> From Saturday to Saturday was as from day to day with the two young women now. In an emotional sense they did not live at all during the intervals. Wherever they might go wandering on other days, on market-day they were sure to be at home. Both stole sly glances out of the window at Farfrae's shoulders and poll. His face they seldom saw, for, either through shyness, or not to disturb his mercantile mood, he avoided looking towards their quarters.
> Thus things went on, till a certain market-morning brought a new sensation.... (12)

A new-fashioned agricultural implement, a horse-drill, appears in the market-place. It attracts an interested crowd. Among them is Farfrae. The two young women decide to go down to look at the instrument. They meet Henchard, with whom they each have an embarrassed exchange. He ridicules the machine and the man who recommends it, Farfrae. He leaves, and the women speak with Farfrae.

> In the silence which followed Farfrae appeared only conscious of her; to have passed from perception of Elizabeth into a brighter sphere of existence than she appertained to. Lucetta, discerning that he was much mixed that day, partly in his mercantile mood and partly in his romantic one, said gaily to him:
> 'Well, don't forsake the machine for us,' and went indoors with her companion. (13)

The significance of the market-place has moved from being simply a bustling, crowded setting for human figures seen from afar to being a place with deep, emotional resonance for the two women through whose eyes it has been presented. The house is no longer architecturally described. It is a home rather than a mansion. It is the focus of threads of interpersonal relations rather than a sign of affluence and social position. The location of High-Place Hall may have been disagreeable to most prospective tenants. To Lucetta and her companion, Elizabeth, it could not have been better situated. At the beginning of the passage just quoted Hardy is quite explicit about the part being played in his narrative by the house and by the market-place.

A new element appears. Commerce is one of the major components of a market-place, and indeed of <u>The Mayor of Casterbridge</u>. Now it is given its significance as the context for the relationship between Lucetta, Henchard and Farfrae. The rivalry of the two men and Henchard's animosity is clearly stated. Here, Lucetta actually comes down into the world of commerce rather than observing it from above, as she did before. But she leaves when she finds Farfrae unable to disentangle his relation to her from his business concerns.

The world of agricultural commerce also envelops the incident which had catalysed Lucetta and Farfrae's mutual attraction in the previous chapter. It encapsulates in a developing sequence of events a transition from an organismic to a role to a relational view of people and place. The two characters' realisation of their new relationship is seen against a recapitulation of the earlier significances of the market-place. To give the full flavour of this transition the passage is cited at length.

It is the day of the great Candlemas fair. Farfrae visits High-Place Hall to see Elizabeth. He finds only Lucetta.

> 'The fair to-day seems a large one,' she said when, by a natural deviation, their eyes sought the busy scene without. 'Your numerous fairs and markets keep me interested. How many things I think of while I watch from here!' ... 'Do you look out often?' he asked.
> 'Yes - very often.'
> 'Do you look for anyone you know?'
> Why should she have answered as she did?
> 'I look as at a picture merely. But,' she went on, turning pleasantly to him, 'I may do so now - I may look for you. You are always there, are you not? Ah - I don't mean it seriously! But it is amusing to look for somebody one knows in a crowd, even if one does not want him. It takes off the terrible oppressiveness of being surrounded by a throng, and having no point of junction with it through a single individual.' (14)

Lucetta herself is made to comment directly on the transition from the market-place as a setting for undifferentiated human beings to its being a place with particular relational meaning. And in doing

Chapter 2

so she admits of her interest in Farfrae, for the first time to his face.

They talk briefly about their previous lives. Then:

> The fair without the windows was now raging thick and loud. It was the chief hiring fair of the year.... In substance it was a whitey-brown crowd flecked with white - this being the body of labourers waiting for places. The long bonnets of the women, like waggon-tilts, their cotton gowns and checked shawls, mixed with the carters' smock-frocks; for they, too, entered into the hiring. Among the rest, at the corner of the pavement, stood an old shepherd, who attracted the eyes of Lucetta and Farfrae by his stillness. He was evidently a chastened man.... He had planted the stem of his crook in the gutter and was resting upon the bow, which was polished to silver brightness by the long friction of his hands.... A little way off negotiations were proceeding which had reference to him....
> The negotiations were between a farmer from a distant county and the old man's son. In these there was a difficulty. The farmer would not take the crust without the crumb of the bargain, in other words, the old man without the younger; and the son had a sweetheart on his present farm, who stood by, waiting the issue with pale lips.
> 'I'm sorry to leave ye, Nelly,' said the young man with emotion. 'But, you see, I can't starve father, and he's out o'work at Lady-day. 'Tis only thirty-five mile.'
> The girl's lips quivered. 'Thirty-five mile!' she murmured. 'Ah! 'tis enough! I shall never see 'ee again!'.... and she turned her face to Lucetta's wall to hide her weeping....
> Lucetta's eyes, full of tears, met Farfrae's. His, too, to her surprise, were moist at the scene. (15)

Farfrae goes down to the group and manages their sorrowful situation by hiring the old man and the son himself. He returns to Lucetta in her house. But the world of work not only brings them together, it intervenes between them.

> ... Farfrae again looked out of the window into the thick of the fair.
> Two farmers met and shook hands, and being quite near the window their remarks could be heard as others' had been.
> 'Have you seen Mr Farfrae this morning?' asked one. 'He promised to meet me here at the stroke of twelve.... he's mostly a man to his word.'
> 'I quite forgot the engagement,' murmured Farfrae.
> 'Now you must go,' said she; 'must you not?'....
> He looked anxiously at the farmer who was seeking him, and who just then ominously walked across to where Henchard was standing, and he looked into the room and at her. 'I like staying; but I fear I must go!' he said. 'Business ought not to be neglected, ought it?'....
> 'What has happened to us to-day is very curious.'
> 'Something to think over when we are alone, it's like to be?'
> ....

'Well, whatever it has been, it is now over; and the market calls you to be gone.'
'Yes, yes. Market-business! I wish there were no business in the warrld.' (16)

In this incident Lucetta and Farfrae reveal to one another, in their different ways, an interest and concern for the romantic. From it can be seen to follow the development of their relationship and their marriage. It is worked out in relation to events in the market-place which is the 'Open Place' of the story and which is successively seen in the three frameworks we are dealing with.

Against the background of the organismic throng, the old shepherd is introduced. Initially he too is simply a figure, read through his posture, a human organism who supports himself on a stick which has been polished by his hand in use. But the stick is a crook - a sign of his occupation, just as the apple-trees of the cider farmers. And his role in society is at the heart of the negotiations which are going on. Finally, the relational or interpersonal aspect of these negotiations is produced. They mean a break-up for the young man either with his father or his sweetheart. Thus, in no more than a page, people at the hiring fair are successively seen in the guises of all three models of Man.

It is the final, relational guise which appropriately evokes the shared emotion and involvement of Lucetta and Farfrae, and which provokes the 'curious' event which will bind them together in their thoughts when the market is over and they are alone and apart. Throughout the episode and at its end the significance of the market as a place of business is clarified. As we have already seen, the theme of business takes on more and more importance as the novel progresses.

A SOCIAL SCIENCE OF 'PLACE'

What might be the significance of such an analysis through models of Man for the relationship which we are discussing in this book between literature and social psychology? From the standpoint of social psychology, or the social sciences generally, it is tempting to see literature as a source of new insights and concepts or as a testing ground for hypotheses. This is the approach which has recently been adopted and developed by a number of geographers for example, specifically in relation to the concept of place which they take as a central, organising concept for making sense of our immersion in or interpenetration with the physical world.

A geographical engagement with literature may be very varied, if we follow one recent commentary. (17) Poets, novelists and their writers can be treated as topographers themselves, exercising a particular skill in word-painting. One might look for the geography or topography which lies behind literature, a landscape which stimulates it or organises it; or trace geographical associations in literature, making an atlas of literary references, or guidebook to a favourite author. Literature may provide much of our indirect knowledge about the environment, and so be a key to understanding people's environmental perceptions and attitudes. Sometimes its influence may be so potent as to exercise social control:

> The consistent negative portrayal, or plain neglect, of the North of England at the expense of the South in novels and poems, has contributed to a Southern-based or -biased perceptual frame of reference among the political, financial and business decision-makers in Britain. (18)

Or more optimistically, imaginative or 'false' geographies, such as occur in the pastoral for example, may give rise to alternative and creative perceptions of familiar surroundings.

Substitute 'social processes' for 'geography' in the last paragraph and we could have a general programme for the social psychological use of literature. Depending on their inductive or deductive bias, social psychologists with an interest in 'place' might use Hardy's portrayal of Casterbridge market-place as a source of different sorts of meaning which 'place' can hold, or as a test of the generality of the models of Man. In the first case, they might arrive at a distinction between 'location' (the where of human behaviour as such), 'setting' (the where of behaviour which is defined exclusively in social terms) and 'place' (the where of human relations). Following our version of the models of Man argument, (19) they might conclude that only 'places' are the proper subject of social psychology: only in 'places' is there an examination of an active and reciprocal relation between people and their environment in a full social context. Social psychology must deal with the social interplay between individuals or individuals and their institutions. Individual behaviour as such is the field of psychology, social behaviour as such of sociology. It is the socio-psychological significance of the market-place which one finds in Chapter 24 of The Mayor of Casterbridge at the crucial meeting of Henchard, Farfrae, Lucetta and Elizabeth-Jane in front of the horse-drill.

HARDY'S USE OF PLACE

The interpenetration of relations between people and their environment is an achievement of Hardy's 'novels of character and environment' which has been insufficiently discussed in the critical writing. There has been a great amount of topographical attention, attempting to locate the events of the novels in actual places in Dorset and other parts of Wessex, providing descriptions of those places and relating Hardy's own experience of them. His skill at portraying Wessex, giving one the feel of the landscape, the villages and towns, has been admired. One critic (20) has recently gone further, to argue that a key to understanding the meaning of the novels lies in appreciating how and why Hardy 'changed' the Wessex landscape, that is in mapping the departures from veridicality of his geography. Elsewhere the environment has been analysed as a character in its right, as a series of metaphors for the states of mind of the actors, or as an 'embodiment' of their experience.

These approaches tend to place the environment in the background of human action. They distance 'character' from 'environment', and deny Hardy's essentially 'ecological' achievement. He deals with character-in-environment, in a way that makes the two inseparable; just as a truly social psychology takes the individual-in-society as its unit of study. Characters, and their relations with one another and with the environment are a 'system'. It is the inevitable 'whereness' of Hardy's narrative events that makes the sense of place which has been so much admired, though in so many different ways. One cannot imagine the events transposed to another location; not because, for example, Egdon Heath 'caused' Eustacia Vye to behave as she did in <u>The Return of the Native</u>; but because an essential part of her behaviour is the fact that it happened on and in relation to Egdon Heath. She is not simply Eustacia; she is Eustacia-in-Egdon-Heath. This systemic whereness makes Hardy particularly attractive for a social psychologist who is interested in persons-in-their-environment.

From this viewpoint it is possible to approach the criticism of Hardy's novels and the concerns of an environmental social psychology as having mutual implications for one another. The social psychologist can find in the novels an outline agenda for the study of 'place'. Hardy deals with 'displacement' as well as place; his places are given a clear social reference, particularly through the roles of working-class characters; places are located in a temporal dimension. These components of place are features which are conspicuously lacking from social psychology generally. It has tended to become fixed at one pole of bipolar concepts: studying leadership independently of follower-ship, conformity but not non-conformity, attraction and not repulsion, attitudes but not the absence of any attitude. Despite its apparent reference, most social psychology to date has proceeded in a social vacuum, giving very little attention indeed to social context. Similarly the historical or temporal element has been neglected, partly because of the convenience of instantaneous experimental studies.

There is a variety of space- and place-themes which recur in Hardy and which would fill out this agenda: for example, the elements, weather, the work-place, inns and churches, the dance. The spatial relations of 'inside' and 'outside', particularly of the home, and of people overhearing one another are again and again used to build the narrative. Although most of these elements have been referred to by critics, they have never been taken together in a concentrated study of the way in which Hardy uses place as a figure through which character and environment essentially interpenetrate one another.
(21)

Chapter 2

DECONSTRUCTING ELIZABETH-JANE

Rather than develop this argument further, or more specifically allow, for example, the treatment of Casterbridge market-place to reflect upon the socio-psychological study of crowding, we will finish this chapter on a more thoroughly critical, 'deconstructive' line, by suggesting that a models of Man approach to place in Hardy can be seen to carry with it a fundamental weakness which undermines its objectives. For this purpose we will make some points about the character Elizabeth-Jane in The Mayor of Casterbridge.

On a first reading the various models through which the Casterbridge market-place is presented act as counterpoints to the development of Lucetta and Farfrae's relationship. This is an obvious reading in view of the important part which their relationship plays in promoting Henchard's downfall; and it is his tragedy which is usually taken as the central subject of the novel. His massive temperament tends to obscure alternative readings. But when we pull out the market-place scenes for particular examination, our attention is more easily drawn to Elizabeth-Jane. What is her part in these scenes, and further in the novel as a whole?

The essence of her part, we suggest, is as a contradictory combination of character and authorial device. As a character, she appears most readily as an unsophisticated girl, whose major standard is 'respectability' and who desperately needs to 'become wise'. Her story is one of the gradual acquisition of 'wisdom' or knowledge, along a path of abasement and suffering. The novel ends with her, in a long passage which indicates her developed consciousness: she learns now from teaching others, whereas previously she had tried to learn from silent observation and solitary study.

It is in this earlier state, creeping 'silently about observing the scene', that she fulfils much of her role as authorial device. More than half of the descriptions of Casterbridge are given as through her eyes; and she provides the major viewpoint for about the first one hundred pages of the novel. More than half of the chapters begin with a reference to her, usually in the first paragraph. This is especially the case in the first half of the novel. For readers of the original serial she would initially have provided an instant point of continuity between instalments.

Her position in the market-place passages reveal something of her development as a character and her simultaneous shift from being an authorial device to becoming a person. But it also exemplifies 'contradictions' which persist because of her dual role.

The first, physicalistic description of the market-place is given as though through the 'unpractised eyes' of a girl 'fresh from the seclusion of a seaside cottage' - a patently authorial means of introducing the reader to a new scene. By the next view she has learnt and is able to comment on some of the social structure of the market-town. She has been made aware explicitly of her own role as the Mayor's daughter, in a development which also makes her reject a predominantly physical identity for herself 'as the town beauty'. Both in her new and convenient role as Lucetta's companion, and in her description of the scene from the upstairs window of High-Place Hall she is again doing the author's work; although some more personal significance for her is briefly introduced in the appearance below of Farfrae's figure.

In the following chapter she is no longer necessary. Some familiarity, on the part of Lucetta and Farfrae, with the physical, organismic and social role aspects of the hiring-fair can now be presupposed. Against that background the relational significance of it for them is developed. When Elizabeth-Jane reappears in the episode of the horse-drill, it is as a character in her own right; her part in the episode is of relational significance.

Although her more infrequent appearances in the second half of the novel tend to present her as a person, there are a number of major contradictions between her position as character and as authorial device. We can find them prefigured in the first description of the market-place. Casterbridge is presented as a set of 'metropolitan novelties to the unpractised eyes of Elizabeth-Jane', in spite of Hardy's extended and practised description of them. The reader is uncertain what Elizabeth-Jane is seeing and what is given by the author. And the contradiction also remains ambiguous in the further uncertainty as to whether it is a strictly authorial contradiction, or itself constitutes a representation of Elizabeth-Jane's own unfamiliarity with and distance from the scene.

To illustrate just one more of these contradictions: a particularly striking example occurs in the context of the visit by a Royal Personage to Casterbridge. A drunken Henchard disgraces himself in front of the assembled company. Elizabeth-Jane is there for the ceremony. Her attention is drawn to her father by the gasps of all the ladies. 'Elizabeth-Jane peeped through the shoulders of those in front, saw what it was, and was terrified; and then her interest in the spectacle as a strange phenomenon got the better of her fear.' (22) The curiosity for the reader is that this reaction should occur at a point in the narrative when Elizabeth-Jane's relation to Henchard appears to be particularly close. After a period of painful estrangement, she has become reconciled with him. She is caring for him and, above all, trying to keep him from drink. The semi-colon in the sentence quoted above transforms an intimate interpersonal relation into a mere 'interest' in a 'strange phenomenon'. One senses a callous reduction of Elizabeth-Jane to her earlier position of observer.

With hesitations such as this Elizabeth-Jane progresses from being a mechanical observer of events, and especially of the environments which are characteristic of a Hardy novel, through a number of social roles, albeit for the convenience still of the narrative (to torment Henchard, or to bring Lucetta more easily into the story), until she is a person in her own right. But in the last analysis she is the 'victim' of the developmental structure which we have identified with the 'models of Man' code. She sustains herself as a person with difficulty. Her struggle for 'wisdom' is inauthentic, because her initial naïveté is contrived. At the end of the story, when she finds rest, she is recognised not to be capable of enjoying the happiness which could be hers. The final chapters read less as a last act of attention to her character, rather as an apology for past authorial abuses, if not a convenient way to round off the tale. The final sentences of the novel again deny her identity by their unacknowledged shift into authorial commentary.

Despite the emphasis which we have been able to put upon her, Elizabeth-Jane is more usually a rather invisible character. She scarcely appears in the critical writing on The Mayor of Casterbridge. The novel is interpreted almost exclusively in terms of the story of Henchard, the man of character. It is as though Hardy's title determines the focus of our attention, in the same way in which a social psychological experiment is always taken to be 'about' whatever topic is specified in the title of its report. Elizabeth-Jane is akin to the experimental subject who does not give positive instances of the behaviour explicitly under examination. When reading a report of an experiment on direction-finding, for example, we are usually not allowed an interest in the processes of those subjects who do not find their way. If a capacity to get lost is the focus, then it is the report of the behaviour of those who do find their way which is inattentive and undifferentiated.

Experimental subjects are also the victims of contradiction. They are essential to the playing out of the experiment; but most of their psychological processes are kept in the background, undeveloped. Because of the conventions of the experimental report, they are not explicitly referred to. The experimenter, as author, needs these characters to allow his story to develop, but he allows them only a marginal identity. Hardy, similarly, is prepared to use a character for authorial purposes and in so doing to deny her her full identity as a person. (23)

We do not need to discuss whether the experimenter or Hardy should be accused of political or moral abuse of the status of personhood. The problem is that both the novel and the experiment appear to rest in important respects on contradicting reasonable expectations of how they will treat persons, expectations which implicitly they establish. Readers appear to be unaware of the contradictions, and so tend to connive with them, in particular if they adopt a realist reading. The antidote is to see both experiment and novel as a construction, and to focus attention on the means by which such constructions are achieved. This we have done for parts of The Mayor of Casterbridge. Whether the means in turn have moral or political correlatives is an important, but here a separate, question.

FRAGMENTATION THROUGH MODELS

It is Hardy's use of a 'models of Man' code in particular which sets up expectations for Elizabeth-Jane which are not fulfilled. Contradictions leave her development as a character in a fragmented state.

The code may be as damaging in psychology. In 1972 when Israel discussed the three models used here, it was exciting to have apparently found a basis for clearly differentiating social psychology from sociology and psychology; and a means of criticising much that previously had passed under the label of 'social psychology', but which was almost exclusively individualistic. If Mead and Marx could be considered as parents of the relational model, that only added to the excitement. (24) But the outcome of following this path is to fragment the human subject under study in quite as damaging a way as occurs in the individualistic or collectivistic theories which implicitly are under attack. (25) The analysis of studies of crowding, (26) referred to at the beginning of the chapter concluded that restricted individualistic or collectivist assumptions actually constituted a large measure of so-called 'problems of crowding'. If the psychologist merely assimilates the assumptions rather than transcends them he cannot hope to counter the problem.

We would not argue that an analytic distinction between different models of Man is fundamentally untenable. The intelligibility of the operation refutes that. The readability of, for example, the opening of The Mayor of Casterbridge and the facility with which our attention is progressively drawn into the tale as it expands through the models suggest that they do offer a readily available framework for reading, for making sense of phenomena. But their separation also produces problems, both in literature and psychology. And its allure conceals what can follow any analytic operation, the demanding and creative task of synthesis.

At the risk of appearing to naturalise such a synthesis, we can refer back to the material cited earlier, in which a woman describes her walk through the Eaglestone estate at Milton Keynes. (27) In the two following passages we indicate what may be organismic, role, and relational components in the discourse.

> In the square on the right side there is a house which the owner has recently painted in yellow and brown, the colours of a Pullman coach, and I really like it. There have been very few houses on the estate painted by their owners.
>
> The second play area on the right, my daughter is a devil to get past with. There are ramps and steps and also it has some lovely cylinders made out of solid concrete. There is also a little climbing-frame for smaller children. My daughter can just manage it.
>
> Coming farther down the path, there is a Japanese lady in the end house whom I often help with her English. Arriving at Market Hill - to the right there is that wonderful slide, which is the greatest amenity of the estate as far as the children are con-

cerned. <u>Nearby there is a place to sit</u>. Probably this would be the place where I would most likely sit and talk to people, because the shop is nearby. Here I could watch Abby go round and round the slide, and look at people come and go to and from the shop. There would also be people waiting for the telephone sitting on the bench.

I can give you more details about the setting and what happens there if you want. <u>Straightaway, coming out of the house into this little square, I am aware of what a shabby state these so-called 'front gardens', Council-maintained, always are</u>. I usually look at mine and Edna's, the lady from number 15, because they are nice. <u>Here, in this space, I am very likely to stop and talk to neighbours because these are the people I live closest to</u>, and I am on first-name terms with almost everybody in this terrace. <u>To get to the Ferndale playground I usually come on this side of the houses. I could go around this way, but this way takes me close to the garages</u> and I do not want to encourage my daughter to go in that direction. And that is actually not the most direct route to the swings.

This analysis is crude, and very far from definitive. Some words and phrases undoubtedly contain more than one component; and the content of some is very much open to question. But the striking feature of the woman's description is not just that it can be read without difficulty as containing all three types of component. She moves rapidly between them at her ease, and does so throughout a transcript which runs to many pages. An effect of this example of everyday discourse is to blur the distinctions between components which in literary and psychological discourse may become fragmented. Thus, there is no inevitable consequence of fragmentation in the models code.

Of course the risk of naturalising a particular interpretation is very real. We are not suggesting that everyday discourse is superior in any sense. Further analysis might well show that the woman's discourse is problematic in its own particular manner of articulation through models of Man. This problem would then become the focus of interest, as it did in the case of Elizabeth-Jane. Similarly the fragmentation of models in psychology, how it is achieved and some of its consequences, is equally interesting in its own right. Indeed the use of the models code in different forms of discourse is more interesting for us than drawing sharp distinctions between those forms.

CONCLUSION

We began this chapter with a hope that literature might yield greater insights into the notion of 'sense of place' than psychology appeared able to do. At first Hardy appeared, in the particular instance of Casterbridge market-place, to be able to present a much more elaborated picture of place than one would find in socio-psychological texts; but one which also was concordant with the relatively advanced meta-analysis of social psychology presented by Israel. At the same time the 'models' code might be taken as a useful socio-psychological resource for clarifying certain narrative devices.

In the latter half of the chapter, however, we detected fundamental 'weaknesses' in Hardy's picture; and weaknesses which are shared by social psychology. These in turn were seen to be a product of reading. The violation of personal identity and the manipulative relation in which the realist reader becomes implicated come from allowing oneself to build up expectations of the novelist and the psychologist which the inherent weaknesses of his practice could never allow him to fulfil.

Our conclusion is that the contiguous study of literature and social psychology may sometimes contribute not so much to substantive insights, as to understanding the ways in which these forms of discourse are constructed, and to defining higher order problems for the analysis of discourse.

PART 2

3 SOME UNSATISFACTORY POSITIONS

There has been no real tradition of interchange between social psychology and literary criticism, although there have been fragmentary attempts by psychologists to draw upon literature and by literary critics to explicitly use psychological theorising. The reason for this poor integration of two disciplines which apparently share a number of mutual concerns is to be found in their basic presuppositions: the causal, individualistic model of influence underlying traditional social psychology and the 'truth and insight' model of writing which underlies traditional literary criticism.

The shortcomings and limitations inherent in these assumptions are displayed in the sorts of interchange that have taken place. For the most part this has followed one of four basic forms. Firstly, studies have examined the influence of various kinds of literary text on readers, trying to assess what sort of effect texts have and how strong it is. Secondly, work has been carried out which tries to explain why texts take the form that they do. Sometimes reference is made to the particular psychological make-up of the author, while in other cases the structure of the text is related to the psychology of readers. Thirdly, literary texts have been looked at as a resource for social psychology, which may assist teaching, theory construction or possibly theory testing. Here texts are treated as exemplars of social psychological work, as social data, or even as fully formed social psychological theories. Finally, traditional literary critics have on occasion drawn upon certain formal psychological theories and models to assist in the construction of interpretations of particular texts or genres.

Before going on to detail their limitations, let us first overview these approaches to the relationship between psychology and literature and describe some specific research examples from each of them.

FOUR MODELS OF INTERCHANGE

1 Literary Influence

The notion that literature can exert a powerful influence on individuals dates back at least to the discovery of printing. Censorship, which implies the possibility of texts having unwanted (to the powerful) social consequences, seems to have existed for as long as literature itself. Much of this early concern about the 'dangers' of literature seems to have been directed at what might be called 'rational influence': the spreading of information and new ideas, for example on religion and politics. From this perspective literature was seen to influence readers through educating them.

Since this time, however, an alternative view of influence has become increasingly predominant emphasising the power of texts to debase and corrupt and to influence the reader's attitudes in other ways. The text is here seen to have a causal power over the reader. Instead of the reader reassessing a belief, say, in the light of new information, the text is characterised as having a direct influence on the belief. Moreover this is seen as lying outside the reader's sphere of agency. This view was encouraged by Puritan thought which treated children's souls as constantly liable to salvation or damnation. Children's literature was thought to take part in this struggle by placing them on the path to redemption or furthering their slide to the devil. (1)

In increasingly more sophisticated garb, this latter view can be traced through to modern times. It appears, for instance, in the Children's and Young Persons (Harmful Publications) Act of 1955 intended to stop the importation of American 'horror comics', which some saw as a damaging influence on unformed minds. It has been adopted in almost unchanged form by social psychologists. Literature is construed as having a causal influence on the personalities and attitudes of people: salvation and damnation are replaced by the promotion of altruism and the instilling of aggression.

All in all, in spite of the fact that research on the influence of literature has been all but abandoned in recent years for the promise of richer pickings in studying film and television influence, this model has probably stimulated more social psychological research on literature than any of the others. (2)

Some of the most extensive social psychological research on the effects of literature was carried out by the American social psychologist David McLelland in the context of his study of people's 'need for achievement'. (3) McLelland used the contents of children's stories as a central measure in a huge study designed to elucidate the relationship between individuals' motivation to achieve and the actual economic development of different societies. It is not a pure example of the literary influence model because the contents of the stories were conceptualised both as indicators of the general emphasis on achievement in education and child-rearing, and as important influences in themselves. Yet children's literature is conceived by McLelland as one of the principal causes of certain personality changes and thereby broader economic changes as these children reach adulthood. (4)

Adapting Max Weber's ideas about the relationship between Protestant values and the rise in industrialisation and capitalism in the West McLelland suggested that instead of the institution of Protestantism itself, certain values underlying it particularly promote social change: the values which place stress on hard work, excellence and self-reliance for instance. These values were seen to lead parents, teachers, children's authors and so on, to socialise children in such a way that they become highly motivated to achieve; they acquire a 'need for achievement'.

McLelland started to test this theory by taking stories used in schools from 25 different countries and categorising them according to the stress they placed on achievement. In turn, these measures of emphasis on achievement were compared with two measures of gross economic development for these different countries: size of national income and total quantity of electricity produced each year. The comparison appeared to support McLelland's theory. A statistically significant correlation was found between stress on achievement in school reading books in 1925 and the economic measures for the period 1929 to 1950. Of course it is this correlation across different periods which is important, because the theory predicts that although the children's personalities will be influenced the economic effects will only appear when they have grown up. Thus it is worth noting that there was only a small, statistically insignificant correlation between themes in 1950s school books and the economic measures of the same period. It seems, therefore, that McLelland's study demonstrates, apparently on a grand scale, the relationship between childhood socialisation through reading and adult personality development.

This broad study of McLelland's seems to have been generally more successful in showing what appear to be influences from literature than the smattering of small scale experimental studies which have been carried out. (5) The typical form these experiments take is to give some specified group, often adolescents, an attitude or personality questionnaire. They are then asked to read some sort of literary material. Subsequently they will be given another questionnaire and the score on this compared with their original score. By these means it is hoped that any effects of the literature can be measured. And, to make sure that these effects are due to the literature, rather than some other feature of the situation, a 'control group' is asked to undergo a similar procedure but with some non-literary material. Several studies of this kind have been carried out. Yet for the most part they have found little or no effect, and in those cases which do claim a positive finding this seems attributable to some factor other than the literature itself. Loban found, for example, that attitude change was only produced when the children being studied discussed the stories in groups; simply reading them, even out loud to the rest of the group, was insufficient for change. (6)

2 The Psychological Origins of Texts

The type of research just described presumes that texts have causal effects on the reader. In the terminology of psychological experimentation, the literary text is considered to be an 'independent variable', while the effect of reading the text is treated as the 'dependent variable'. Thus, for the McLelland study, the degree of emphasis on achievement themes in school reading books was the independent variable, while national income and electricity production were the dependent variables. The close relation between the two was taken to indicate the causal effect of one variable on the other. Without altering this general approach, it is possible to reconstrue the literary text as a dependent variable and ask why it takes the particular form it does; i.e. what influences the make-up of the text.

Generally this sort of research has looked for parallels between the structure or content of the text and features of the author or reader. It is then inferred that the text duplicates these features in some way. Parallels are established by using a particular psychological theory to pick out and emphasise certain crucial features of the text and other similar features of the author or reader. In particular the theories of Freud and Piaget have been used in this way.

The classic Freudian approach to the social origin of literature treats the text as a direct product of the unconscious mind of its author. Events depicted in the text are understood to be representations of the author's personality dynamics; that is the symbolic fulfilment of wishes or the resolution of conflicts. To take a rather simple example, Goldschmidt has analysed <u>Alice in Wonderland</u> in the light of the supposedly neurotic personality of Charles Dodgson/Lewis Carroll, its author. (7) A number of writers have claimed that Dodgson was unable to form satisfactory relationships with mature women, but had strong affections for certain young girls, notably the girl who served as the model for Alice herself. For Goldschmidt, this regressive behaviour is clearly represented in Dodgson's text by the activities of Alice in the 'hall of mirrors'. After she has tried a tiny key in many large locks in the hall without success, Alice finds that she can use it to unlock a small door which lies hidden behind a curtain. And when it is opened Alice is able to look through the door and into a garden. Goldschmidt relates this sequence directly to Dodgson's unconscious personality dynamics. The key not fitting the locks on the large doors represents his lack of sexual satisfaction with adult women; while the key fitting the small lock stands for his potential sexual gratification with children. Furthermore, the curtain represents the child's skirts and the garden the pleasure that may be obtained underneath them. In this way, Goldschmidt argues, Dodgson's text outlines his repression and his hidden sexual desires are symbolically gratified within it.

The Piagetian version of this model is directed, not surprisingly, at children's literature. Instead of explaining the text by reference to the psychological make-up of the author it attempts to explain the contents of popular texts by reference to their readership. The contents of popular texts are seen to parallel the psychology of children who enjoy reading them. Indeed, it is this parallel which is seen as directly responsible for the work's popularity. This type of explanation has been suggested by Favat to explain why fairy tales are still so widely read and by Singer to explain why the same is true for Winnie-the-Pooh books.

Favat notes that fairy tales are suffused with magic and animism - objects are endowed with human powers - and the predominant constraining force is moral rather than causal. In addition, the hero is depicted as standing in a strongly egocentric relationship to his or her world. These features of the tales are exactly the ones Piaget identifies as important in children's thinking. Thus, Favat concludes, fairy tales are popular because they accurately mirror features of children's developing minds. (8) Singer's argument is very similar. She catalogues a whole panoply of Piagetian phenomena which are found in the make-believe world of Christopher Robin and Pooh Bear: egocentrism, time confusion, animism, ludic symbolism, immanent justice, non-conservation of volume and so on. Pooh at one point explains that the only reason bees make honey is so that he can eat it. Singer sees this as a classic example of egocentric thought in the Piagetian sense, and argues that constant repetition of such features of childish thinking is what makes the books so popular with young children. (9)

It is interesting to note that a form of this model has dominated traditional sociological thinking about literature. In this case, however, the origin of the text is explained by reference to the structure of society. Thus Lukács and Goldmann have used versions of Marxist theory to identify certain homologies between structural features of capitalist society and features of the organisation and content of literary texts. Just as the text can be seen to recapitulate the unconscious personality dynamics of its author so it can be seen to replicate the exchange relationship of market economies. (10)

3 Literature as a Resource

In the past two decades it has become increasingly popular, particularly amongst humanistically orientated social psychologists, to talk of novels as being a storehouse of rich and sophisticated social knowledge, as embodying important truths about society and its members. We have already encountered this perspective in Chapter 1. At its weakest, this approach gives to literature only the subsidiary role of illustrating different social psychological theories for the purpose of teaching. Literature is used because it retains the interest of students or because it displays and dramatises psychological processes situated within their natural human context. Stronger versions, however, suggest that literature can be treated as data which embodies valid descriptions of human action in varied social contexts. Or, more strongly still, literature can be treated as proposing social psychological theories at either an implicit or an explicit level.

In an example of the weaker version of this model Fernandez presents extracts from novels as documents of an inventory of social psychological notions. (11) Each section of this book is labelled according to the usual chapter headings in social psychology textbooks: socialisation, conformity, leadership and so on. Yet, below these headings and after a brief introduction to each concept, lie not discussions of experiments and reviews of findings but stretches of literary prose from 'great' novels. These are intended to dramatise and illustrate central social psychological ideas in terms of the actions of specific characters depicted in the text. Their status as knowledge is, however, left rather vague. In a sense the veracity of psychological concepts is warranted by the text and, in turn, the acuteness and truth of the text is justified by the extent to which it exemplifies scientifically verified theoretical notions.

In stronger versions of this perspective literature is taken not only as an illustration of theories and concepts but actually as a way of enlarging upon them or showing their inadequacy. On the whole there have been more statements of intent than actual analyses of this type. Two researchers, Merrill and Finkelstein, however, have notably gone further than most. Although working broadly within sociology their work also indicates the direction a more distinctively social psychological approach might take. According to Merrill, 'literature is an important *source* of *knowledge* about groups in interaction and the individuals who play their roles in this process. Novels are living *sourcebooks* to which we go for valid *insights*.' (12)

Novels are seen to contain knowledge about a plethora of central social phenomena in the form of penetrating truths which may be retrieved by consulting the appropriate literary text. If the social psychologist only bothers to look, there is a ready-made storehouse of social knowledge openly available in every library. While not attempting any detailed analysis of particular texts, Merrill outlines a way in which such an analysis might be approached. A literary text, she suggests, should be treated as a sort of experiment, with different characters interacting in varied social situations. In this way, literature may expand upon the very limited realm in which social experiments can be carried out in practical circumstances. Social psychologists can certainly set groups simple tasks to solve, or can generate certain minor disturbances in the social fabric; but they cannot so easily design controlled situations in which people's responses to sudden death or heights of emotion can be studied.

Concentrating on Emile Zola's accounts of his own writing, Merrill argues that the novelist invents characters and then lets them interact with each other. The author, from this perspective, thus verifies theories or hypotheses by placing characters in certain situations and studying their reaction. Of course, these characters are not real, flesh and blood human beings; nevertheless, Merrill suggests, their interactions embody valid insights and have a reality which is comparable to that of ordinary people. For great novelists are deeply concerned about the empirical value of their work, and thus wish it to properly represent and illustrate actions which real people placed in similar situations might perform. For Merrill, then, novels embody social theories which are tested out in the symbolic realm of literature.

In a similar vein, Finkelstein stresses that novels are a repository of data, particularly data pertaining to people's subjective experience. As she puts it,

> novels give access to human consciousness in the form of biographical experiences; patterns of interaction; perspectives on self and others; and the process of constructing social meanings. The novels as data allow entry into the lived reality of others, as well as outlining typifications which can be more broadly applied. (13)

Finkelstein illustrates this argument by way of a brief analysis of Susan Sontag's novel <u>Death Kit</u>, which, she argues, demonstrates the link between actions, shared meanings and social values. Yet Finkelstein never seriously addresses the issue of how Sontag's text can be read 'literally' in this way, as a document of psychological connections, nor how her own interpretation is superior to possible alternatives.

4 Psychological Theory in Criticism

In the last approach to the interrelation of psychology and literature we shall consider, psychological theories are drawn upon in the explication and evaluation of literary works. The rationale behind this is that knowledge of the actual way in which people interact, or the structures of their minds, or the organisation of social groups within society, will facilitate an improved understanding of the text and its significance. As opposed to previous lines of investigation the issue at stake here is interpretation not influence. What had seemed opaque, confused or was only partially understood about a text, may be made intelligible through the application of pertinent psychological knowledge.

On the whole, the only formal psychological theorising that literary critics have seriously taken up and applied to different forms of literature has been psychoanalysis. Freud himself, of course, had a considerable interest in applying psychoanalytic theory to literature. He produced studies of <u>King Lear</u> and Wilhelm Jensen's <u>Gradiva</u> and, in probably his best known literary exploration, used the play <u>Oedipus Rex</u> to illustrate one of the central stages in child development. (14) Freud's use of Shakespeare's plays subsequently initiated a virtual industry of psychoanalytically based exegeses of Shakespeare's work, where the changes of intrafamilial desires and conflicts were rung many times. This probably reached a pinnacle of achievement in Ernest Jones's <u>Hamlet and Oedipus</u>, but this style of work still continues. (15)

Traditional psychoanalytic criticism tries to explicate the psychodynamics of the characters which appear in the text. This is seen, for instance, in the considerable literature speculating about the existence of Hamlet's Oedipus complex. Interpretation may then lead into discussions of the text's effect upon readers and, adopting the kind of model we have seen used with Piagetian theory, the psychoanalytic critic may try to explain the popularity of certain literary texts. From this perspective literature is treated as engaging the emotions of readers by metaphorically or covertly presenting the fulfilment of childish, primaeval desires. For example, Holland characterises the role of all literary works as being to 'transform the unconscious fantasy discoverable through psychoanalysis into the conscious meanings discoverable through conventional interpretation.' (16) Often conclusions about reader impact depend upon the previous analysis of the characters' psyches. Thus the reader's repressed wishes are fulfilled through identification with characters who are acting out those particular wishes. (17)

More recently a distinctly different form of psychoanalytically orientated criticism has emerged, which draws upon the semiologically informed theories of the French analyst Jaques Lacan and his followers. (18) However, this embodies very different assumptions about literature, language and analysis from the traditional work. We will not discuss this work directly in this text, although it has influenced some of the newer approaches to criticism discussed in later chapters.

In relation to literary critics' use of psychological theories, it is worth emphasising that it is impossible to draw a clear line between their explicit use of theories and their use of implicit theories, which have become embodied in the everyday discourses of a culture. For instance, Moscovici has shown that psychoanalytic terminology has come to permeate everyday, non-technical accounts of people's actions. (19) In so far as literary criticism inevitably draws upon assumptions about motivation, character, interaction and so forth, it cannot avoid drawing upon explanatory categories which may have originated in the technical discourses of earlier times, a point discussed in Chapter 8. In this sense social theory will enter criticism whether it is invited in or not.

Occasionally psychologists have themselves attempted to look at the process of literary criticism and evaluation. For example Harding has tried to look experimentally at the role of familiarity in the evaluation of poems. (20) He suggested that when no explicit social guides are present the appreciation of poetry would follow the same pattern as the appreciation of any other 'aesthetic object'; namely initial puzzlement and difficulty, followed by enjoyment, and eventually boredom and even dislike. His procedure was to get a large number of undergraduate students to read poems or extracts from poems (presented anonymously) of varying degrees of difficulty. They had to repeat this on a number of occasions, each time providing the experimenter with an evaluation of the poem.

Harding interprets his findings as being in line with his model.

Thus the poems which were initially rated as liked and understood were more likely to be described as not offering much more on further readings, while poems which were seen as too difficult at first were often later described as liked and understood. Furthermore, over a number of readings the participants' evaluations stabilised. These findings, Harding suggests, show that individuals are able to produce stable evaluations in the absence of the external social norms usually provided by experts and authoritative opinion. And he concludes that the educational potential of this form of individual, experiential learning of literary evaluation should be explored. It must be remembered, however, that Harding's work is unusual. In general, psychologists have paid very little attention to literary appreciation and understanding. Harding's work is of interest because it demonstrates how psychologists, using traditional assumptions, might approach literature. (21)

SHORTCOMINGS AND LIMITATIONS

It is hardly surprising that no really successful programme of research has developed from these fragmentary beginnings and that researchers' statements of intent outweigh in number their actual analyses. For each of the kinds of interchange discussed above embodies assumptions which lead to fundamental and unavoidable difficulties. It is only when these tacit assumptions can be explicated and abandoned that a more productive cross-fertilisation may take place. For the sake of clarity only three such assumptions will be highlighted here: the notion that people's actions may generally be explained from a purely individualistic standpoint; that people are passively influenced by literary texts; and that 'reading' texts is a straightforward process of receiving certain 'meanings'. The first two of these assumptions became important topics for dispute in social psychology during the 1970s, when a number of commentators began to question many of the previously tacit presuppositions of the discipline. At the same time a thoroughgoing critique of the assumptions of traditional literary criticism has stressed the complex issues involved in making sense of literary texts. We will discuss each of these assumptions in turn and show how they underlie the work discussed above.

Individualism

Several European social psychologists, notably Moscovici and Tajfel, have suggested that mainstream social psychology has to a large extent underestimated the social dimensions of action and experience. (22) It has done this in a number of ways, but principally by attempting to explain group behaviour in terms of processes which occur solely within or between individuals. Take, for example, the phenomenon of racial stereotypes and prejudice against minority groups. Social psychologists have often treated this as a by-product of purely cognitive processes, in which the operation of various mental strategies for information processing and synthesis artificially and mechanically exaggerate the infrequent, undesirable,

and hence noticeable, actions of minority groups. Despite a low
actual frequency of occurrence the perceptual and informational
salience of action may result in them being seen as more representative of a particular social group than they are in practice, thus
producing a racial stereotype: 'all Jews are shrews and money conscious'. (23) This explanation, based in the cognitive psychology
of individuals, fails to explain exactly those aspects which are
crucial for the understanding of prejudice; namely why particular
activities and social groups are salient in the first place and,
moreover, why out of those salient activities some are given such
derogatory significance. By trying to explain the phenomenon purely
in terms of an individual's cognitive processes the stereotyping
process is mystified. For crucial features of the phenomenon can be
explained only by understanding broader social processes such as the
function of derogatory stereotypes for majority groups and the
socio-political context in which racial categorisation takes place.
(24)

We can see this sort of individualistic bias writ large in McLelland's work on achievement motivation. He treats gross economic
features of whole societies as aggregates of the actions of their
individual members. In turn these individuals' actions are conceived of as produced by a single personality trait internalised in
childhood: the so-called 'need to achieve'. Thus, instead of looking for any distinctively social explanations for different levels
of economic productivity, such as the particular political or economic structures of a country, the level of investment, exploitation
of natural resources and so on, McLelland attempts to produce a
purely individualistic explanation. Moreover, it is not enough to
simply point to the size of McLelland's correlations, for without
some satisfactory model to explain them they stand as mere anomalies. Indeed, it is tempting to invert McLelland's explanatory
schema and view his research as a social product of 1950s America,
as a scientific rationalisation of the ideology of aggressive individualism.

Harding's experimental work on the role of familiarity in the appreciation of literature embodies a second basic individualistic
assumption. This treats the 'individual' and the 'social' as two
separate influences on action. Thus Harding attempts to produce an
experimental situation where people make evaluations of literature
without any social pressures on them. Such pressures are seen as a
distortion of the more natural individual process of evaluation.
The experiment is characterised as one in which the reader naively
engages with the text 'as it is', free from the worst influences of
fashion and orthodoxy. Yet this implicit bias in favour of 'pure'
individual evaluations is based on a false dichotomy. Whether
literature is presented anonymously or not, evaluations will be made
with the aid of certain interpretative resources and criteria (some
diffuse, some specific) which people will have acquired within specific social contexts. Withholding certain information from the
experimental subjects, as Harding does, may make the use of certain
literary assumptions more difficult; it will not, however, prevent
the use of systematic and conventional forms of sense-making.

Traditional psychoanalytic theory also tends towards individualism. Although it does emphasise the construction of people's personalities through interaction, primarily with their parents, on the whole, broader social and ideological processes are ignored. Furthermore, outside the field of early personality development, its explanations stress the determinate role of particular personalities on activity and pay very little attention to other aspects of the social context. Thus, in the example discussed above, Goldschmidt explains the structure of Lewis Carroll's text exclusively by reference to the (abnormal) structure of Carroll's unconscious personality. No reference is made, for instance, to the possible significance of the sexual mores of Victorian England.

Mechanism

Allied to this discussion of individualism in social psychology have been questions of the role given to human agency in social psychological explanations. This debate has involved some highly technical issues in the philosophy of action and explanation, but can be characterised, without doing it too much violence, as being between the attempt to explain behaviour by reference to causal processes which operate in an automatic and lawlike way and attempts which emphasise the necessity of considering people's particular beliefs, reasons and interpretations. (25) Harré and Secord have argued at some length that the prevalence of the former explanatory style in social psychology is to a considerable extent a product of the predominantly experimental approach to behaviour adopted by psychologists. (26) They see the technique of studying changes in people's activity in response to the manipulation of a very restricted range of environmental 'events' as leading directly to the study of people as if they were information processing machines and therefore implicitly excluding the more active model of Man. It is important to stress, however, that this emphasis on the active powers of individuals does not lead back to an individualistic form of explanation. Although thinking and acting are not simply determined by social 'forces', they are both limited and enabled by social resources and the available stock of interpretative systems for making sense of the world.

The experiments on literary influence, both on the small scale and McLelland's large scale study, epitomise this causal approach. They treat the text as a dependent variable which the experimenter manipulates (or finds a natural analogue of that manipulation in the case of McLelland) to produce a causal effect on people's behaviour, personality or attitudes. There is no space left in this kind of analysis for the reader's own activity. This is often characterised as the 'hypodermic' model of influence: attitude change is taken to be 'syringed' into the individual by the text. Indeed, it is not easy to escape from this form of explanation while using the traditional experimental format. For this format is precisely designed to elucidate specific causes through the manipulation of discrete variables.

One result of the adoption of this format is that the researcher's attention is directed away from the text and the process of reading. These things are construed as 'intervening variables'. The important causal relation is that between exposure to the text and change in attitudes or behaviours. In the experiments discussed above no attempt is made to examine what parts of the text people attended to, how they interpreted it, or whether, given the choice, they would have read it at all. Nor did McLelland seriously consider the way literature may be understood differently in the various countries in which his study was done.

The traditional psychoanalytic approach also presupposes an overly simplistic causal model, although of a rather different kind. Take Goldschmidt's explanation of the structure of <u>Alice in Wonderland</u>. He sees the writing of this text as being beyond Carroll's conscious control. Instead it is taken to be a product of his unconscious motivations and repressed desires. There is a sense, then, in which the text, or at least its particular structure, is seen as caused by the tensions within Carroll's unconscious. From this perspective the unconscious is viewed as a kind of causal mechanism.

Reading

In the last few years a number of literary critics, such as Roland Barthes and Julia Kristeva, have produced a sustained and wide-ranging critique of their discipline. (27) They have questioned commonly taken for granted assumptions about the pre-eminent role of the author in literary production and the unity of individual literary texts. In particular, they have attacked the idea that literary works are passive descriptions of reality (albeit a sometimes imagined reality). Instead they have stressed the constructive nature of texts and the possibilities of varied yet equally viable readings of the same text.

We have already discussed some features of the model of literature that these critics are attacking in Chapter 1. This 'expressive realist' view is concisely described by Belsey. 'This is the theory that literature reflects the *reality* of experience as it is perceived by one (especially gifted) individual, who *expresses* it in a discourse which enables other individuals to recognise it as true.' (28) This traditional view underpins those studies that we have outlined which treat literature as a resource for social psychology and those which use psychological theory as a basis for criticism. Fernandez, for instance, summarises his perspective on literature and suggests why it is important to social psychology.

> The aim of literature is to depict reality as it is lived, or at least as it should or might be lived. Moreover, when we encounter good literature, when we are dealing with an artist who is really familiar with the essentials of his time, there is no doubt that in some manner we are able to participate with the characters in the interaction being described. (29)

Chapter 3

In this extract Fernandez emphasises exactly those features crucial to expressive realism: that literature depicts reality (real or imagined); that a great artist is familiar with the truths of 'his' time; and that we can recognise these truths through vicarious identification with the characters in the novel.

Fernandez goes on to exemplify this perspective by proposing that an extract from du Gard's The Thibaults can be explained by, and can illustrate, the psychologist Festinger's theory of 'cognitive dissonance'. Put simply, this is the theory that a person holding contradictory views or beliefs (cognitions) will find the situation aversive and try to alleviate this feeling by reducing the 'dissonance' between 'cognitions'. (30) Fernandez's reading of du Gard's text is guided by his expressive realist assumptions. Thus he concentrates on the descriptions of a particular character's crisis. This concerns whether, as a doctor, he should relieve the suffering of a dying child by killing her. In his discussion Fernandez presupposes that the character can be treated, for all intents and purposes, as a 'real' person who has 'real' cognitions, which are 'really' dissonant and which he consequently tries to change. In effect, he treats the author as having an implicit insight into the process of dissonance reduction which is displayed in his presentation of character. Yet Fernandez nowhere justifies this particular reading of du Gard's text, or shows that alternative readings, for instance those readings in which the character is not seen to hold contradictory cognitions, are not to be preferred. He sees the text as merely a passive record of events; similar perhaps to a sequence of experimental observations or a videotape of activity. The text itself ceases to be important, and the analyst concentrates on the events depicted by the text as if they were somehow separable from it. However, this approach becomes quite untenable when it is shown, as a number of recent literary studies have, that texts cannot necessarily be taken as straightforward descriptions of this kind. (31)

Merrill and Finkelstein, in their arguments for literature as a source of social theory and data, are rather more sophisticated than Fernandez; yet they adopt basically the same underlying model. Like Fernandez, each reifies 'literary characters' and treats them as in practice analogous to 'real people'; and each treats novelistic accounts of social situations, values and so on, to be analogous to the real thing. Thus, although they accept that literary characters are not 'real', nevertheless they are treated straightforwardly as such for analytic purposes. Their special discursive quality does not enter into the analysis. Instead of questioning the varied ways in which we assign 'character' to different networks of symbols combined under proper names, or examining how a complex of congruent and contradictory textual figures lead to an appearance of 'personality' (as we start to do in Chapter 8) they take these crucial and theoretically interesting steps as unacknowledged presuppositions of the analytic process. In short, both Merrill and Finkelstein take reading a literary text as something unproblematic; reading is what the analyst does to lay bare the truths derived from the insights of the author and embodied in the text. Furthermore, much traditional psychoanalytically orientated criticism, despite its emphasis on the symbolic function of texts, adopts these same basic presuppositions.

All in all, we have documented the significance of three central problems which beset traditional research at the interface of literature and psychology. It is clear that there is a need for work which properly takes into account the social dimensions of reading and literary production, but which, at the same time, accepts the existence of people's active interpretative powers. Furthermore, we must face up to the complexities of the process of reading and get away from the limited commonsensical model which consistently prevented coherent analyses being performed. In the next chapter we will try to tease out the implications of such an analytic practice.

4 FROM ACTION TO DISCOURSE

In this chapter we wish to look more positively at possible solutions to the three basic problems raised in Chapter 3, namely individualism and mechanism, which are pervasive features of social psychological research, and the overly simplistic view taken of the process of reading. In particular we will discuss work by Rom Harré and Paul Willis which faces up to the first two of these faults, and thereby forms a potentially more fruitful basis for constructive interchange between literature and social psychology. However, we will argue that the very sophistication of Harré and Willis's analyses starkly highlights, yet does not solve, the problem of reading. Both in their approach to everyday talk and to specifically literary texts, the issue of how to make sense of discursive material becomes so acute that it can no longer be avoided. We will argue that only a thorough reappraisal of the process of sense-making and reading can provide a firm foundation for a properly constructive analytic practice. Such a practice is clearly important for the study of literary texts; yet it has a significance beyond that. For it is a necessary prerequisite for a social psychology which pays serious attention to people's everyday discourse in its many different forms. In the process of discussing these issues it may seem at times that we are forgetting our purpose of relating social psychology to literature in preference for problems intrinsic to one discipline or the other. However, it should become clear that, while they are expressed in different ways, a number of issues significant in one discipline have important implications for the other.

First of all, however, let us examine in detail Harré and Willis's approaches to social life which stress the crucial significance of social resources and the social context in human action, while not consigning actors to the role of mere passive victims of their circumstances. Harré's 'ethogenic' theory of social behaviour will be examined as it has been applied to the study of football supporters, and it will be compared with Willis's work on the complex reasons which lead working-class boys to take manual working-class jobs.

ETHOGENICS AND RULES OF DISORDER

The basis of the ethogenic theory, overviewed in Harré's book Social Being, is a distinction between 'competence' and 'performance'. (1) This distinction was originally used by Chomsky to contrast the speaker's or hearer's knowledge of language with the actual use of language in concrete situations. (2) If we understand a speaker's knowledge of language we can also understand how certain utterances made by the speaker are possible, although understanding how they are possible does not explain the performance, how a particular sentence is produced. Thus it is, claims Harré, with social life. We can explain action, whether it be through talk or otherwise, by reference to the actor's 'social competence'. Put another way, the possession of a certain social competence is a necessary requirement for the correct performance of certain acts and at the same time sets limits on the acts it is possible to perform. Yet many more things than the social competence will be involved in the specific performance of those acts.

The central ethogenic hypothesis, then, is that people possess a store of social knowledge which enables them both to act and to give accounts (explications, justifications, etc.) of their actions. This hypothesis has important methodological consequences. As the same set of cognitive resources are seen to underlie both actions and the description and justification of those actions, then it should be possible to elucidate the nature of particular actions by using accounts of them given by the actors. The analysis of accounts will reveal features of people's social competences which, in turn, will reveal the significance of their acts.

Unfortunately, according to Harré, it is not possible to avoid this roundabout route to the explication of action. The actions of human beings within a culture are far more than mere movements, because they only take on meaning in the context of specific, and often very local, social conventions. Thus, to reiterate a well worn example: it may seem obvious to an observer that two people shaking each other's hand are greeting one another. But this obviousness is derived from a social competence shared between the handshakers and the observer. Each understands the appropriate social convention which allows them to see the movements of hand shaking as an act of greeting. There is nothing necessary or intrinsic to hand-shaking which means that it can only signify a greeting. An observer would certainly not have the same ease in identifying the greeting ceremony of a very different culture; say that of Maoris or football fans. Here the observer might confuse the act of greeting with an expression of intimacy or the passing of insults, or perhaps the movements would simply appear enigmatic and indecipherable. Actions thus have a semiological character. That is to say, their meaning is not derived from the brute movements themselves, but from a network of social conventions which allow certain movements to be seen as the performance of a particular act and distinguish that act from different but related acts.

The analogy with Chomsky goes even further than this basic distinction between competence and performance. Chomsky equates the idea of linguistic competence with the mastery of an underlying system of rules. Similarly, Harré suggests that an essential part of our social competence is knowledge of social rules. It is these social rules which to a large part enable people to act proficiently and rationally, and furthermore to display that proficiency and rationality. (3)

The social conventions mentioned above are seen as interpretative rules by Harré: they enable social actors to assign meaning to movements and events. However, there is also another important class of rules which is used not for the assignment of meaning but for the regulation of activity. These regulative or prescriptive rules enable people to choose correct or legitimate courses of action in particular situations. Harré's suggestion, then, is that people draw upon cognitive resources, a shared social competence, to produce effective and proper social activity and also enmesh that activity with that of other social actors. Interpretative rules enable people to define situations while regulative rules, in turn, enable them to produce actions legitimate within these situations. These actions, of course, may further change the nature of the situation, and so on. (4)

It will make the practical and methodological implications of these ideas clearer if we briefly describe a specific research example taken from Marsh, Rosser and Harré's analysis of the social worlds of football fans. (5) In part of their analysis Marsh, Rosser and Harré attempt to show that the apparently unrestrained aggressive behaviour of the fans is in fact tightly structured and rule bound, that is, these seemingly disorderly actions are guided by a shared social competence.

Using the fans' accounts and observations of their behaviour the authors suggest that in the various confrontations between opposing fans there operates a complex structure of rules which, except in very unusual circumstances, prevents fans being seriously injured. For instance, fights may be terminated by the loser ceasing hostile action and looking downwards and away from his opponent. This display of submission would, in most instances, stop the aggression before either party was seriously hurt. Furthermore, in many confrontations no actual physical conflict took place at all; both sides could satisfy the requirements that their honour be retained in a chase. Those fans who did the chasing would achieve a highly visible victory by seeing the opposition off; while those being chased would not lose any face from such a patently tactical retreat. Indeed, there may be very little desire to actually catch the fleeing fans. To do so might actually constitute a breakdown of the conventions which constrain serious violence, and therefore lead to fans getting hurt. Chasing thus becomes a more expressive than practical activity. It demonstrates the willingness to fight without the damaging consequences which would result from actually fighting.

68 Chapter 4

In addition to exhibiting in their accounts this orderly view of life on the terraces the fans presented another, very different view. This suggested that a great deal of actual violence takes place, that many people get hurt, and that football matches are inherently dangerous places. Sometimes, as the following extract shows, these two sorts of account are closely intertwined.

> Questioner. What do you do when you put the boot in?
> Fan A. You kicks em in the head don't you? ... Strong boots with metal toe-caps on and that.
> Questioner. And what happens then?
> [Quizzical look]
> Questioner. Well what happens to the guy you've kicked?
> Fan A. He's dead.
> Fan B. Nah - he's all right - usually anyway. (6)

In this extract Fan A formulates a picture of violent and dangerous struggle, while Fan B interrupts with a much more placid picture. Marsh, Rosser and Harré want to suggest that the violent, disorderly version does not give an accurate representation of football supporting, and also that the fans themselves know that it is not really that dangerous. They claim that the fans, in part of their talk at least, have adopted the exaggerated account of violence constructed by the mass media. Moreover, they suggest that it is the combination of the two accounts, the one which stresses disorder and violence and the other which focuses on order and safety, which maintains the specific activities of the fans. For the accounts which emphasise violence and destruction keep up the fans' excitement when they become involved in the action, and also open up the possibility of constructing 'glorious' and exciting stories of the events afterwards. Yet, as they 'know' it is safe, they are able to take part in the activities without reservation. Thus, paradoxically, the fans' accounts of disorder can be seen to play an essential and purposeful part in the maintenance of their local social order. They form a functional rhetoric, which the authors contrast with the fans' more descriptive talk emphasising order.

For Marsh, Rosser and Harré, then, the fans' accounts have a crucial place in the analysis of their activities. Through these accounts the researchers are able to reveal the structure of rules which regulate and give meaning to the fans' actions. What is not clear, however, is how it is possible for Marsh, Rosser and Harré to identify one set of accounts as mainly descriptive, as elucidating the structuring of interaction, and another set as mainly rhetorical, used to excite and glorify the fans' lives. We will explore this issue in more detail shortly, but first let us examine Willis's work.

LEARNING TO LABOUR

In his book _Learning to Labour_ Willis set out to address the issue of how manual working-class boys get working-class jobs. (7) How is it that, without obvious physical coercion, and despite poor economic rewards, an undesirable social definition and the intrinsic meaninglessness of the work, working-class boys still let themselves take working-class jobs? Willis followed a group of adolescents through their last two years of school and first year of work to try and get at the specific processes taking place within the boys' local culture. The group were working-class boys from the 'oppositional subculture' of a secondary modern school in a large Midlands industrial town. Willis attended their classes and spent time with them, around the school and during the evenings, gathering individual accounts and recording group discussions.

Willis used this data to argue that the idea that manual working-class boys are the bottom end of a continuum of decreasing ability and confidence is false. Instead, he suggests that the working-class boys in the study exhibited a radically different cultural form with its own processes, definitions and accounts of other social groups. And it is the specific features of this culture - understood within the broader social/institutional context - which must be used to explain the choice of working-class jobs.

It is at a point between their second and fourth year at school that some of the pupils begin to take part in the school's oppositional culture. (8) In the process of joining this culture they adopt a new social perspective for understanding and evaluating the school: its authority is undermined and opposed, and they sharply differentiate themselves from those pupils who they see as accepting the school's official ethos. Those pupils who join 'the lads' (as they call themselves) thus take on a new and clearly defined set of social conventions, or rules, for understanding their situation and ordering their activities.

The lads continually express opposition to the authority of the school through their interactions with staff in and out of lessons. They undermine and invert the school values of diligence, deference and respect through endless minor displays of insubordination. Willis describes the lads in class.

> Settled in class, as near a group as they can manage, there is a continuous scraping of chairs, a bad tempered 'tut-tutting' at the simplest request, and a continuous fidgeting about which explores every permutation of sitting or lying on a chair. During private study, some openly show disdain by apparently trying to go to sleep with their head sideways down on the desk, some have their backs to the desk gazing out of the window, or even vacantly at the wall. There is an aimless air of insubordination ready with spurious justification and impossible to nail down. If someone is sitting on the radiator it is because his trousers are wet from the rain, if someone is drifting across the classroom he is going to get some paper for written work, or if someone is leaving class he is going to empty the rubbish 'like he usually does'. (9)

Those pupils who are seen by the lads as conformers they label 'ear'oles'. They oppose these conformers, partly because they feel superior to them. This sense of superiority is maintained through a number of features specific to their oppositional culture. For instance, in their view the lads have a good time, 'a laff', while the ear'oles do not, for they have far too much invested in the traditional teaching model and its definitions of their world to spend time having fun.

The lads feel especially superior in matters of sex; they were the ones, they believed, who could successfully 'chat up birds' and were fully sexually experienced. This sexually attractive and potent image, along with further opposition to the school's authority, is reinforced by the consumption of cigarettes and alcohol and the adoption of current clothing fashions in place of the uniform. Willis argues that these things are significant not so much for their practical value or for the direct pleasure they bring, but because of what they express. Fashionable clothing certainly makes the lads more attractive to the opposite sex; yet, because of its contrast with school uniform, it also differentiates them from the ear'oles and symbolically questions the legitimacy of the school culture. With cigarettes, similarly, the important thing is to be seen to smoke; smoking is a highly visible way of expressing disdain for the strictly enforced rules on smoking, and it becomes a site for further conflict with authority. In these activities and styles, the lads thus draw creatively on certain cultural meaning systems from outside the school to express the distinction between their particular culture and the official culture of the school. (10)

Willis suggests that through participation in this oppositional culture within the school the lads develop an understanding, at least in practical terms, of the true role of the school and the career guidance that it offers. The members of this culture 'see through' the school's official rhetoric of educational opportunity and career choice. For instance, they are very sceptical about the value of qualifications. They see them as making little difference in the kinds of manual jobs they are likely to get. With this view, Willis argues, they have penetrated, at least partially, the common educational myth that opportunities can be made by education and the qualifications it provides, rather than the upwards pull of the economy.

The lads see qualifications as offering a maximum upward mobility which reaches only to apprenticeships and clerical work. But they view these jobs as encroaching on their lives in the way manual labour does not. Mental work is seen as bound up with obedience, childhood and the authority of the school; in contrast they see a number of direct continuities between the specifically oppositional culture of the school and the aggressive, adult culture of the shop floor. Moreover, because it is not the intrinsic features of manual labour that are important to the lads, but the particular culture it offers and what that culture represents, the idea of job choice is irrelevant. The significant categories of choice for the lads lie in the simple binary opposition of manual work and 'penpushing'; and they had firmly elected to take the former path.

Willis thus concludes that there is a period, perhaps only a moment, in the development of these adolescents' culture when the lads have a partial insight into the nature of their social situation and when their active choice of manual labour is both an expression of opposition and transcendence and at the same time their entry into a system of exploitation. In the adoption of these jobs they are displaying their rejection of the spurious ideology of educational opportunity, with its empty promise of mobility, yet at the same time consigning themselves to a lifetime's manual labour. The choice of these jobs, then, does not arise from some simple internalisation of a dominant ideology, or because the boys are too lacking in intelligence to know any different, but from the understandings, conventions and values that arise in their specific culture.

SOCIAL ACTION IN HARRE AND WILLIS'S WORK

In the last chapter we suggested that the constructive interpenetration of social psychological and literary approaches to social life has been restricted by three basic shortcomings in the research of social psychologists and traditional literary critics. Furthermore, we suggested that the elimination of these shortcomings could provide a sounder theoretical and analytical basis for addressing the social psychological implications of literature. We have discussed Harré and Willis's work in general terms above. Let us now overview the ways in which this work has dealt with the first two of these flaws before going on to address the remaining difficulties posed by the third.

In many respects Harré and Willis's work emphasises the social dimensions of interaction in very similar ways. For Harré, social knowledge is presupposed in the notion of 'social competence'. This consists in the categories and rules of a specific culture. As people are initiated into that culture - for instance novice football fans into the group of full-blown supporters - they are initiated into its specific set of categories and rules. In other words, they become socially competent members of the group. According to Harré, the very existence of a social order, be it of football rowdies or people making small talk at cocktail parties, presupposes a very high degree of consensus about the appropriate rules. Social organisation and interaction are not derived from biological necessity, or the information processing skills of asocial beings, but from culturally constructed social conventions.

Like Harré, Willis emphasises the importance of the local conventions and values which are shared by the group. It is not their individual insights which lead to partial understanding of their social circumstances, but the practical knowledge which arises out of their activity in the group. In fact Willis found a relative suspension of individual interests. The important social dynamics could only be understood by treating the group as having a specific identity. No amount of aggregation of individual characteristics would make the group activity and insight intelligible.

72   Chapter 4

This emphasis on the social dimensions of activity has important methodological implications. It means that it cannot be taken for granted that the crucial features of the groups' attitudes and behaviour can be pieced together out of interviews conducted individually with its members. And although both Willis and Marsh carried out individual interviews, many of their most interesting and informative findings are derived from exchanges which took place within the group.

The approaches set out in <u>Social Being</u> and <u>Learning to Labour</u> both place a great deal of emphasis on the role of participants' activity and understandings. Rather than taking these things to be irritating noise, whose effects must be minimised in a 'proper' psychological explanation, Harré and Willis view participants as continually and creatively initiating action in the light of their practical goals and understanding of their specific context. Thus Marsh, Rosser and Harré did not view the football fans in their study as caused to act in certain ways by features of their environment; instead he took them to be using the various cognitive resources which make up their social competence to guide their actions and enmesh them with others'. There is, then, no causal relation between the rules and the actions they guide. Indeed, deviations and breakdown of rules are a persistent danger on the football terraces, often resulting in uncharacteristically serious injuries. Similarly, in Willis's study, the lads' choice of unskilled, manual jobs is explained as an active and creative - although ultimately ruinous - response to their penetration of the official accounts of schooling and career choice. These approaches contrast strongly with a great deal of traditional social psychology and sociology, where action is customarily seen as under the direct, causal influence of the environment or to be blindly governed by institutional or ideological forces. (11)

Both Harré and Willis, then, adopt a qualitative approach which emphasises the crucial importance of people's accounts for the proper explanation of their activities. In fact they argue that no satisfactory explanation will be possible without access to the categories which the participants use to characterise and make sense of their own social worlds. It is clear that this approach, which uses participants' discourse as its basic data, deals more adequately with social and intentional aspects of behaviour and ought to be able to address specifically literary issues in a way denied to more traditional perspectives in social psychology. And indeed Harré has used this approach to draw on literary examples in a way which we will discuss shortly. Yet, in analysing discourse, whether in the form of participants' accounts or literary texts, there is, as we have seen, a third problem to be faced. It is to this we now turn.

READING AND REALISM

One of the points that Harré has repeatedly emphasised is the wide variety of purposes to which accounts can be put. (12) For instance, a person's account of a particular act - buying a car, say, or killing someone - may be meant to explicate those actions, to explain why they did it. However, it is also possible that the account is intended to warrant or justify the act, to show that it is right and proper. Furthermore, the account may be directed towards practical ends; perhaps it is used to achieve a particular goal, such as obtaining money or a better job. On the other hand, it may have the more expressive purpose of simply displaying the speaker as skilful or innocent, or perhaps worthy in some other way. Clearly, these are all viable conceptual distinctions; we have no problem in seeing them as different. But can they be reliably made in practice?

Much of Harré's work has been concerned merely to stress the significance of these distinctions. However, in the research on football rowdies with Marsh and Rosser he has attempted to apply them to actual data. We saw in the earlier discussion of this work that the fans' activities on the terraces were seen to be maintained by the operation of two distinct kinds of accounts: one which depicts events as 'orderly and rule bound' and another which characterises them as 'disorderly and dangerous'. The former characterises the terraces as in fact safe, while the latter, in contrast, increases the excitement and creates many expressive possibilities for the fans who are ever keen to demonstrate their valour. Now, Marsh, Rosser and Harré claim that they are not trying to determine the truth of these accounts. For there is no one true, literal account of an event; any event may be accounted for in many ways. Nevertheless, they treat the accounts which depict order as if they explicate the genuine structure of the fans' interactions, even though they do not see them as directly veridical. This portion of the fans' discourse is taken to reveal a social reality beyond itself. '[The] apparently disordered events on the football terraces [...] can be seen as conforming to a very distinct and orderly system of roles, rules and shared meanings. Action is neither chaotic nor senseless but rather is structured and reasoned.' (13)

In contrast, the alternative set of accounts, which emphasise senseless violence, is treated as rhetorical, i.e. these accounts are treated as more important for what they 'do' than for what they 'say'. The authors suggest that they are 'conspiratorial' accounts, derived largely from press reports, which the fans use to retain an exciting sense of danger and as a resource for valorous display. In the following extract what the fans really 'know' about what goes on is contrasted with their rhetorical 'construction' of events.

> Since fans 'know' that this is not the case - they are aware and can tell you that few people get hurt even when things 'get out of hand' - they must conspire to construct disorder. And because there is an easy rhetoric to hand - the rhetoric of the media which insists that events at football matches are *in fact* disordered, the conspiracy is an easy one to conduct. (14)

For Marsh, Rosser and Harré, therefore, certain sections of the fans' talk are treated as literal, or at least intimately bound up with the realities of life on the terraces, while other sections of talk are treated as rhetorical.

Willis, similarly, comments on the contradictory and fragmented nature of the accounts he analyses in his study. However, as is clear from the way he uses accounts to document his conclusions, he too separates out accounts into those which have a 'true cultural resonance' from those which are simply given as attempts to please the investigator or out of politeness. Just as with the football study, accounts which are supposedly literal are sifted from those which are seen as rhetorical or false. And Willis's explanations depend on his ability to make judgments of this sort.

This raises, in an acute form, the problem of reading. How is it that these analysts can apparently select, from what they themselves point out is a contradictory and variable corpus, certain accounts which reveal the actual nature of the actions, attitudes, social groupings, etc. under study? How is it, in other words, that these analysts are seemingly able to read one set of accounts realistically, as genuine social indicators, in contrast to another set of accounts which are rhetorical or ironic?

One reply might be that the analyst can do this through observation of the participants, which would serve as a check on the literal accounts and show the others to be rhetorical. However, if it were observation that enabled the analyst to do this there would be no need for the complicated and time-consuming process of account gathering. The analyst would be able to observe and then record the observations as 'what really went on'. Yet, as we noted earlier, Harré himself stresses that accounts must be used to give meaning to observations, that observations on their own are insufficient. And Willis also emphasises the crucial role of participants' accounts. Furthermore, at no point in their respective studies do Marsh, Rosser and Harré or Willis attempt to show how observations might be used as a reliable basis from which to evaluate the facticity of accounts.

In fact the issue of how accounts can be divided into the genuine, realistic and the rhetorical, ironic or merely polite is never explicitly raised in these works. Categorisations of this kind are taken as unproblematic. Yet we wish to suggest that the analysis of accounts must be given a much more systematic basis than this. Analysis should pay much closer attention to the specifically discursive properties of verbal data. However, before we go on to tease out some of the detailed analytic implications of this position, let us examine Harré's approach to specifically literary discourse.

HARRE, TOLSTOY AND SHAKESPEARE

As we might expect from our argument up to now, Harré draws on literature to a much greater extent than is common in social psychology. And he also draws on it in relation to central social psychological issues rather than as a separate and somewhat esoteric topic on its own. Nevertheless, in some respects his approach to literary texts is more traditional than his approach to everyday accounts.

As part of a broader discussion of certain issues in social psychology, Harré has examined Tolstoy's War and Peace and Shakespeare's Love's Labour's Lost, each in similar ways. (15) Drawing upon Tolstoy's appendix, which gives a detailed characterisation of the book's social implications, Harré takes War and Peace to embody a theory of the social properties of collectivities (which he goes on to criticise). This theory suggests that the only genuine properties of large scale social groups are simple, gross features such as migrations from country to country. In contrast, smaller scale groups have no genuine, intrinsic properties at all. Indeed, this disorderliness leads people to look to historians and such like to provide them with representations of the events which are orderly, although ultimately fictitious. For example, Tolstoy's description of the Battle of Borodino is treated as showing the typical formlessness of small scale collectivities. It is depicted as an accidental and thoroughly chaotic event, which was a victory for neither army. Yet the historians on each side characterised the battle as orderly and, moreover, as skilfully directed by the army armies' leaders, Kutusov and Napoleon.

In the case of Love's Labour's Lost, Harré identifies a number of social psychological theories which are features of the play's plot. In particular, he stresses the importance to the play of a theme concerning the relationship between people's reason and their emotions. He warrants this interpretation of the play by reference to a historical investigation by Frances Yates. (16) This suggested that the play is a commentary on contemporary discussions of the connections between the intellect and the passions, and most especially on an essay about this topic by the Earl of Northumberland. Harré suggests that Shakespeare provides a detailed explanation of this theory in Love's Labour's Lost, and shows that 'the possibility of actually achieving a real domination of the passions is a fantasy'. (17)

Two traditional assumptions are embedded in Harré's approach to literary texts. Firstly, he takes as especially privileged certain authors' interpretations of their own work: in the case of Tolstoy his interpretation of War and Peace outlined in the appendix; in the case of Shakespeare his interpretation as revealed in Yates's historical research. Secondly, Harré treats these texts as having a single, coherent meaning which expresses certain social psychological theories. In fact, he treats literary texts as unified in a way which he does not assume for the football rowdies' accounts. Harré was happy to emphasise the heterogeneity and contradictions in their representations of life on the terraces. Yet he seems reluctant to extend the same licence to literary texts. As we will see, both these assumptions impede a fruitful analytic practice both in studies of literature and other kinds of discourse.

Harré's justification of literature's significance for social psychology stresses its role in 'reflecting' social life.

> Literary works ... reflect, to some degree, the actual psychological processes, personality types, rhetorics etc. available to the folk of their time. I presume that in a play, the psychology of the characters which did not reflect that of the audience in a considerable measure would be unacceptable. (18)

This warrant is interesting because it lies uneasily at the intersection of two rather different perspectives on literature. One of these falls squarely into the expressive realist model discussed in Chapters 1 and 3. It takes the importance of literature to lie in its true and acute depiction of reality. As an argument for the use of literature as a resource for social psychology it has severe limitations. For, in equating acceptability to readers with psychological reality, it seems to imply that all popular literature will be realistic in some way or other. Yet this type of claim does not advance analysis very far, because it ultimately throws up the very same problem that this criterion was meant to solve, namely that of deciding what aspects of a text are realistic or not.

Take, for instance, a study by Middleton which finds a strong correlation between family-size in the USA and in the popular literature of that country during three separate periods. (19) The implication of this research is that literature can embody accurate social knowledge. However, this correlation is only a contingent fact. There is no theory of literature which suggests that correlations of this kind must continue, and therefore that literature might be used as a reliable indicator of family-size in other eras and other countries. Moreover, such a perspective condemns literature to the status of a highly imperfect form of social assessment.

There is, however, a more interesting way of reading Harré's warrant of the significance of literature. If it is stripped of its expressive realist language, which formulates literary texts as reflections of reality, the warrant can be seen from a different perspective. This stresses that texts, like people, are not islands divorced from their social contexts but are crucially dependent on systematic forms of sense-making and codes of interpretation.

As Barthes has most effectively shown in the analysis of a 'realist' text by Balzac in S/Z, texts do not derive their significance from being 'copies of the world' but are dependent for their intelligibility upon other signifying systems or codes of presuppositions. (20) To take one of the simpler examples from S/Z: the sentence 'Midnight had just sounded from the clock of the Elysée-Bourbon' appears early in Balzac's text. Barthes suggests that its significance derives not from what it denotes but from what it connotes. Readers with the appropriate background knowledge will know that the Elysée-Bourbon is in a wealthy neighbourhood of Paris noted for its popularity among the nouveaux riches who became wealthy through speculation and similar means. (21) The literal, denotative meaning of this sentence comes to be of secondary importance, and indeed could be replaced by many different sentences. What is crucial is what the sentence - or any possible replacement - conveys through its connotations, namely the information about wealth which is structurally needed for making sense of Balzac's text.

Chapter 4

From this second perspective, which we wish to develop in this book, the justification for examining literature does not lie in its acute reflection of reality but in its embodiment of conventional forms of sense-making. If we are to analyse these forms, and start to compare them to forms of sense-making used in social psychology, we will need to develop an analysis of discourse.

ANALYSIS OF DISCOURSE

In order to address the problems raised by our examination of Harré and Willis's work let us now look in more detail at the recent developments in literary criticism referred to in Chapter 3 and their implications for the analysis of both literary and non-literary discourse.

Literary critics have traditionally considered a number of tasks to be appropriate to their role: explication of the biography of the author and possibly his or her social and intellectual context, delimiting the different literary allusions in the work and so on. More recently, partly because of what Culler has described as the hegemony of the New Criticism, the central task of literary studies has been seen to be the production of interpretations of individual texts. (22) What was held as important was the unitary meaning of a particular text, which could be revealed through the reader's experience. Nevertheless, its meaning was seen to be a property of the text itself, rather than to reside in the experience of the reader.

More recently there has been a significant shift away from these traditional approaches. This shift has centred on the role of interpretation and the way meaning is assigned to texts. It is proposed that instead of looking at the sense of the text as a given, pre-existent entity, emphasis is placed on the way sense is 'made' of the text. With this shift the central analytic question ceases to be 'what is the meaning of the text?', or 'what is its correct interpretation?'. Instead it now becomes: 'how is the meaning of the text produced?'. Or, put another way, 'What is the process by which readers assign specific meanings to particular texts?'. As a consequence, the proliferation of interpretations characteristic of traditional criticism is no longer taken to be the end-point of analysis; instead it becomes the 'topic' for analysis. The goal of such a transformed perspective on literature, then, is to explicate the varied 'reading practices' of authors, critics and 'ordinary' readers and to elucidate the semiological processes through which texts acquire meaning. (23)

Let us clarify the distinctiveness of this perspective by making some of its implications more explicit. One direct consequence of this shift is that literary texts are not to be considered to have a particular, enduring meaning. In fact, meaning is not considered to lie 'within' the text, but to be a product of specific context-dependent readings. In this way the aim of analysis is not to strive after some hypothetical 'real meaning' of the text, but the more modest, yet analytically more viable, aim of examining the way specific versions of the text's meaning are constructed for particular purposes. The meaning of the text is thus seen as continually 'achieved' via reading practices, which may be highly disparate, depending on their goals and context. (24)

Furthermore, the text is not to be considered as necessarily coherent and unitary. For coherence and unity are not somehow immanently present 'within' the text, but are resources for certain conventional styles of reading and at the same time the apparent outcome of those same readings. Thus in traditional criticism it is typically assumed that seemingly contradictory features of the text are 'meant to express a deliberate tension' or are 'not *really* contradictory at all': and as a consequence an interpretation becomes a document attesting to the unity of the text. Yet this is unsatisfactory from our present perspective since, clearly, interpretative resources, and the devices that go with them, need to become a topic for study in their own right. (25)

In the same way, the intention of the author cannot, as formerly, be taken as an unproblematic resource for legitimating particular interpretations of texts. For not only is the 'real' intention of the author as elusive as the 'real' meaning of the text, but in addition there is no reason to suppose that the author's intended meaning is necessarily more correct than the meaning given by readers or critics. Consequently, analytic interest has refocused on the way particular 'characterisations' of an author's intentions may be drawn on by different readers in the construction of interpretations of the author's work. Barthes expresses this well.

> It is not that the Author may not 'come back' in the Text, in his text, but he then does so as a 'guest'. If he is a novelist, he is inscribed in the novel like one of his characters, figured in the carpet; no longer privileged [...] He becomes, as it were, a paper-author: his life is no longer the origin of his fictions but a fiction contributing to his work. (26)

The topic for study thus ceases to be the intentions themselves (even if they could somehow be isolated) but the way in which particular versions of 'the author's intentions' are constructed and drawn upon to make sense of the text.

As Jonathan Culler has been one of the most successful Anglo-Saxon commentators on these developments, and has done much himself to articulate a coherent semiological approach to literature, it is important to distinguish his perspective from the one we are proposing. This will also serve to further clarify our position.

Culler has tended to view the proper semiological approach as a search for people's (generally critics') social competence, where 'competence' is used in a sense similar to Harré's above. (27) This would lead the analyst to search for psychologically encoded sets of norms or rules which would enable people to assign certain meaning to particular texts. There are, however, two obvious difficulties with this. Firstly, by calling for an analysis of sets of norms, Culler appears to take as unproblematic the relationship between norms and the particular interpretations they feature in. Norms are treated as having fixed meanings and acting as an inflexible constraint on interpretation. Yet this ignores the way in which norms making up a person's literary competence may be flexibly interpreted to fit particular circumstances. (28) Instead of looking at norms as an abstract system and presupposing their constraining role we suggest that attention should be paid to the particular practices in which norms are used. To have reading practices instead of norms as the focus of the analysis is far better, because it stresses the equal importance of the conventions which are available and how they are used in practical contexts.

The second difficulty is the sharp distinction between literature and other modes of discourse implied by the notion of a specific literary competence. Culler talks of literary conventions as quite distinct from broader social conventions. (29) Yet this reifies the category of 'literature' and prejudges the possibility of separating literary understanding from everyday understanding. There is nothing self-evident about this separation. Indeed, many of Culler's sources, in particular Barthes, have claimed the existence of an unavoidable and thoroughgoing interpenetration of literary and everyday form of understanding. (30)

In this present work our aim is not to sharpen the distinction between literary and other forms of understanding, nor to overemphasise the division between literary and other kinds of discourse. On the contrary, we wish to suggest that problems of literary interpretation should be seen as part of a more general issue of the interpretation of all sorts of discursive material. Or, to put it another way, 'reading' practices should be seen as a subset of more general interpretative practices. Accordingly, any specific features of literary understanding should be allowed to emerge through analysis rather than be stipulated beforehand. What is required, then, is a broad analysis of discourse, whether that discourse is spoken, written or literary.

Let us now return to our discussion of Harré and Willis's analysis of accounts. We suggested that the way that they have read their accounts is a central, yet unexamined, issue. If we look at this in the light of the general analysis of discourse which we have proposed above, we can view Harré and Willis's readings as a 'topic' for analysis; i.e. we can elucidate their interpretative practices by a close examination of the way certain participants' accounts are read as literal and others' as rhetorical or ironic. In other words, we can treat their categories and ways of organising accounts as interpretative practices which are an essential, but unexamined, basis for their conclusions. (31)

More importantly, we can extend this to look at the interpretative practices of the participants themselves by examining the organisation and context dependence of their discourse. For instance, it would be possible to look at the various circumstances in which the fans used the different accounts of their activities. Certain questions would be pertinent to this. Are 'violent and disorderly' accounts always used in the same interpretative context? What marks a particular speaker's shift from one sort of account to another? Do the fans themselves distinguish two sorts of account? Through asking questions such as these we can start to address the issue of what the fans' accounts are being used for, i.e. we can elucidate what the fans are doing in this sort of talk. Marsh, Rosser and Harré, of course, do speculate on the function of certain of the fans' accounts; yet they do not try to reveal this function through analysis. Instead they introduce the notion of a functional rhetoric to resolve the analytic problem raised by the variable and contradictory nature of the fans' accounts. For it is only by treating certain accounts as rhetorical, and sifting from them other, more literal accounts, that Marsh, Rosser and Harré are able to produce an orderly analytic version of the 'activities' of the fans. This analytic problem can be avoided, we suggest, by paying detailed attention to the interpretative practices of the fans as revealed in their discourse. (32) Some analyses which try to deal with participants' discourse in this way will be discussed in the next chapter.

Broadly speaking, then, there is a parallel between developments in literary criticism and in social analysis which can be summarised as follows. The central aim of literary criticism has been the production of the definitive, or at least the best, interpretation of a particular text. Likewise Harré and Willis, although in many respects more sophisticated than traditional social psychological approaches, still attempt to produce a definitive portrait of participants' attitudes and behaviours. The difference is that while traditional social psychologists try to do this via experiments and questionnaires Harré and Willis use participants' accounts. The new perspective suggests instead that analysis concentrated on explicating the varied interpretative practices by which versions (of a text's meaning, of some football supporters' actions) are constructed out of certain bodies of discourse (literary texts, participants' accounts).

It should now be apparent that this new approach is not vulnerable to those criticisms which suggest that social psychologists will have to abandon their critical, scientific objectivity if they are going to study literature. These criticisms relate wholly to those perspectives in psychology which adopt wholesale the expressive realist view which treats literature as a repository of true and valid insights into social life. However, our interest in literature does not derive from the possibility that great authors may have acute insights into our social existence. As we have seen, in literary criticism there has been a sustained critique of the idea that literary texts should be seen as the personal expression of certain highly gifted and creative individuals. For this 'commonsensical' notion simply impedes analysis by treating the production of texts as if it lies in an unanalysable realm of 'human creativity'. Our approach, therefore, is not 'subjective' in the sense of trying to deify novelists' perspectives on social life. It is exactly these perspectives which, we argue, should become the 'topic' for analysis and explanation.

A further important implication of our present approach is that it is not strictly accurate to say it is reading which is the subject of analysis. The analyst is faced with one or more stretches of discourse. Conventionally we might say that one passage of discourse is a 'reading' of another; yet this should not be taken to imply that this discourse in some way encapsulates an elusive 'inner' experience of reading. For our concern is with shared processes of sense-making and not primarily with any conventional differences which might exist between, for instance, an everyday account of a novel, a critic's interpretation, and the text of the novel itself. For analytic purposes, then, the question of reading becomes one of 'intertextuality', of the similarities and differences between texts and the way that one text draws upon others. (33) It is through documenting these similarities and differences, and carefully explicating their relationship to different discursive contexts, that we can start to elucidate the varied interpretative practices underlying the production of discourse. This is not to suggest, of course, that there are not interesting differences between a stretch of discourse in a novel, which may have been reworked many times, and the ad hoc utterances about the novel made by a first time reader. But these differences are not central to analysis. The task of the analyst should not be to emphasise the polish on one of these forms of discourse, but to expose the varied ways in which each constructs and naturalises versions of social reality.

LITERATURE AND SOCIAL PSYCHOLOGY

Having addressed these issues concerning reading and interpretation it is now possible to draw the threads of these last two chapters together and elaborate on the central aims of this book. Both literature and social psychology can be considered as a body of texts (albeit with different goals, conventions, etc.) which contain accounts of actions, identities, and a myriad of other features of people's social lives. In each of the analytic chapters (1,2,7,8) comparisons are made between various kinds of literary and social psychological discourse. These chapters examine the way social life is made sense of and, moreover, depicted as real and natural in these two realms of discourse. We therefore treat 'realism' as an effect of the language used in these texts, rather than their grounds or cause. This involves examining the many devices, assumptions and accounting systems which are used to achieve the effect of literal description of the social world. It might seem that this is a futile task with scientific texts, which after all are usually taken to be the ultimate form of descriptive literature. Yet it would be wrong to think of them as exempt from such processes. As we shall see in Chapter 5, there is a growing body of work concerned exactly with the complex forms of 'reality construction' in various kinds of 'factual' discourse.

It should not be thought that our intention is solely to apply the insights derived from modern literary criticism to social psychology. At the same time as emphasising the important role of these theoretical developments in elucidating certain central issues in social psychology, we wish to stress the significance of theoretical and empirical developments in social psychology for the study of literature. For too long literature has been treated either as if it exists in a purely sealed ascetic environment or as if it is a direct product of large scale social structures. Although recent literary criticism has rectified this to some extent by moving towards a systematic analysis of sense-making in literature, it has paid very little attention to the growing body of relevant research in social psychology and interpretative sociology. Theoretical work on social action (discussed in this chapter and the previous one) as well as empirical developments in discourse and conversational analysis (discussed in the next chapter) have raised issues which lie at the very heart of modern literary criticism. (34) A serious analysis of discourse can only benefit from a mutual interchange between disciplines that has been absent until now.

This attempt to elucidate the mutual implications of literature and social psychology can be seen in Chapters 1 and 2. There the juxtaposition of very different forms of discourse, which share certain common topics, allows the analyst to expose the contingency of certain taken-for-granted interpretative practices in both literature and social psychology, and thereby to document the way particular features of social life are depicted as obvious and natural.

In Chapter 1 a comparison is made between notions of femininity used in social psychology, literary criticism, and in the literature of Barbara Cartland, Jilly Cooper and Doris Lessing. In both the social psychological and the literary critics' work there is a tendency to treat femininity as a preconstituted entity which is merely described, in different ways, in social psychological and literary discourse. In many respects Barbara Cartland and Jilly Cooper, of course, are even more guilty in this respect. Yet Lessing's work can be read, on one level, rather differently. For it seems to take the Cartland/Cooper model of femininity and undermine it, substituting a more diverse and complex language of feminine subjectivity, although one which still reifies certain sexual categories.

In Chapter 2, on the other hand, the use of implicit models of Man is compared in three different kinds of discourse. In the case of social psychology we can see that such models are statically used to organise entire categories of discourse; while in Thomas Hardy's Mayor of Casterbridge, and in an 'everyday' account of someone's walk through their housing estate, such models can be used discretely, as with the social psychological discourse; but they can also be fluidly enmeshed to suit particular contexts and create certain effects.

In this chapter we have discussed some of the complex issues raised by studies which are based on participants' discourse in one form or another and we have argued that a proper response to these issues is a thoroughgoing analysis of discourse which is not constrained by traditional and unquestioned assumptions concerning the role of texts in social life. In the next chapter we will discuss in more detail the complex interpenetration of participants' and social psychologists' ways of making sense of social life in the context of analyses of certain 'factual' texts.

5 DISSECTING FACTUAL TEXTS

In the last few years a number of literary critics and social scientists have suggested that many of the supposedly obvious differences between various kinds of texts might be rather less interesting than their similarities. Indeed, they have argued that the development of our understanding of the way texts make sense may be strongly hindered if we unthinkingly adopt everyday classifications such as 'literary', 'scientific', 'journalistic' and so on, and thereby take on the baggage of assumptions which go with these categories. Culler, for example, has suggested that any special distinctiveness awarded to literary texts cannot be taken for granted but must be left to emerge through analysis. If this is done 'literary works will appear not as monuments of a specialised high culture but as powerful, elegant, self-conscious, or perhaps self-indulgent manifestations of common patterns of sense making'. (1) The literary theorists Terry Eagleton and Roger Fowler have adopted similar positions. For them the traditional and largely unquestioned assumptions about the unique and humanistic nature of literature should be purged from analysis. (2)

At the end of Chapter 4 we referred to the major goal of this book, which is to contrast some of the different ways of making sense of social life adopted in literature and social psychology and to reveal some of the regularities underlying both approaches. The literary theorists mentioned above argue for a general analysis of texts which is not constrained by the traditional guidelines imposed by the category 'literature'. However, it may not seem obvious why an analysis which included non-literary discourse would be interesting; particularly an analysis which examines scientific and other factual texts as we do. Yet, just as a serious analysis of literary texts is undermined by the expressive realist myth which sees literature as a residue of universal human truths, so the study of factual texts has been constrained. In this case, however, the problem has been social psychologists' overriding concern with what texts are about, or represent, at the expense of any serious study of how they are constructed and how they function. Discursive material of various kinds has almost inevitably been used by social psychology for the documentation of actions, beliefs or other aspects of social reality. The central analytic concern has thus been with the reliability or validity of the text in its task of representation. (3)

Traditionally, then, the paramount analytic question for social psychologists has concerned the relation between texts and what they depict. Moreover, when this relation has been properly elucidated the text itself has generally ceased to be of interest. It is largely for this reason that so little attention has been paid to literature by social psychologists. For they have seen the relation between literary texts and what they depict as highly problematic and lacking acceptable means of validation. Furthermore, as we have commented, the attention that has been paid comes mostly from humanistically orientated thinkers who are prepared to adopt expressive realist assumptions to warrant the unique acuity of literary texts. In either case texts are seen as important because of what they depict; not, as we argue, because of how they give the appearance of depicting the social world or because of their relationships with one another.

In this chapter we wish to extend this argument and look more closely at the ways in which versions of social life are actively constructed in different kinds of discourse. At the same time we will examine some of the ways in which traditional approaches to texts, which attempt to recover the actions, attitudes, etc. which they depict, can become parasitic upon the specific interpretative practices which are involved in the construction of texts. For people are inevitably and continually utilising lay social psychological notions when constructing accounts of their social world. Thus it is only through fully explicating the relationship between analysts' and participants' discourse that analytic findings can be successfully distinguished from the systematic systems of accounting which are apparent in discourse of all kinds.

We will illustrate these points by discussing some studies using conversational and discourse analysis which show that participants' versions of their own and others' actions and beliefs are regularly constructed in ways which parallel a number of basic theoretical issues in social psychology. Indeed, they suggest that certain of the basic analytic categories that social psychologists use to explain social behaviour are also deployed in participants' discourse for a variety of highly situation-specific purposes. Without a full understanding of these processes which occur at the level of discourse about social life, there is a constant danger of the analyst simply adopting participants' implicit social psychologies as apparently general theoretical characterisations of their actions. It is the explication of this issue which is the main reason why our present enterprise is of more importance to social psychology than merely providing a new subject-area for the discipline. Its full implications will become clearer as we discuss specific studies of the construction and organisation of discourse.

RECONSTRUCTING IDENTITIES

Social psychologists, and indeed psychologists in general, have spent a good part of their time in both professional and academic contexts classifying people as prejudiced, intelligent, neurotic, extrovert and so on. One common classification which has important repercussions is 'mental illness'. The officially ratified use of this categorisation can have far-reaching and sometimes destructive consequences for a person's prospects and life style. Of course, an enormous amount of research has been carried out on this issue of diagnosis and psychiatric classification and some emotive debates have ensued. Yet very little attention has been paid to people's everyday notions of mental illness. How do lay persons come to identify people as mentally ill and warrant these identifications?

This was the question which Dorothy Smith took as her initial perspective on an account of a particular girl, K's, mental illness. (4) This account was obtained by one of Smith's students for a class project. It is a reconstruction, from memory, of an interview in which a girl called Angela describes the onset of K's illness. In a sense, then, it is a joint product of Angela and the interviewer; although much of it appears to consist of remembered direct quotations from Angela's original oral description. These features, which from a methodological point of view are serious flaws, do not diminish the interest of Smith's analysis. For such features are a chronic aspect of everyday accounting, and as Smith does not use the interview to provide an objective picture of social reality they should not be seen as imperfections.

On a first hearing of the account, when it was read out in class, Smith took it as a literal, unproblematic rendering of the onset of K's illness. However, on closer inspection of the written text, Smith became less sure of its acuity. An alternative and radically different version of K's difficulties soon, in fact, became apparent. Smith's analysis seeks to show how the original, 'authorised' version made sense, but how it may also be dismantled to present a new and contrasting version in which K's mental illness no longer seems obvious and unproblematic.

It is worth describing the account in some detail. It starts by describing the admiration that Angela felt for K, whom she met at university. 'Here was a girl, a year older, of such a good family, a good student, so nice, so friendly, so very athletic, who was willing to befriend her. K suggested outings, and they went skiing, swimming, playing tennis together.' (5) However, Angela noted that 'nearly every morning' on the way to university K would cry about 'little things'. She also started to have problems with her courses. At this time Angela gradually came to recognise that there was something wrong. She tells that her admiration turned slowly to bafflement.

> K is so intense about everything at times, she tries too hard. Her sense of proportion is out of kilter [...] When you meet her,

> you are struck, by a sweet girlish appearance. She will sit
> quietly in company, smiling sweetly at all times, and seems disarmingly appealing. But when there were young men in the company she would find it harder than ever to carry on a conversation, and would excuse herself and leave very soon [...] It was obvious that she was terrified of anyone getting too near to her, especially men. And yet she used to pretend to us (and obviously to herself too) that she had this and that guy really keen on her. (6)

At a later date Angela and another girl asked K to share an apartment with them, partly because Angela 'felt responsible' for K. However, before moving in K stayed with Angela's family for a few days. Angela recounts the difficulties which arose: for instance, K ate her mother's breakfast on one occasion, and on another was embarrassed when the family openly displayed emotion. Once together in the apartment, the girls 'had to face the fact that K was definitely queer'. Problems arose over washing, cooking, budgeting and other domestic activities. Finally things came to a head over dinner at a friend's flat.

> Conversation was lively, but she did not take part. A boy was discussed, but K had not met him. However she suddenly cut in: Yes, isn't he nice. Everything was quiet for a moment, but I carried on talking sort of covering up for her. A few minutes later she cut in again, with: Oh yes, and the little black sheep and the lambs.... This was really completely out of touch. (7)

At this point the girls started to take action; they contacted a friend of the family for advice, who admitted that the social circle of parents and relations 'had silently acknowledged' that K was not well for some time. It was arranged that K should see a psychiatrist.

In many respects this is an unremarkable story, apparently documenting the tragedy of one girl's progressive mental disorder. However, by examining in detail the various mechanisms for sense making utilised in the account, Smith is able to throw its straightforward factual basis into doubt. The first of these mechanisms draws on the general interpretative frame in which the account is placed. In various different ways it is indicated to the reader that the correct approach is to read the account as a factual record of K's mental illness. The fact of K's illness, stated at the outset, is available for use by the reader as a resource for interpreting the information which is subsequently presented. Furthermore, the account is privileged in the sense that the key participant, K, is absent from the scene of accounting and is thus unable to present her version of events (although the very fact of her mental illness, once established, suggests that K's version would anyway be suspect).

A second and related process that Smith analyses is the construction of the account's 'objectivity'. The account treats the fact of mental illness as something existing prior to its being 'admitted' by the various characters referred to. They are depicted as having no part in its construction. Furthermore, each of the characters - Angela, Angela's mother, etc. - is treated as positively disposed towards K: they either liked or admired her. Thus their gradual 'realisation' of her illness can be seen as reluctant; it is not something they wish, as they might if they disliked her. The reader cannot easily 'explain away' their views as being a product of their specific interests; for her illness is displayed as contradicting these interests. Moreover the account treats each individual 'acknowledgment' of her condition as quite separate and based on some form of direct observational evidence; her illness' factual status is therefore depicted as having been independently verified. Yet, when closely examined, various aspects of the account cast serious doubt on this independence. The account is thus organised in a manner which prejudges its conclusion, or as Smith puts it:

> If the collection is viewed as a problem, then we have been told what the solution is. The problem presented by the account is not to find an answer to the question 'what is wrong with K?', but to find that this collection of items is a proper puzzle to the solution 'becoming mentally ill'. (8)

A third mechanism which displays K as mentally ill is apparent in the detailed descriptions of K's behaviour. These are, it seems, provided to give the reader a chance to judge K's mental state independently of the various claims made about it. As such they reinforce the general appearance of objectivity. Yet it is in these descriptions that Smith is able to reveal much of the 'work' of the account taking place. Smith identifies a device for characterising action which she calls a 'contrast structure', which is used repeatedly throughout the account.

Contrast structures are two-part sequences of discourse in which the first part provides a context for making sense of the second. For instance:

(i) When asked casually to help in a friend's garden,
(ii) she went at it for hours, never stopping, barely looking up. (9)

In this structure, K's behaviour, depicted in part (ii), is made to seem anomalous or bizarre by the implicit instruction or rule suggested in part (i). (10) Thus the 'casual' request for help results in inappropriately 'singleminded' labours by K in the garden. Of course, in another context, where the reader has not been led to read the account as a document of mentally ill behaviour, this might merely appear as an example of excessive zeal. Yet in this context the deviation from the normal, required behaviour represents an anomaly. It cannot be fitted into the framework of everyday normative behaviour or common deviations from that behaviour.

Some contrast structures have a more complex structure:

(i)   We would go to the beach or pool on a hot day and
(ii) I would sort of dip in and just lie in the sun,
(iii) while K insisted that she had to swim 30 lengths.
      (11)

In this case parts (i) and (iii) of the structure are on their own insufficient to display K's behaviour as anomalous. What is bizarre about swimming, especially on a hot day when interested in athletics? However, part (ii) suggests the behaviour which is appropriate or normal when visiting the beach. This associates the hot day with lazing around and relaxing - not swimming 30 lengths. The sense of bizarreness is further heightened by noting that K 'insisted' on swimming this much, which implies that she is acting in an obsessional manner, rather in the way that she 'barely looks up' while gardening.

Other contrast structures are very simple:

(i) She would wash dishes
(ii) but leave them dirty too. (12)

This appears to be an achievement that exceeds normal incompetence. As Smith notes, dishes can be washed badly so as to leave bits of food on them; but to leave them 'dirty' after washing them is 'almost Dada and an achievement in itself'. (13) Again the sense of anomalousness is created by presenting a norm and showing how K's activity bore no sensible relation to it.

Smith claims to have identified at least 11 contrast structures in the account, out of 23 discrete items of behavioural description. The account as a whole achieves its effect through multiplying these structures over a wide variety of different situations. Any weaknesses in particular structures are obscured by the overall effect, which prevents the reader from formulating any kind of rational story which can make sense of K's behaviour other than that she is becoming mentally ill.

We can see, therefore, that Smith has modified her initial question, which asked how lay people come to identify mental illness, and replaced it with a different sort of question: how is an account organised to display the fact of mental illness and to undermine alternative classifications? The site of interest is no longer people's actions, and how they come to understand that someone is abnormal, but the organisation of the text itself. Smith's analysis undermines the impression that accounts can be a neutral rendering of actions and instead displays a complex, layered discursive structure which is responsible for the apparently unproblematic classification. Smith herself goes on to argue that an alternative explanation of K's problem is available in the text if it is analysed closely, an explanation which suggests that K is being 'frozen out' of a particular social circle. She reassesses the idea that Angela is K's friend, and suggests instead that Angela and her flatmate are trying to exclude and victimise K. Smith is thereby able to reread K's comment about the black sheep and the lambs (line 123) as a rational description of this process of exclusion, and not 'out of touch' at all. However, we do not need to follow Smith down this avenue where she begins to speculate back beyond the text to the real nature of the actions it depicts. (14) For our purposes what is interesting is the illustration of the contingency of this seemingly straightforward account, and the demonstration that key social psychological issues are being largely pre-packaged.

If analysts are to use such accounts as this as the basis for research they must be aware that they are produced in the light of participants' implicit and situation-specific social psychological understanding. What Angela's account embodies is not simply a description of the onset of illness, but a set of inferences and conclusions organised in such a manner that K's mental illness appears obvious and inevitable. It seems, then, that if social psychologists are to produce fruitful analyses with data of this kind, which do not simply reproduce participants' own folk psychologies, we must treat accounts with great care and attempt to lay bare the techniques by which they legitimate or undermine particular versions of the social world.

ATTRIBUTING CAUSES

Dorothy Smith's procedure when presented with the account of K's illness was to expose an alternative version of K's problem which was available in the text but initially much less apparent. The descriptive contingency of the text was thus revealed by showing that it could not be taken as a coherent, unitary account of action but should be seen as a more fragmentary, heterogeneous account which, although 'authorising' one version by the use of a number of textual devices is, nevertheless, open to alternative readings. In other cases the contingency of accounts of action can be demonstrated by comparing versions of events presented in different texts. This is what Tony Trew has done in an analysis of two contrasting newspaper accounts of the violence at the Notting Hill Carnival of 1977. (15)

Trew has examined in detail 'on-the-spot' reports and editorials concerning disturbances at the annual carnival in the <u>Sun</u> and the <u>Morning Star</u>. These are, of course, strongly contrasting newspapers: the <u>Sun</u> has one of the largest circulations in the UK while the <u>Morning Star</u> has the smallest; the <u>Morning Star</u> is the official newspaper of the Communist Party of Great Britain, while the <u>Sun</u> is not formally at least tied to a political party in this way. These differences are not, however, presupposed in the analysis, which centres on the descriptive and evaluative language the papers draw upon. In particular Trew examines the way the news reports of the events at the Carnival are shaped to mesh with the evaluation of those events in the paper's editorials.

Two brief extracts from the reports will serve to give a flavour of their contents. They are broadly similar, for the most part mentioning the same events. However, as Trew's analysis makes apparent, there are some important differences.

> Sun   30 August 1977
> INTO BATTLE! Riot shields out as the police storm Carnival mob
> Two hundred police carrying riot shields and truncheons last night charged a rioting mob of black youths at London's Notting Hill Carnival [...]
> An eye-witness said 'At one point the police were pinned down. The mob stoned them and they used their riot shields to protect themselves' [...]
> The violence started early in the afternoon when small groups of youths used the gaiety of the Carnival for an orgy of crime.
>
> Morning Star   30 August 1977
> FIGHTING MARS END OF CARNIVAL AFTER DAY OF PEACE
> Police observers hovering in a helicopter above the huge crowds at London's Notting Hill Carnival yesterday estimated between 200,000 and 250,000 people were taking part [...]
> The two sides sparred amid a hail of missiles, and from there on the police adopted streetfighting tactics [...]
> When they broke into one shop from where missiles had been coming, those inside were knocked about by truncheons. (16)

Trew's style of analysis is rather different to Smith's. He uses fine grain linguistic categories taken from the socio-linguistically orientated work of Halliday to examine the complex ways in which participants and processes are depicted in the two texts. (17) To properly understand Trew's study it is important to have some understanding of the way these categories operate. They have to be treated very carefully. Things which are depicted as having agency at certain places in the text may not seem much like agents in ordinary life. For instance, it is a regular feature of both texts that they treat items like 'truncheons' and 'missiles' as if they were active agents rather than passive objects, and they are thus categorised as 'participants'. Conversely, many nouns are depicted in these texts as processes with duration, end points and so on. For instance 'riot' is used both to depict a thing and a process.

When this classification scheme is used the texts can be broken down into two sorts of clauses. 'Transactives' represent processes which include one active participant and one passive, who is merely involved or acted upon. An example of such a clause is 'A gang of youths attacked a group of press photographers.' In contrast, 'non-transactives' represent processes in which there is just one participant involved and no causal process taking place. An example of this sort is 'a man of 21 was in a critical condition with a stab wound'. When these two stages of classification are carried out the analyst is able to highlight the distribution of agency and interaction within these accounts. This form of analysis thus makes explicit who is initiating action and who is being acted upon.

Using this technique dramatic differences are revealed between the two accounts. The Sun article includes many more transactive clauses than the Morning Star article, indicating that it depicts more agents and more causal interaction. Furthermore, much of this contrast is concentrated in the category of 'young people / thugs'. The Sun depicts processes as occurring between groups of participants and as being most predominantly initiated by 'gangs of youths'. On the other hand, the Morning Star report takes the processes themselves as focal, rather than the initiating participants. Only the police are depicted as initiating action to any degree.

A second important difference occurs in the description of the Sun's most active participants. The Morning Star article describes these as 'groups of youngsters'. The Sun, however, uses 'youths', 'black youths', 'gangs of youths', 'thugs', and 'a mob of black youths'; thus contrasting 'gangs' and 'mobs' with the Morning Star's 'groups', and 'youths' and 'thugs' with the Morning Star's 'youngsters'. Similar sorts of contrasts occur in the terminology used to define the processes in which the 'gangs'/'groups' were involved: for instance 'riot' in the Sun for the Morning Star's 'trouble'. Yet in the descriptions of other groups and other processes the papers share almost identical terminology. Exactly why these very specific differences in the reports should occur can be seen when Trew examines the editorials associated with each report.

In each paper's editorial the events at the Carnival are explained and placed in the context of broader social groups and processes. Suggestions for appropriate action are made in the light of these explanations. Furthermore, the form of these explanations arises naturally out of the descriptive terminology of each newspaper. Thus, in the Sun, the violent events are depicted as the actions of 'thugs' and 'hooligans', and these terms provide their own explanation. It is in the nature of 'yobs' and 'thugs' to be violent and produce disruption; nothing further need be said to make sense of their actions. (18) However, in the Morning Star, the violent actions are presented as more enigmatic because they are either carried out by 'young people' who are not identified as special in any way, or they are seen as disembodied processes such as 'hooliganism' or 'thuggery'. Such things need explaining, and the Morning Star indicates a number of possible causes, such as deprivation and the inadequate financing for the Carnival. Trew summarises this relationship between the description and explanation of events as follows:

> From these different forms of classification and their implicit explanations, flow, with all logic, different remedies; 'punish them' says the *Sun* editorial - 'improve the conditions', says the *Star* editorial. 'These people are our enemies,' says one, 'it's the yobs against the rest of us.' 'These young people are our young people', says the other, 'we must remove the causes of their anger.' (19)

It is clear, therefore, that these two newspaper reports cannot be

considered to be literal depictions of events. The apparently
straightforward descriptive terminology of each article can be seen
to be part of a more comprehensive system of discourse which provides also for explanation and evaluation. Each newspaper draws
upon a different system for explicating action. By closely comparing the accounts in the different papers certain orderly features
of their specific versions of actions and events may be made explicit. The Sun emphasises 'internal' or dispositional factors,
while the Morning Star emphasises 'external' or situational factors.
It is through fine grain analyses such as this that we can put some
flesh onto our intuition that certain newspapers take a different
ideological 'slant' on events and we can start to reveal the detailed processes through which these political versions are constructed.

It is interesting to view the social psychological research concerning lay people's attributions of causation for behaviour in the
light of Trew's analysis. This research ought to be of great relevance here because it is specifically concerned with the way people
draw upon implicit social psychological notions when explaining
their own and others' behaviour. Each of the newspaper accounts can
be seen to embody an implicit social psychological analysis of the
behaviour of certain participants at the Carnival. However, research on attributions has traditionally treated explanatory categories such as dispositions and environmental influences (or internal versus external causes) as part of the organisation of
people's perceptual schemes or as a feature of their information
processing. (20) That is, this research has adopted the individualistic, asocial approach typical of much American and British social
psychology. (21) Yet it is clear from Trew's analysis that we can
only make sense of the use of dispositional and environmental influences when we understand the social context of the different accounts and, ultimately, the different ideologies which they imply.
(22) Far from being essential categories of information processing
and perception the newspaper accounts are organised, as was the
account of K's illness, to inexorably lead to one particular explanation. The innocent appearance of straightforward explanation
arising from literal description must therefore be seen as an
'achievement' of each account.

MAKING RULES AND ACCOUNTING FOR CONSENSUS

So far we have looked at the way certain social psychological notions are used in two very different sorts of discourse. A 'theoretical' issue for the social psychologist - is this person mentally
ill? were this group of people caused to act in this way? -
becomes a 'practical' issue for the participants. Just as psychologists draw on technical notions of mental illness and social influence in the construction of their theoretical versions of events,
so people themselves draw upon similar notions when producing versions of their own and others' actions which are appropriate for
particular occasions. Psychologists who ignore these overlapping
aims do so at their peril. Texts and talk, such as are discussed

above, do not merely describe various features of actions and understandings which make up people's social worlds but they are an active part of the construction of those worlds. Only through properly understanding the practical functions and organisation of participants' discourse can it be ensured that it is not merely reified as social psychological theory.

One form of discourse which is often considered to be a paradigm example of precision and literal description is scientific discourse. Yet even here a number of recent analyses have shown that neither scientific talk nor writing can be considered as straightforwardly literal. (23) Here too, issues of theoretical interest to the social psychologist present themselves as practical problems to the participants being studied. The way these participants depict these issues in their discourse is similarly closely bound up with the pragmatic constraints inherent in specific social situations. We will discuss two examples to illustrate this relation between the form of the scientific discourse and its function.

As we noted in Chapter 4, the notion of a rule and the idea of rule following have become important in more recent, qualitatively based approaches to social psychology. However, there has been considerable debate over the exact status of rules: how they function and how they may be used to explain behaviour. Harré has tended to see rules as templates for guiding activity. (24) In this view, a given rule allows the participant to produce the correct actions in any appropriate circumstances. In contrast to this idea of rules as guiding frames for action is a second, rather different view which claims a much looser connection between rules and activity, and implies that rules are inevitably open to various different interpretations when applied to complex real situations. Indeed, from this perspective rules may be treated as devices used for making sense, justifying or condemning behaviour as much as for guiding it. They are seen as members' ways of creating the 'appearance' of order by 'accounting' for behaviour, rather than creating 'actual' order by 'guiding' behaviour. (25)

This debate may seem far removed from the everyday realities of scientific life. Yet there are situations where this sort of distinction can become a crucial practical issue. Such a case occurs where scientists use criteria to explain the selection and rejection of theories. A number of philosophers and historians of science have suggested that broad criteria such as accuracy, consistency and testability play an essential role in the choice between competing theories. (26) And indeed such criteria are regularly drawn upon in scientists' discourse about their theory choices. However, there are important and systematic differences in the way they are characterised.

A detailed study has been carried out of the way in which the criterion of testability is used in the transcript of a psychology conference. (27) This demonstrates that in both general accounts of theory choice in psychology and in accounts of the role of this criterion in the selection of particular theories, different versions of its importance are produced. There are two primary versions, both of which are formulated by a number of different psychologists. The first depicts testability as a determinate criterion of selection which states that no theory which is untestable should be selected. Accordingly any scientist who supports an untestable theory is misguided or even unscientific. The second version depicts testability as rather unimportant for theory selection. This may be because the real reasons for a scientist's theory choice are seen to lie in diffuse social processes; or it may be because the relationship between theories and data are thought to be too vague to enable a definitive decision about whether a theory is testable or not.

Where scientists give accounts of the role of testability in both the selection of their own theory and the selection of competitors' theories an interesting asymmetry becomes apparent. When characterising the choice of their own theories they tend to use a notion of testability much like the first view mentioned above. Testability is represented as an effective constraint on choice which is not significantly influenced by social processes. It is outside the speaker's sphere of social control and it seems purely to select those theories which may be related to bodies of data in a clearcut fashion. On the other hand, when accounting for the selection of competitors' theories, testability is described as ineffective in constraining scientific activity. For it is open to different interpretations which may be strategically made by scientists to give a spurious aura of legitimation to their theories. Thus accounts given by competing scientists who characterised their own theory as selected because of its testability are taken to be rhetorical rather than literal.

We can now see how these different accounts are related to the theoretical dispute about the nature of rules. If criteria for theory choice are treated as a type of rule for choosing correct or appropriate theories, it is clear that psychologists draw on different versions of this rule in different contexts. When talking of selecting their own theories they describe the rule as a template for guiding action. When talking of competitors' choices the rule is characterised more flexibly as a rhetorical presentation which is dependent on other scientists' interpretations. This asymmetrical accounting can be viewed as an essentially practical resource for the scientists concerned. They draw flexibly on the criterion of testability to do two very different things: firstly to display their opponents' views as problematic, i.e. not directly and necessarily constrained by criteria but influenced by a number of social factors; secondly to characterise their own decisions as being forced by the impersonal, determinate operation of criteria. Thus, by way of these accounting techniques, they legitimate their own position and undermine alternative, competing positions. We cannot, therefore, use accounts of this sort to decide which view of the function of rules is the correct one because the scientists, in different contexts, draw upon each of them. Moreover, while parts of the discourse appear compatible with a theory which treats rules as determinate templates other parts treat them as essentially flexible and indeterminate.

As a last example, let us look briefly at the use of notions of consensus in scientific discourse. A large amount of research, both in social psychology and other social sciences, is underpinned in one way or another by the idea of consensus. Yet the central role this notion plays in making sense of research findings is rarely acknowledged. For example, in the studies we examined in Chapter 5, Willis and Marsh produce a number of categorisations of participants which are treated as stable, unproblematic features of their social worlds, and taken to indicate their possession of agreed sets of rules or consensual beliefs about school or football culture. However, Willis and Marsh devote very little space to a discussion of the exact sense in which these groups 'share' rules or beliefs. This is despite the fact that in each case their final explanation is dependent on the broadly consensual nature of these phenomena.

A study of scientists' use of notions of consensus by Nigel Gilbert and Michael Mulkay illustrates some of the serious problems which can arise when using this apparently straightforward notion. (28) These authors looked at a group of biochemists' responses to a description of increasing theoretical consensus in their field. This description was contained in an honorary lecture given by Spencer, an eminent member of the field, which was subsequently published. (29) The description was accompanied by a graph purporting to illustrate the increasing acceptance of the speaker's theory by relevant experts in the field.

A number of biochemists responded that the graph represented an accurate, veridical description of the increasing consensus in the field. However, other scientists responded very differently. They raised various problems with the veracity of the graph. For instance, some suggested that Spencer had wrongly identified the membership of the field; leaving out certain important figures and mistakenly including others. Further scientists suggested that beliefs had been wrongly attributed, in fact that certain participants characterised as believing in the theory did not do so. Thus, for these scientists, consensus was a point of contention. Although some accepted Spencer's diagram, others suggested that it was flawed.

Without going any further into the details of this study, it is clear that claims of consensus such as that made by Spencer, whilst being a ubiquitous feature of science and other areas of social life, cannot be taken as a stable basis for social psychological analysis. To do so would be to implicitly take sides with certain participants' versions of their social situation at the expense of others'. All of these scientists cannot be right about the state of consensus, because their accounts contradict one another. Despite this, accounts of consensus are regularly used by the scientists in the construction of accounts of broader aspects of their field. Thus Spencer's graph can be seen as a way of showing that some members of the field are acting in a dogmatic, closed-minded fashion and that his theory is increasingly being seen as correct by those scientists with open minds. While those who gave accounts which questioned Spencer's consensus claims often did so in the context of arguments in support of competing theories. In this way the overall weight of support for Spencer's theory could be shown to be less than claimed by Spencer.

It seems, then, that as with accounts of the criteria used for theory choice, we can make more sense of these accounts by treating them as fashioned for particular interactional purposes than by treating them as veridical descriptions of consensus. Of course, the fact that claims to consensus are controversial and orientated towards practical ends is not at all a surprising one. Yet it has immensely important implications for social psychology in cases where representations of consensual social groupings - be it of biochemists, the middle class or football hooligans - are constructed using participants' discourse. For it is only too easy for the analyst to produce research which incorporates and sustains certain participants' sectional interests as an unnoticed baggage brought in with their versions of collective belief.

PARTICIPANTS' AND ANALYSTS' DISCOURSE

Each of these analyses of spoken and written discourse is to some extent preliminary. On the whole, they and others like them have only been conducted in the last few years; although linguists' and conversational analysts' interest in this topic goes back rather further. (30) There is as yet no unitary method or fully agreed set of presuppositions. Some studies, such as Smith's, try to explicate the organisation of discourse within single texts, and thus try to reveal how they accomplish the impression of 'mere description'. Others, such as Trew's, attempt to show the inconsistency of different accounts of the same phenomena, and how variations in the accounts are related to the social context in which they are produced and, ultimately, to their different functions. In each case, then, we can start to see 'factual' accounts as contingent social products organised to achieve certain practical goals.

Despite this diversity and the provisional nature of these studies, they raise questions that are of central methodological and theoretical importance to social psychology. They illustrate, for instance, how basic social psychological notions such as 'identity', 'motivation', 'rules' and 'consensus' are very much the currency of participants' discourse (although they will not necessarily be formalised in this particular way). Moreover they demonstrate that ordinary discourse is recurrently organised in such a fashion that explanatory and evaluative categories appear as descriptions which merely document the genuine, observable features of social life. The danger, as we have stressed, is that what are really participants' explanations, participants' lay social psychologies, will become implicitly incorporated into the analysts' explanations. This can easily happen when members' discourse is treated as a straightforward document of social actions as it is regularly constructed to appear. (31)

This sort of methodological confusion between the interpretations of the analyst and the people being studied is evident in the work of Harré and Willis discussed in Chapter 4. For instance, as we have noted, a central feature of Willis's research is a comparison between the behaviour of two groups of school pupils. These groups are chosen by Willis to represent pupils who conform to the school culture and those who oppose it. Throughout his text Willis adopts, however, the descriptive terminology used by just one of his groups. He used 'the lads'' label for themselves and also their label for the conforming group, 'the ear'oles'. Yet it is clear that the ear'oles would not use this label to describe themselves. For it carries with it a negative evaluative baggage which becomes increasingly apparent as Willis outlines the detailed differences between the two groups.

For the most part the ear'oles are described from the perspective of the lads, who continually contrast their own daring, sexual prowess and social maturity with that of the ear'oles, whom they see as lacking these things. The ear'oles' perspective on themselves hardly enters into Willis's text. Indeed, the occasional quote from a member of this group is used only to reinforce the lads' account by seemingly illustrating an unquestioning acceptance of the school's version of reality. Thus, although the lads are viewed as rounded characters, riven through with contradictions and able to take an ironic stance on their activities and surroundings, the ear'oles come over as ciphers who are fully institutionalised into the school culture. It seems that Willis has adopted, at least in part, the dominant system of interpretation used by the lads, and this inevitably penetrates and sustains his analytic conclusions. Although his study is intended to undermine those explanations which treat participants as passive victims of social and institutional processes, Willis ends up explaining the behaviour of the ear'oles in exactly this way.

We do not wish to suggest, returning briefly to the theme of Chapter 4, that analyses of formal texts and discourse like those discussed in the majority of this chapter should entirely replace studies of people's different ways of reading. These analyses are meant to reveal the strategies by which certain texts 'manage' reality and thereby construct the social world in ways appropriate to each occasion of use. The question of how they are read (or heard) is a quite separate one. It is not, however, a logically prior question. Studies of reading cannot underpin particular textual analyses because 'readings' are subject to the very same social contingencies as texts and must therefore be approached in the same way. A rigorous analysis will eventually need to examine both those sections of discourse which are conventionally designated as readings, and start to tease out the complex interrelations between them.

Throughout this chapter, then, we have been concerned to illustrate the complex organisation and function of certain 'factual' texts and some of the ways in which they can embody participants' lay social psychological understanding. Moreover we have emphasised the danger of analysts reifying this understanding and incorporating it into their research findings. In the next chapter we will look closely at one particular attempt by a social psychologist to use certain 'factual' texts as a data base for developing social psychological theory. This example will illustrate in greater detail the way that analytic conclusions are dependent on certain systematic, but unacknowledged, techniques for dealing with discourse as a record of events.

6 VICTIM OF REALREAD

In this chapter we shall develop several points from the two previous chapters, through an examination of the use by a social psychologist of texts on the John Kennedy presidency. Irving Janis's Victims of Groupthink presents an analysis of some of the major US foreign policy fiascos in recent history, in terms of the psychological dynamics of small-group decision-making. In each case he relied for evidence of the relevant events on accounts written by officials, historians, political scientists, biographers, and so on. It is rare for social psychologists to use texts of this kind. Janis's work enables us to extend our explication of reading practices with a most interesting example which is frequently referred to, sometimes at unusual length, in textbooks of social psychology.

We shall limit our analysis to one of his case-studies, the incident of the Bay of Pigs. One textbook (1) introduces its significance for the study of groups as follows:

> There is perhaps no better analysis of how these normal groups interfere with effective problem-solving than Irving Janis' (1972) analysis of decision-making during the Bay of Pigs invasion of Cuba. President Kennedy's advisers included Dean Rusk, Robert McNamara, Douglas Dillon, Robert Kennedy, McGeorge Bundy, Arthur Schlesinger, Jr., and Allen Dulles - 'one of the greatest arrays of intellectual talent in the history of American Government' (Janis, 1972, p.43). They decided to send CIA-trained Cuban exiles to Cuba to overthrow the Castro government. The invasion proved to be a disaster. The exiles were captured or killed, the United States was embarrassed, and Cuba solidified its relationship with Russia. 'How could we have been so stupid?' President Kennedy asked. Janis argues that it was not stupidity, but *groupthink* that led to the fiasco. The main principle of groupthink is 'The more amiability and esprit de corps there is among the members of a policymaking in-group, the greater the danger that independent critical thinking will be replaced by groupthink, which is likely to result in irrational and dehumanizing actions directed against outgroups' (p.44). Among the processes that led to the invasion decision was the

illusion that the policy advisers were unanimous in their approval of the plan. Schlesinger (1965) wrote, 'Our meetings were taking place in a curious atmosphere of assumed consensus. Had one senior adviser opposed the adventure, I believe that Kennedy would have canceled it. Not one spoke against it.' There were strong pressures toward conformity among the advisers, so that those who had doubts about the policy remained silent.

The case-study will be examined here in terms of certain features of texts which Janis used as sources and the way in which he read them. His principal references were Arthur M. Schlesinger Jr's A Thousand Days and Theodore Sorensen's Kennedy. His aim was to produce an account, broadly consistent with his socio-psychological theory, of how matters really stood in the decision-making processes which led to the Bay of Pigs. Our argument in its simplest form is that in constructing his account he tended to read his source-texts as documents which represented social reality straightforwardly and unproblematically. In doing this, he seems to have been unaware of the variety of purposes which texts may fulfil, and to have assumed the possibility of their having a real meaning rather than meanings constructed by varying interpretative resources. We shall try to show how he achieved this and what some of the consequences are. The way in which Janis gives a privileged status to his sources, and in particular to parts of his sources selectively, recalls the difficulties discussed in Chapter 4 surrounding Harré's and Willis's use of 'accounts'.

We will draw attention to three features, in particular, of Janis's work, each at a different level of analysis. Firstly, it reveals rather tenuously (in the preface and footnotes) a conflict over the validity of historical material as data for a social psychologist. This seems to be resolved by a polarisation between 'fact' and 'myth' which inhibits 'interpretation' of the material and gives it its privileged status. Secondly, the realist position contradicts itself. The evidence for Janis's main thesis is contextualised by passages in the source text which lead one to doubt the feasibility of a valid realist reading. To achieve his conclusion he has to assume that a quite imperfect account is sometimes given by his source, and that this can be treated realistically as sufficient evidence. Thirdly, Janis's text can be read as having an ideological objective, which is not only not made explicit, but which can be seen as reflecting the ideology of his sources - there is an 'intertextual' component. We shall see that ideology emerges as a function both of Janis's scientific goals (to insist on a group, as opposed to an individualistic or structural, explanation of events) and of the way in which he reads his sources.

Several emphatic cautions are in order with respect to the argument in this chapter. Although we adopt a critical analysis of Janis's work, this chapter is not a critical review, in the sense of attempting to discount it. The work is entirely consistent with our claim that social psychologists might make more use of literary and other texts. And it is a highly original, interesting and fruitful use. We are not concerned with the scientific status of Janis's thesis; nor do we wish to comment on group dynamics theory nor on associated empirical research. (2) Our critique is not from within group psychology, political science, or history. What we do wish to discuss is the way in which he achieves his thesis through a particular type of reading of anterior texts. But we do not consider, except by implication, how Janis might alternatively have read his sources. Several indications may be picked up in other chapters of the present book. But it is not our intention to offer 'rules for reading' to social psychologists nor to anyone else. In ourselves adopting a particular reading, both of Janis and his sources, we are quite aware that our text, like its subject-matter, is open to alternative interpretations.

Finally by way of introduction, we wish to fend off interpretations arising from our and Janis's identity as psychologists. In what follows we do not intend to say anything 'psychological' about the motives and so on of Janis, Schlesinger and others. Anything which suggests such intentions should be re-read as being a proposition which emerges from the text and not from the author's psychology. Similarly in criticising Janis, we are not saying that he failed, as a psychologist, to detect the hidden motives of his authors; but rather that he failed, as a reader, to respond to certain features in the construction of his texts which we would interpretatively highlight. He was guilty, however, of psychologising, in so far as he derived his thesis 'a priori' from the psychology of group dynamics, rather than as emerging from the texts as texts.

PREFACING

Janis's <u>Victims cf Groupthink</u> is presented, indeed, as 'a psychological study of foreign-policy decisions and fiascoes'. The main theme of the book occurred to the author, he says, as he read the chapter on the Bay of Pigs incident in Schlesinger's account of the Kennedy presidency. The disastrous conduct of the CIA-organised invasion of Castro's Cuba by exiles based in the United States seemed to him to be so incredible as to be inexplicable in terms of the apparent stupidity of the President and his advisors. He was led 'to wonder whether some kind of psychological contagion, similar to social conformity phenomena observed in studies of small groups, had interfered with their mental alertness.' (3)

Subsequently, Janis found himself [sic] suggesting in a group psychology seminar that the behaviour in the White House on that occasion might illustrate a tendency in people to be more concerned with retaining the approval of fellow-members of their work-group than with coming up with good solutions to the task which faces them.

> Shortly after that, when I reread Schlesinger's account, I was struck by some observations that earlier had escaped my notice ... (which) began to fill a specific pattern of concurrence-seeking behavior that had impressed me time and again in my re-

search on other kinds of face-to-face groups, particularly when a 'we-feeling' of solidarity is running high. (4)

Other accounts of the Bay of Pigs incident strengthened Janis's impression that detrimental group processes had crucially affected the decision to invade Cuba.

Case-studies of other foreign policy decisions, which are also described in the book, provided further indications of the detrimental consequences of concurrence-seeking in a cohesive group. Janis's claim is that the psychology of group dynamics enables one to interpret historical facts about such cases in a way quite different from that employed by interested historians and political scientists. At the same time, his book is presented as a stage of hypothesis construction from 'imperfect', though the 'best available', historical materials: (5) the hypotheses are to be tested and rechecked by conventional social scientific means. And the book is also intended to make people more aware of and armed against 'groupthink' phenomena in the decision-making process.

A final note for scholars: this book is obviously at the intersection of three disciplines - social psychology, political science and history. I hope that the interpretations and theoretical conceptions suggested in the case-studies will add something to the thinking of scholars in each of these disciplines. (6)

The development and rationale of Janis's study is cited rather fully here, because it illustrates a number of issues in the relationship between social psychology and literature, or texts. But first we should refer to the theoretical function of the preface itself. At first reading its anecdotal and autobiographical tone is highly appealing - particularly to the psychologist reader, who will be unused to such revelations by a colleague as to how he came to choose his field of work or of the external influences upon it, and who may think it apposite in such an unusual study. But a closer look shows that it is not as historical or innocent an account as it may claim to be. For example, the aura of initial coincidental revelation of the theme cloaks its strong predetermination by the existing scientific, and ultimately political, interests of Janis. While the statement of objectives appears to open up the reader's mind to the wide potential of a novel, psychological attention to historical material, it can also be seen as a means of directing the reader to a particular interpretation of the book, and implicitly away from alternative interpretations. We shall suggest such an alternative ourselves; while at the same time arguing that Janis himself might have considered the possibility of interpretations, rather than simply a naturalistic reading, of his source texts. However, it should be emphasised that, if we make a contrast between explicit and implicit purposes in the Preface, we see these only as emergent from the way Janis's text is organised, and not as saying anything psychological about the subconscious or hidden intentions of Janis, the author.

One of his explicit objectives is to promote the use of 'alien', non-psychological documents as a way of putting across psychology. This approach has expanded considerably (7) since his book appeared. And the intersection of disciplines is one of our own main objectives, and indeed strongly attracted us to the book. It is difficult, however, to see what Janis intended to achieve in this respect or why he restricted its interest to 'scholars'. There is no discussion, no examples of what the intersection constitutes, and virtually no reference to principles, procedures or substantive results in the other two disciplines. The two remaining purposes - psychological interpretation of historical data and the formulation of new psychological hypotheses on the basis of reading historical material - are uneasily related, and there is no suggestion that each could be used critically to unmask the other. The starting and finishing points rest in the current state of psychological knowledge. The impetus was less a wish to find out more about the psychology of group dynamics, than to demonstrate the power of social psychological analysis using existing concepts. And, as we shall later claim, this is carried through for quite distinct purposes which are not referred to in the Preface. One could argue that Janis's failure to achieve the purposes set out in the Preface is no more than apparent, and is due to the unreflective manner in which he proceeds. But we would rather suggest that the significance of the multiple objectives is not in whether they are attained, but in their rhetorically directing our attention away from the implicit agenda of the book. What this agenda is we shall examine through a scrutiny of the way in which Janis uses the texts which are his source materials.

THE SOURCE ACCOUNTS

For his analysis of the Bay of Pigs incident Janis relies predominantly on his original source, Schlesinger's <u>A Thousand Days</u>, with supplementary information from Sorensen's <u>Kennedy</u> and several other books. His interpretation of this material rests on his dissatisfaction with what he calls the 'official four-factor explanation', his sense of its incompleteness. Dissatisfaction arises from his belief that the failure of Kennedy and his advisors to question and invalidate the 'assumptions' on which the Bay of Pigs invasion was based and which were subsequently shown to be faulty, and the advisors' failure to voice strong objections to the policy, is not accounted for.

The main thrust of the source accounts is that structural, organisational factors (for example, the inheritance of the basic plan from the Eisenhower administration, the untried nature of Kennedy's team, CIA secrecy) were responsible for the decisions made. Janis, on the other hand, finds in the accounts six symptoms of groupthink, without which these factors would not have been influential. Neither he nor his two principal sources pinpoint individuals as to blame for the decisions; or, rather, they engage in various manoeuvres to draw attention away from individuals. Janis establishes the focus of his thesis quite explicitly in his introductory chapter: 'The concept of groupthink pinpoints an entirely different source of trouble, residing neither in the individual nor in the organizational setting.' (8)

Most of Janis's evidence for the operation of groupthink in Kennedy's team comes from Schlesinger's account. Sorensen's is used almost entirely to document the role of the misinformation (variously termed 'miscalculations' or 'assumptions') which were subsequently seen to underlie the decisions made, and which formed the basis of the 'official' explanation. This disparity between his use of sources does not seem to be taken as noteworthy by Janis, presumably on the grounds that the two accounts represent equally reliable and authoritative, if different, samples of the total historical fact. But a less naturalistic reading of the texts suggests quite readily that they have conspicuous and crucially different agenda; and that this difference reflects on their potential usefulness for Janis's thesis.

Sorensen is open about the extent to which his book is not a neutral account, neither detached nor a-partisan. It is his substitute for the book which Kennedy himself would have wanted to write. In that spirit he attempts to be as candid as possible, portraying 'warts and all'. He is aware that his account is only one of several possible: 'Recollections differ, opinions differ, even the same facts appear different to different people.' (9) Although Schlesinger, in the foreword to his book, makes somewhat more play of its historical authenticity he, too, insists that it is a personal memoir, a partial view rather than a comprehensive history. We shall see later that Janis treats historical material as imperfect sources for psychological work; but he does not seem to respond to the implications of these particular avowals.

Admittedly Sorensen's prefacing may be no more open-hearted than Janis's. His account may well be interpretable in terms other than those which he sets out. But we are not interested in Sorensen's intentions as such; rather in the intertextuality of his, Schlesinger's and Janis's accounts. Janis neglects his sources' purposes and does not distinguish at any level between their differing claims. He actually deletes Sorensen's preface in an interesting 'mistake'. He displaces his intentions into the form of a comment by a third party: it is a <u>New York Times</u> reviewer who is allowed to describe Sorensen's book as 'the nearest thing we will ever have to the memoirs Kennedy intended to write'. (10)

In Sorensen an agenda of justification is explicit.

> John Kennedy was capable of choosing a wrong course but never a stupid one, and to understand how he came to make this decision requires a review not merely of the facts but of *the facts and assumptions that were presented to him*. (11)

The assumptions originate with the CIA and the military, who were responsible for the operation's planning and execution. In Sorensen's account, Kennedy and his advisors were given grossly untenable information by those whom they were prepared to view as the 'experts'. Blame thus emerges implicitly as lying with the CIA and the military, and with the contingent fact that the plan was 'inherited' from the Eisenhower administration (the word is repeated three times in one paragraph). (12)

Sorensen's justification comes to a climax in the final pages of his narrative, in which he insists on Kennedy shouldering the blame while simultaneously signalling both that for Kennedy to have taken the right decision would have entailed more qualities than one man might reasonably contain, that Kennedy's own outspoken and insistent assumption of blame was a part of the man's unique character, and that the ultimate triumph was that he entirely overcame this early setback to his tenure of office. There is not the space here to spell out the rhetoric which is used to achieve this goal. The account is subtly orchestrated both to acquit Kennedy of stupidity and blame and to extract the maximum heroic potential from what has otherwise been called a 'perfect failure'.

SCHLESINGER'S SELF-JUSTIFICATION

Schlesinger's agenda is more complicated. In both books Kennedy's image has to be protected, not only because of the authors' acknowledged admiration for him, but also because they connive in Kennedy's own public refusal to make the CIA or military out-and-out scapegoats for the fiasco. (13) Schlesinger's text adds self-justification to the justification of Kennedy. This component bears critically on Janis's use of A Thousand Days. But nowhere does he allude to it. The oversight is a feature of a reading practice which is devoted to a realistic use of texts. What follows is an alternative reading which draws attention to the text as constructed, often for purposes of social influence, and as concealing a far from innocent or authoritative author.

In the months preceding the invasion Schlesinger had written a White Paper on Cuba, and unlike Sorensen had taken part in many of the relevant policy discussions with Kennedy's team. (14) He was involved in the episode and makes no effort to conceal the fact. He is not reluctant to present himself in a favourable light. He describes, for example, Senator Fulbright's denunciation of the plan: 'He gave a brave, old-fashioned, American speech, honourable, sensible and strong; and he left everyone in the room, except me and perhaps the President wholly unmoved.' (15) This is followed immediately by a section headed 'A Personal Note', in which Schlesinger summarises two memoranda giving his opposition to the plan. But the self-justification is cloaked in a double-bind:

> These memoranda look nice on the record, but they represented, of course, the easy way out. In the months after the Bay of Pigs I bitterly reproached myself for having kept so silent during those crucial discussions in the Cabinet Room. (16)

And later when Bundy has to remind Kennedy that Schlesinger opposed the expedition, the President is quoted as saying, 'Oh, sure, Arthur wrote me a memorandum that will look pretty good when he gets around to writing his book on my administration.' (17) The reference in the next sentence to Kennedy's 'high sardonic humour' is a nice instance of displacement! What we read as Schlesinger's need for justification is fuelled both by self-reproach and by Kennedy's hurtful forgetfulness.

The impression of that need and of Schlesinger's self-interest is constantly reinforced in Chapters 10 and 11 of A Thousand Days.

> More than once I left the meetings in the Cabinet Room fearful that only two of the regulars present were against the operation; but, since I thought the President was the other, I kept hoping that he would avail himself of his own escape clause and cancel the plan. (18)

The very first description of the Cabinet Room group is given a rhetorical edge in Schlesinger's favour:

> I was summoned to a meeting with the President in the Cabinet Room. An intimidating group sat round the table ... and appropriate assistants and bottle-washers. I shrank into a chair at the far end of the table and listened in silence. (19)

This anticipates later excuses:

> It is one thing for a Special Assistant to talk frankly in private to a President at his request and another for a college professor, fresh to the government, to interpose his unassisted judgement in open meeting against such august figures as the Secretaries of State and Defence and the Joint Chiefs of Staff, each speaking with the full weight of his institution behind him. (20)

Both passages are set immediately in the context of Schlesinger's opposition to the plan.

The six pages devoted to his 'Mission to Miami', (21) when he was dispatched to placate the Cuban Revolutionary Council, add to the autobiographical flavour of his account of the Bay of Pigs. Beyond introducing Kennedy's compassion for the Cubans, and referring yet again to their expectation that they would receive direct US military support, (22) the episode adds little to our understanding of the 'thousand days'.

The foregoing details from the Schlesinger text have been read as strongly suggestive of an agenda of autobiography and self-justification, in part by ceasing to assume that the account is authoritative or privileged. This reading is consistent with the view put forward in our two previous chapters of texts as being organised to 'do work', notably to justify or persuade, rather than simply to describe. It seriously undermines Janis's project in the form in which he presents it.

It is not that he failed to see that his source, according to traditional criteria, might be 'inaccurate' or 'biased'. Nor is it the case that he got 'his facts' wrong through paying inadequate attention to Schlesinger's own close involvement in the events of the Kennedy presidency. Such criticisms would rely on traditional notions of realism and subjectivity which Janis himself might subscribe to, but which run counter to the position advocated in this book. The point is rather that his naturalistic reading prevents him from taking A Thousand Days as an 'account'. He does not interpret Chapters 10 and 11 in sum, (23) as a total persuasive achievement, set in its own social and value-laden contexts; but, apparently, as a string of independent 'facts'. This enables him to select out certain passages as containing the 'truth'. Like Harré and Willis he treats just one part of his material as explicating the genuine structure of social reality, in this case group decision-making processes. Even if Janis denied any claim to identify 'truth' in Schlesinger, he has still failed to give grounds for favouring what he cites as evidence. Again, like Harré and Willis, his reading practice can be seen to rest on ignoring the discursive integrity of quite particular constructions of social reality.

EVIDENCE FOR GROUP-THINK

Having discussed something of what is missing from Janis's reading, what of the evidence which he does bring forward for the group-processes which are so crucial to the evolution of his thesis? The symptoms of 'groupthink' which he detected were: an illusion of invulnerability in the group to the dangers of its actions; the replacement of critical thinking by consensual validation and an assumed unanimity; the suppression of personal doubt; the suppression of deviating points of view in others through social pressure; the maintenance of docility in the group by 'suave leadership'; and a taboo against antagonising valuable new members. Schlesinger's account is cited by Janis as giving evidence of all six symptoms. In most cases reading Schlesinger as a text, and particularly as an 'open text', permits interpretations which do not support Janis. (24)

For example, the main manifestation of the illusion of invulnerability is the sense of unlimited confidence, of euphoria which is said to have characterised the initial weeks of the Kennedy administration. In A Thousand Days the main description of this state occurs in Chapter 9, immediately preceding the Bay of Pigs narrative. But despite its title, 'The Hour of Euphoria', only one-third of the chapter is taken up with this theme - the rest is devoted to setting the scene in Cuba, Castro's rise to power and 'communization'. The chapter's structure suggests that the euphoria is placed to contrast with the gathering trouble in Cuba and the administration's subsequent setback with the Bay of Pigs. There may have been a euphoric mood in the administration. (25) But here it acquires dramatic emphasis, with a suggestion of hubris before a fall.

Janis treats the information as separable from its context and as quite literal. It is preferable, however, to see it as inevitably embedded in and structurally related to a wider text, and thus open to a range of alternative interpretations, one of which refers to this textual device of contraposition.

In the scope of <u>A Thousand Days</u> as a whole, the Bay of Pigs fiasco is counterbalanced by the triumphant handling of the Cuban Missile Crisis more than a year later. The significance of the former episode, in a diachronic reading of the text, cannot escape the latter. Janis does refer to the missile crisis in <u>Victims of Groupthink</u>; it is a case-study for demonstrating the non-incidence of groupthink and of successful group problem-solving. Although he inevitably makes contrasts - that is his purpose - they are between events and not between texts or parts of a text. The different way in which Schlesinger reports them and their particular roles in his text as a whole are not examined by Janis. They are not seen apparently as an essential part of what he has available as source material. His synchronic reading is characteristic of social psychology's more general reluctance to engage with temporally extended processes.

The evidence for an illusion of unanimity also looks different if one takes account of the immediate context from which it is drawn. The two principal citations are set in passages which attribute the unanimous decision to go ahead with the plan to the relative inexperience of the administration, to the CIA's domination of discussions, and to Kennedy's trust in the experts - that is, to several components of the 'official explanation'. There are at least three ways in which we might view Janis's reading of these passages. From a traditional social scientific viewpoint it is unparsimonious. Janis can be seen as invoking an additional group characteristic to explain what might quite reasonably be assumed to have occurred because those who were involved did not have enough confidence to doubt the experts. Also from a traditional standpoint, it is an invalid use of evidence. One part of a set of data is rejected and a contradictory claim is built up on another part of the same set. Furthermore, this procedure is only justified by intuitive misgivings, by Janis's assumption that intelligent advisors could not have failed to doubt the CIA experts unless some other force had intervened - that is, groupthink. A third version of what Janis is doing might claim that he is critically interrupting Schlesinger's text, by demonstrating the historian's consciousness of his own involvement and responsibility even at the point when he is explicitly attributing the cause to structural factors. But, as we have seen, Janis does not in fact exhibit any interest in Schlesinger's involvement except as a 'historical fact'. Thus on both a traditional as well as a more radical reading Janis fails to bring home his evidence at this point.

The allegedly naturalistic evidence for the illusion of unanimity is clearly adorned by Schlesinger's own rhetoric: 'the massed and caparisoned authority of his senior officials' echoes the earlier self-deprecating description of his first encounter with the Cabinet

Room gathering; and the phrase 'curious atmosphere of assumed consensus', which is such an important part, if not a direct reflection, of Janis's thesis of deluded unanimity, comes from one who was perhaps the only man who in fact did not share the consensus. Indeed, to be the only one in the right is an awkward position, as Kennedy sardonically hinted.

In the light of this, the symptom of suppressed personal doubts is far from obvious. Although Sorensen's post-mortem concluded that people had had their doubts, the only manifest doubter is the self-confessing Schlesinger. Janis suggests that group members may have been inhibited in their doubts by fears of seeming 'unvirile', echoing Salinger's claim that 'virile poses were conveyed in rhetoric used by the representatives of the CIA and The Joint Chiefs of Staff'. (26) But the rhetoric is in fact Schlesinger's, and perhaps only serves to underline his shame at not having spoken out.

One final comment may be made on the evidence for symptoms of groupthink: that for the taboo against antagonising valuable new members. Here Janis is hoist by his own petard. Schlesinger expresses admiration for Bissell and describes how the group were 'fascinated by the workings of this superbly clear, organized and articulate intelligence'. Their high regard for him, Janis claims, prevented them from adequately criticising the CIA-plan which he and Dulles advocated throughout. But this is Janis's own tactic. He begins his analysis with a two-page, glowing summary of the qualifications of the core members of the advisory group, and starts from the explicit standpoint that individuals of such considerable intellectual talent could not be capable of reaching the decision which was made - their failure was collective. Contradictions such as this critically expose the way in which Janis's reading of Schlesinger is guided by his prior purposes.

Our argument so far has focused on the way in which Janis read his sources, and in particular on his failure to see Schlesinger's account as being significantly different in kind from other possible accounts. The fact that the best part of his evidence for groupthink symptoms comes from the account of a participant, while that of a non-participant, Sorensen, does not apparently contain similar evidence is by-passed. The references to assumed 'groupthink' are never unequivocal; more importantly, they are embedded in passages which more centrally appear to be dealing with Kennedy's or the CIA's role in the decision-process or with Schlesinger's own part. Since Schlesinger has reasons for diverting our attention from a head-on confrontation with these awkward issues, the possibility exists that Janis's evidence is a part of his source's diversionary rhetoric, a deliberate or subconscious hinting at another agency at work than the President, the author, or the organisational fabric of government and defence. (27)

In the terms of our previous chapter Janis may be failing to detect the social psychological constructs which are deployed in the discourse he takes as evidence. What for him is a theoretical issue, is for Schlesinger a practical and social issue. His reading thus becomes parasitic upon Schlesinger's interpretative practices and he does no more than incorporate those elements of social events which he would seek to explain.

EMERGENT MOTIVES AND IDEOLOGIES

Janis's text actually gives rise to a similar set of emergent motives as Schlesinger's. The form in which Schlesinger's text appears in Janis's reveals analogous processes of sense-making to those which one finds in Schlesinger's itself. <u>Victims of Groupthink</u> shows a notable reluctance to ascribe blame either to individuals or to organisations. Apart from a mild reproof to Kennedy's over-suave leadership (for which at the same time Janis holds the Cabinet group partly responsible), the President's image is not tarnished. (28) An additional guard is erected in a concluding chapter where Janis is at pains to contradict the 'myth' of sole presidential responsibility in decision-making (both in government and other corporate bodies) and restates what he believes to be the crucial role of advisors. (29) (In doing so he by-passes the extremely interesting rhetoric of Sorensen, which we have already referred to, whereby Kennedy is allowed sincerely to accept responsibility and thereby heroic status, without acquiring any of the blame for the episode.)

Janis's group thesis is protective of individuals at the outset, in his outright incredulity at the apparent stupidity of those involved. The indisputably central and harmful role of the intelligence and military organisations is constantly blurred by him in his translation of matters of misinformation and secrecy on their part into illusory assumptions on the part of the advisory group (which included members of those organisations). The teacher in group dynamics at Yale makes no bones about his wish to promote a group thesis. He chooses to do this by giving an exaggerated impression of the insignificance of individual and structural components of the episode. Although he makes a formal gesture at the necessity of considering these components in an integrated way with the group explanation, there is absolutely no indication of how this might be achieved. And his actual suppression of two of the components, which we have suggested he has to carry through to achieve his particular reading of Schlesinger, as well as to highlight his thesis, is akin to a denial of any such integration. Several chapters in the present book argue that this absence of integration is characteristic of much socio-psychological analysis.

Ideologically, the texts of both Janis and Schlesinger can be seen as having the same protective goal. For the United States, neither the state and its apparatus, nor its symbolic head, nor the mystical virtues of the individual can easily be held responsible for an episode which shamed them before the world, and made them a laughing-stock. Far better that the responsibility should be 'collective'. Janis's Preface adds his peculiar purpose as a social psychologist who wishes to reinterpret history and show the relevance of his discipline to phenomena which it normally reflects.

In achieving that purpose the text intersects on frequent occasions with the more hidden agenda of its source. While it misses Schlesinger's self-justification, it connives at other parts of what his text can be read as achieving.

RHETORIC AND REALISM

Janis has his own rhetoric to help establish his thesis, which prevents one reading it, if one ever could, in quite the scientific light suggested for us in the Preface. Thus, the 'group' whose behaviour is analysed is treated as a self-evident entity, something other than a collection of men; and yet there is little evidence as to exactly what that collection constituted and what sort of group it was. The six case-studies are all, allegedly by 'happenstance', of United States' policy decisions; the thesis thus becomes firmly embedded in an unquestioned set of cultural presuppositions. Only in the penultimate chapter are 'candidates for a casebook of European fiascoes' introduced; and then only for the purpose of generalising the groupthink hypothesis. We have already referred to the way in which Schlesinger is referred to as 'authoritative'; and to the translation of 'misinformation' into 'miscalculations' or 'assumptions'. The possibility of the advisors questioning those assumptions, the voicing of opposition and the expression of mild misgivings tend to be elided with one another, though these are by no means the same things as far as the operation of groupthink is concerned. In either case, these expected reactions rest on the particular assumption about the role of Kennedy's advisors, and a presupposition about the shaky grounds for the information which they were considering. Janis is 'incredulous' of their apparent stupidity; he has a 'sense of incompleteness' about the 'official explanation' of the decision process, but cannot articulate it. He concedes that the groupthink hypothesis supplements that explanation, but gives no indication of how it might be integrated or what essential difference it would make to the structure of the official explanation. The disparity in weight between components of the latter, which are on the face of it highly reasonable and straightforwardly attested to in a number of sources, and Janis's recondite inferences, which are built up from a few small details, is never confronted.

If Janis does consider the nature of Schlesinger's text at all critically, it is only indirectly and in a footnote. (30) He recognises there that all pro-Kennedy authors may have introduced subtle distortions and biassed reporting. But the only solution to what he evidently sees as a problem

> is to take the position that *if* the facts reported by Schlesinger, Sorensen and the authors are essentially accurate, my analysis of the converging pattern of this 'evidence' leads to the conclusion that the groupthink hypothesis helps to account for the deficiencies in the decision-making of the Kennedy team.

A further note, on the source material for the fifth case-study, the

Cuban Missile Crisis, also recognises the possibility of bias and in a most interesting way. 'As usual ... all the observations ... come from participants who have a stake in presenting the group's actions in a favourable light.' (31) This discounts, by implication, the possibility that participants should wish to dress up their own individual actions, thereby preserving some basis for the validity of their accounts at the same time as keeping attention directed at the group level. Furthermore, 'This bias ... becomes most serious when we are dealing with supposedly well-worked out decisions (such as the Missile Crisis) rather than with the erroneous ones that led to fiascoes (e.g. Bay of Pigs).' No reason is given for this asymmetry, which does so much to preserve the analysis of the earlier case-study.

The same note contains an excellent illustration of how Janis's realist position sets him firmly against the possibility of interpreting texts. He fends off the problem of bias in this particular case-study by referring to the impressive consistency of his evidence. '... to be *that* consistent, the participants must be either describing accurately what they actually observed or presenting a myth that they collectively worked out in a conspiracy to mislead the public about what really went on.' There seems to be no alternative position. The polarising status of myth appears again in a later chapter, in a section on 'The leader's role: Fact versus myth.' (32) In order to discount individual responsibility, for example of the President, it is labelled a myth; group decision-making through the participation of advisors thus becomes a matter of 'fact'.

Janis expresses more general worries in his Preface about the 'errors of written history'. (33) A multiplicity of documents entails controversy and partisan distortion. Participant historians will have an eye to their own place in history. The best interim solution is 'to start off on solid ground by selecting the best available historical writings and to use as my springboard those specific observations that appear to be solid facts in the light of what is now known about the deliberations of the policy making groups'. Ultimately, 'the psychological explanations inferred from the imperfect historical materials will have to be checked carefully' by conventional social scientific means. The only secure means of 'testing group dynamics hypotheses are verbatim records of formal group meetings and of informal conversations among the members'.

In adopting these attitudes, Janis raises a number of issues about the status of 'texts' for a psychologist. Multiplicity of texts is taken as problematic, but not as interesting in its own right, as precisely the point of interest. If it is soluble, it is by reference to notions of 'fact', authority and criteria of excellence. These are not discussed; but are presumably the conventional, consensually based criteria of the scientific (or historical) élite. No data are perfect; the only defence against chaos is the judgment of good and true men through generations of the search for truth. The notion that it is the very 'imperfections' of the data which constitute their interest, that the 'holes in the text' reveal both sides of its meaning, does not commend itself to psychologists. They prefer to believe in some alchemical test of the soundness of one's inferences, and presumably also of the original data, by experimental means; and in some ultimately perfect data. But how one text (observations in a laboratory experiment on group dynamics) reflects on another (inferences from a historical account) is obscure. Concordance is looked for at a high level of conceptual abstraction. But there is no theory to justify the implicit equation of the process of inferring the linking concepts from, in his case, historical observations with that of operationalising them in the laboratory. Our doubts are compounded when the inferences are made by a social psychologist who is highly experienced in making such operationalisations. The reading of the historical text is probably guided by the dictates of that experience; and the text of the laboratory experiment becomes privileged. Verbatim records also take on a privileged form, protected by their customary inaccessibility or resistance to conventional, crude quantification. Why should they be more interesting than the indirect speech and reports which form so significant a part of social process? And can we avoid the regress of taking them in turn as a 'partisan' or 'biased' gloss on what the speakers knew was really going on between them? They are equally imbued with the problems of textuality and reading which we discuss in this book.

CONCLUSION

None of this discussion of <u>Victims of Groupthink</u> and of <u>A Thousand Days</u> is intended to suggest that Schlesinger's account or Janis's interpretation of it is in any sense 'wrong' or 'inaccurate'. We would wish to emphasise also that more and different readings of Schlesinger and Janis are quite possible. What we do question, however, is the notion that certain texts are privileged to be taken at face value, that they say what their authors claim. Thus, Janis's text appears to us to have been taken in by Schlesinger's: by accepting the overt message it has accepted the hidden agenda, but has then connived by withdrawing it and erecting it to a position of potential 'truth', rather than seeing it as a manifestation of the author's unease. Janis further invites us to read his text according to a specific format, as being the work of a social psychologist seeking after truth and offering preventive advice, rather than as the reproduction of a particular ideology.

The thesis of 'groupthink' is not invalidated nor made redundant by the criticisms of Janis's reading, which are that he adopted a realist rather than interpretative approach. In doing so he fell victim to the complexity of his source: the evidence in Schlesinger for the groupthink thesis is, we claim, contextualised by material which leads one to doubt the feasibility of a straightforwardly realist reading. In exposing Janis's approach, we ourselves interpret the texts. We do not suggest an alternative, more definitive realist position, as regards Janis's intentions or Schlesinger's motives. Drawing attention to the vocabulary of justification is a means of exploring Janis's reading practice and of suggesting what can emerge when one reads 'between' texts. Groupthink may still legitimately be treated as a phenomenon which can be found in certain texts with certain characteristics; interpreting those characteristics synthetically produces 'groupthink'. It is not an independently existing and operating entity to be unearthed from data or deduced from prior psychological knowledge. It is a construction by Schlesinger, Janis and the readers of Janis's text. Nor even should self-justification have been identified as a psychological entity in Schlesinger; it is a feature of the text which Janis sought to use.

PART 3

7 ELITES AND STEREOTYPES

> In the re-creation of such themes as ... groups both big and
> small, their nature and the way they work; the relationship of
> the group and the individual; the formulation of group decisions
> and the importance of jobs in a bureaucratic society - Snow is
> undisputedly a master. He speaks with authority and conviction,
> doubtless because he has himself held office in several different
> fields. (1)

Janis's starting point in the previous chapter, the study of groups, is a major area of social psychology. One introductory textbook (2) has even been subtitled 'People in Groups'. Some of the most interesting recent advances in the discipline, (3) to which we shall refer in the latter part of this chapter, focus on processes between and within groups. If a group psychologist of the 1960s or 1970s had taken an interest in literature, similar to that of Janis in political biography and historical writings, he would probably have found himself reading the novels of C.P. Snow. Most likely he would have followed one of the approaches discussed in Chapter 3.

We shall very briefly outline how these approaches might run; and argue, not on this occasion that they are inadequate in themselves, but that Snow's novels despite their realistic allure are a poor basis for such an enterprise. The refutation is then pursued by a detailed examination of one of Snow's essays. In reading this alternative form of discourse from the novel as a veiled justificatory account by Snow of his treatment of élite groups in his <u>Strangers and Brothers</u> novel sequence, we question the status and sophistication of the social thinking and observation which lies behind his highly polished and realistic tale. Reading Snow in this way, in our guise as social psychologists, in turn suggests certain criticisms of 'élitism' in social psychology. These are followed by further critical 'inter-readings', between Snow and social psychology. For example, we draw attention to problems of fragmentation in the two sets of discourse, and to authorial problems. Finally, we shall use some recent developments in the socio-psychological study of stereotypes, both to suggest common features in the 'sense-making' which occurs in Snow and in everyday social processes and discourse, and also on that basis to criticise Snow's social representations and ultimately the socio-psychological analysis itself.

GROUPS IN SOCIETY

If Snow's novels had been taken as a potential resource for social psychology it would almost certainly have been because of the recurrent and dominant treatment of group themes such as decision-making in organisational settings. No doubt the allure would have been increased by the setting of several novels in academic life and the world of science. (4) In The Masters or The Affair, for example, those themes are repeatedly represented, as a small Cambridge college attempts to resolve its difficult task of appointing a new head or adjudicating a case of alleged scientific fraud. The closed community must act alone to reach a decision and does so through a central series of groupings and re-groupings, anxious meetings of different sizes and levels of unanimity, and full-scale battles between opposing sides around the table. In The New Men and Corridors of Power the stories largely hinge on the ways in which ministers, civil servants and scientists work together or apart. In these high reaches the formal nuances of committee procedure express as much as actual substance. In all these novels the more minor characters have little more than a passing identity except in relation to one or more groups; and for all the characters their work and their consequent involvement in, or alienation from, formal institutions constitutes the major part of their lives.

If one accepted the claim which has been made that Snow was a master of political and social realism the novels might be read by psychologists to improve their social insight or as a source of more ecologically valid processes in need of scientific explanation. Or one might use psychological models of group processes, for example, as a means of giving an independent or 'objective' structuring to the content of the novels. From the viewpoint which is interested in the social influence and persuasiveness of literature, one might ask about the impact of The New Men, a novel frequently prescribed as a text in secondary schools, or Corridors of Power, both of which deal with the development and use or interdiction of nuclear weapons. Attitudes on such potent issues might well be influenced by highly naturalised, and perhaps authoritative accounts of how they are dealt with by scientists, civil servants and politicians. Alternatively, Snow's own psychological state could excite attention, because, for example, of the avowedly autobiographical basis in the main character of the novels, Lewis Eliot; or the unusual combination in one person of successful academic scientist, civil servant and literary figure.

At the same time Snow seems to achieve what is scarcely to be detected in laboratory experiments on groups. His observations are situated within fifty years of English social life. He might be seen as a commentator on the social scenes which were contemporary with the events of each of the sequence of novels: from the early provincial life in the twenties (George Passant), the life of Anglo-

Jewry (<u>The Conscience of the Rich</u>) and attitudes towards and detachment from war with Germany (<u>The Light and the Dark</u>) in the thirties, to the affluence and permissiveness of the 1960s (<u>The Sleep of Reason</u>) and later the idealism and restiveness of youth (<u>Last Things</u>). To quote one of his chief admirers again:

> Outside the novels he has lectured on important public affairs and social issues, and within his fiction he has caught the changing tenor of half a century in Britain with a niceness and accuracy which must compel admiration from the most grudging critic. (5)

When Snow himself says that 'the moment you extract man from society you don't make him more interesting, you don't make him deeper, you make him in the long run trivial' (6) he might be joining recent critics of 'social psychology in a vacuum'. (7) He describes his novels as attempting a resonance between man and society and wished to write a novel in which neither society nor the individual played a pre-determining role over the other. If he was successful his novels should provide a model for a social psychology which does avoid predominantly organismic-individualistic or role oriented-collectivistic imbalances, of the kind to which we drew attention in Chapter 2 and shall return to in the next chapter.

Our argument here, however, is that Snow should not be used for these purposes. Despite his intentions and the claims made for him by critics, he fails at those very points where he might be used as a resource and precisely at those points. If he has a significance for social psychology it is to illustrate its weakness; and to demonstrate the unavoidable intertextuality of products which come from related intellectual traditions.

We discuss him here to suggest that a too instant recognition of the potential relevance for psychology of particular literary works should be taken as an indication that they may only be mirroring one another, with no more than incidental differences. We foreshadowed this conclusion in Chapter 1, in doubting the extent to which Lessing's novels give more insight than psychology into the nature and practice of sex-role.

We would argue, for example, that Snow restricts himself almost entirely to the examination of élitist groups, and in doing so adopts a consensual, reactionary and uncritical approach to their operation. His apparently competent treatment of the social scene is for this reason necessarily partial, and even within his self-imposed limitations the wider social situation is superficially presented. Rather than achieving a balance between the individual and society, he introduces an artificial discontinuity between them. This is reinforced by a thematic series of analogous polarisations, such as worldly success vs. self-knowledge, morality vs. aestheticism or the demands of office vs. idealism.

These shortcomings are both revealed in and created by a number of procedural failings. The novel-sequence is mortally fragmented:

resonance or integration between different aspects and levels of lives is inhibited by the gaps between those novels which refer, whether explicitly or implicitly, to the same characters or events. The operationalisation of themes and concepts is very thinly managed. An examination of anything which loosely comes within the scope of a social term, for example, is allowed to stand as an examination of the content of that term, without any prior analysis of its centrality or weight. And, finally, the use of the autobiographical narrator and character, Lewis Eliot, produces continual implausibilities, immodesties and incongruities, which considerably hinder the attainment of Snow's other purposes.

THE JUSTIFICATION OF ELITES

Little of this argument is original. Most of the points can be found in published comments and criticisms on the eleven novels of Strangers and Brothers. Rather than repeat them at this stage, we prefer to look in some detail at an article (8) written by Snow not long after he had completed the sequence. In a brief span it gives an impression of what we might be taking on if we accepted Snow through his novels as an especially insightful and skilled commentator on the British social scene. He produced many articles and lectures on public affairs and issues; and the article discussed below was published at the time that a collection of this work was appearing. (9) It is especially revealing for our purposes because the commentary so closely, if implicitly, involves Snow's own role as a novelist, and throws light on the status of his novels as social commentary. The pseudo-social scientific form of the article perhaps makes it a riper target for social psychologists than for literary critics.

'In the communities of the elite' sets out to justify an attention to élites in literature. Snow sees élites as likely to become ever more prominent in advanced societies throughout the world, despite a counter-tendency towards egalitarianism. Their mere presence legitimises their treatment in literature, provided that it is handled without self-consciousness. A prime example, Snow suggests, was Proust's artists. A major question about all élites concerns their social constitution. This is discussed in relation both to the academic élite, which has appeared in literature, and to the scientific, which has only rarely. Administrative élites can and have often been introduced, unproblematically. The final justification for this theme in literature comes from two artistic rewards: it introduces lucidity or comprehensibility, and it enables the writer to study characters - members of élites - who are 'freer spirits' than the rest of mankind.

Although it is precisely those élites which Snow refers to in the article which also lie at the heart of Strangers and Brothers, he does not refer to his novels. Readers of The Times Literary Supplement would not need to be reminded of them. Yet there is the gap in the text. This, together with the article's generally de-

fensive tone, allows one to read it as a justificatory account in
which Snow constructs answers to implied criticisms which might be
levelled at his novels. We are first lulled with a brief discussion
of the inevitability of egalitarianism in advanced industrial societies. But then we are immediately told that there is a nasty and
destructive as well as a benevolent source to this trend. Furthermore, there is a fight between egalitarianism and its counter-force,
(10) the specialisation which advanced society also demands:
'Psychologically it tends to aim at maximum mixed-up-ness; func-
tionally, it needs people, or at least significant groups of people,
to become more differentiated, not less.' These groups require
specific abilities and develop each a common sub-culture. 'So that
the groups become élites. Whether we like it or not, that is a fact
of life.'

The polarity which Snow introduces, between psychological and functional modes, parallels polarities in his novels, to which we have
already referred and will return. The special sense which Snow at-
taches to these terms is apparent. He is never an elegant writer,
but 'maximum mixed-up-ness', repeated later in the article, is pe-
culiarly and unnecessarily jarring; its emotional connotations are
plain. The restriction of functional differentiation to a small
minority of the population is glossed over and taken for granted by
the innocuous 'or at least'. The non-sequiturs and misplaced col-
loquialisms of the two sentences 'so that the groups ... fact of
life' reveal just how much Snow is likely not to discuss in his
article: namely how and why differentiation leads to élitism,
and what its consequences are.

What he turns to instead is a discussion of a particular élite:
'The elite of self conscious artists, and the whole romantic conception of the artist, is a neat example.' This, with excursions
into academic and scientific élites, takes up most of the rest of
the article. It is, of course, a neat example. In so far as
artists are especially self-conscious and conform to the romantic
image - generally, a highly dubious proposition - they are quite
distinct from those élites from whom our attention is being di-
verted, the administrators, politicians, businessmen, engineers,
lawyers and other professional groups who hold the majority of
power in advanced industrial societies. More particularly they
conspicuously lack, in their romantic guise, those characteristics
which epitomise members of the élitist groups who inhabit Snow's
novels. They are more akin to such sensitive, pathological, doomed
individualists as Roy Calvert, who is persistently set against each
group he encounters. The focus on artists as an apposite example
of élites gives Snow the advantage of having to deal only indirectly with his treatment of élites in his novels.

Administrative élites, which are the most central thematically in
the novels, are actually shrugged aside later in the article.

> Many less specific elites, such as administrative ones can be
> and have been written about with no difficulty at all. You can
> see this in detective stories, which, for a purely artistic

reason, have been able to apply themselves to elites with more
certainty of touch than have higher forms of art. ... a detec-
tive-story ... can incorporate its social material, as it were
without looking for it deliberately.

Administrative élites are tamed by being arbitrarily labelled as
'less specific', and popularised through an association with detective stories. Even their purely artistic application is suspect.
We understand that these are only 'stories', and a humbler form of
art than the novel. The extraordinary association of administrators
with detective stories at first conceals their importance in Snow's
novels, but ultimately reveals his unease about their status there.

Despite the inevitability and rewards of writing about élites, Snow
wishes it to be achieved with a minimum of fuss; rather, he suggests, in the way in which the Victorians held class naturally in
the background. (11) 'No one ought to pick out an elite, study it,
and write about it as end in itself ... he has to do it naturally,
not self-consciously, as part of an altogether deeper and uncon-
nected impulse.' This 'impulse' is not further explained. It seems
to entail a lack of critical appraisal. One is reminded of Bergonzi's comment (12) on Snow's literary technique, which he sees as
'very much part of the English ideology, which regards writing
novels as something one just *does*, like breathing or walking, without any need for conscious thought'. A similar comment could be
made on Snow's attitude to the substance of the novels, when he
says, in the context of this natural impulse: 'The social world,
for a writer, is what he is presented with.' Elites are a part of
the world, let's face it, whether we like it or not, a fact of life.
So we must write about them, do research on them, just like that,
as we find them.

Fortunately for Snow, however, there is some recompense for an
innocent, unblinking openness to the social world as it actually
is; there are artistic rewards. One is lucidity or comprehensibility, which is so hard to produce 'in a world of maximum mixed-
up-ness'. Elites are 'small patches of order'. Jane Austen and
Trollope used them to express a 'social comprehensibility' which
'gives their readers confidence and perhaps subliminal peace'. It
would be difficult to find a more direct statement of Snow's con-
sensualist and reactionary aims for literature.

The other reward is 'a little odder'. Indeed! For it is an outright contradiction of one of the most persistent themes in Snow's
novels: the incompetence in social organisations of the free
spirit, the sensitive and idealistic individual, and the superiority
of the steady and moral group. Members of an élite are a gift to a
writer because they are 'slightly freer in personality than the rest
of us ... they are that much different from the rest of us'. Passing over the unconvincing dissociative use of 'us', one can only
repeat that all the characters who are relatively freer in personality, and in Snow's terms more conformable to the stereotype of
the romantic artist - the most obvious being Calvert, Passant and
Martineau - are those who reject the rewards of élite group-member-

ship. In part, this extravagant contradiction is sprung upon Snow by his own use of artists as the prime example. But both the contradiction and the inconsequence of the example help us to read the integral flaws in a body of writing which is celebrated for its smooth urbanity.

Further difficulties arise in the central part of the article, where Snow deals with academic and scientific élites. Although they play a major role in more than half of the novel sequence, they are discussed here in rather a disassociated way. Indeed, the interest of scientific élites is that they have received little literary attention. But uppermost in this passage is Snow's feeling, or anticipation of his readers' feeling, that a particularly problematic element of élites is class-membership. (13) He has previously associated writing about élites with Victorian writing about class. He ponders on the class origins of academic and scientific élites.

He notes the relatively developed status of the academic novel (Malamud, Bradbury, Amis), and wonders how accurate its social physiognomy is. 'Sociologically, probably not far off: it ought to be possible to discover.' Indeed, but how many established [sic] university staff in the US or UK are by origin middle-class? Perhaps ninety per cent. 'It would probably be at least as high in France or Germany, but there does not seem much literary evidence.' Snow has been hooked by his own naturalising tendencies into apparently believing that the representations of the academic novel can be discussed in the same sense as quantitative sociological data.

At the same time, by reducing the matter of class in academic novels to a potential question for sociology its political content is kept in the background. The power of the élites which appear in Snow's novels derives to a marked extent from class-membership. Yet their power is not mentioned in this article. They are seen as receiving advantages, but not as being in an unique position to control them: '... elites anywhere get various kinds of special treatment, sometimes privilege, sometimes material rewards, and as a rule, and most important the chance to carry on with their idiosyncratic professional life' ('idiosyncratic' appears to attach itself to the artist élite which has just been referred to by Snow. The far from idiosyncratic practices of, for example, administrative élites are thereby discounted).

Snow does actually express a wish to know, in a conventional empirical manner, what are the family backgrounds of Fellows of the Royal Society, and whether they vary with age and subject. But characteristically, given his apparent disregard for the wide range of sociological and psychological research relevant to his interests which had been completed in the US and UK by 1971, he would find it instructive to have no more than a 'little simple investigation' of the question. His apparent ignorance of the research, though perhaps not his disdain, is, in a Civil Service Commissioner, unconvincing. Perhaps he does not wish to know the answer. Thus, he can immediately go on to assert that 'One of the most genuinely

classless elites on earth is to be found in the Institute of
Theoretical Physics at Trieste', with a director born in a poor
village in Pakistan. The single case seems to make the irrelevant
point more neatly for Snow, that élites are not class-bound. One
is reminded of the only real attempts at a working-class character
in the novels, Walter Luke, son of a Devonport dockhand, who rises
to be head of the fictional equivalent of the Atomic Energy Research
Establishment at Harwell and Lord Luke of Salcombe.

It is difficult after reading 'In the communities of the elite' to
have confidence in Snow as an authoritative and percipient source of
issues to be examined in contemporary society. If issues are raised
they come from the contradictions and gaps of his text. What is
raised by Snow's writing are not critical questions about the internal processes of élitist groups as such, or about how they acquire and exercise social influence over other groups in particular
social circumstances. The questions which stand out concern the
ways in which he constructs his various discourses. How do his
novels work to conceal the uneasiness which is so apparent in other
writings? (14) In part it is because one is carried along by involvement in an apparently realistic story, by admiration for his
persistent ability to make some recognisable connection with fifty
years of life in England - novel sequences seem to win attention
and respect automatically today - and by our ready professional
identification with the academic, scientific and civil service
worlds. The force of the realism which Snow so much admired (15)
carries one over the difficulties which appear in more obviously
abstract texts.

REFLECTIONS ON PSYCHOLOGY

If we consider the practice of academic psychology as a form of
discourse in the light of these remarks about Snow, (16) a number
of analogous observations suggest themselves - not about what social
psychologists have to say about the behaviour of élite or any other
groups, but about how they achieve what they say. (17) The apparent
ease with which psychology, like other sciences, maintains itself as
a practice through highly persuasive discourse can be disrupted by a
reflexive reading of 'In the communities of the elite'.

The assumption of ultimately realisable laws which are universally
generalisable is psychology's version of egalitarianism. But it has
been made less convincing by, for example, a largely ethnocentric
practice; (18) and, more fundamentally, by theories and methods
which rely on principles of differentiation. The principal practical fields of psychology not only service élitist professions
(managers, teachers, doctors), but do so extensively through the
application of modes of functional differentiation. Academic social
psychology has been almost entirely élitist, both in its audience
and its subject-matter. There is rarely an attempt to study representative samples of the population; ever-present students are used
as subjects. Their marginal status may be admitted; but it is used
in turn to gloss over their privileges and natural expectation of

power. The availability of student-subjects is taken as naturally as the ready availability of topics for study - albeit in the psychological literature.

The social world is taken as given, rather than being self-consciously analysed. Like Snow, few psychologists would think of picking out an issue, studying it and writing about it as an end in itself. There is no accepted critical apparatus for selecting issues. As basic a social question as the psychological significance of employment, for example, has been almost entirely ignored until very recent crisis conditions, when unemployment begins to cripple the middle class. Even now it is studied with palliative rather than critical motives. Class itself is simply not an issue in most social psychology, perhaps because of the dominance of North America in the discipline until recently. One cannot detect even the unease of Snow. Though if class ever does intrude it tends to be shrugged off as 'sociological', neutralised in the shape of a classificatory variable - as sex was until the feminist movement was heard.

Underlying these complaints are issues of order. Science is typically presented as a means of ordering an otherwise chaotic view of a chaotic world. But the contingent features referred to above carry with them quite separate rewards of orderliness. The strong warranting of practices in the scientific community brings as much confidence and peace to most of its members as Jane Austen or Trollope could give Snow. The achievement of that peace through the neglect or control of those outside the community may be overlooked. The other artistic reward which élites can offer the writer - their distinctive psychological natures - is reflexively incorporated, because writers are also an élite. But curiously psychologists rarely study themselves or reflect their explanations back upon their own behaviour as scientists. Perhaps for that reason they are the most free in spirit of Snow's élites.

All these points would probably be contested by a large number of psychologists. (19) They would feel equally uncomfortable with the kinds of ideas which sociological studies of science are introducing - such as those touched on in Chapter 5. (20) The ideology of science has become so strongly naturalised that most of its practices seem beyond question, if science is to be preserved at all. The central means for transmitting the ideas of psychology is the journal article. It is the convention of that form of discourse which is largely responsible for glossing over the doubts which we can read out of Snow's article. His highly realist novels conceal his ideology, which is only revealed when he tries to justify them in abstract terms. Similarly, when scientists, including psychologists, talk about their work, in distinction to writing schematically about it, their practices and criteria do not seem quite so inevitable, (21) and doubts once again emerge about their formal practice.

READING 'BETWEEN' SNOW AND PSYCHOLOGY

The observations above arise from our reading as social psychologists of Snow. As social psychologists we inevitably re-read social psychology through Snow. The immediate text and the texts presupposed by our assumed role become interwoven. Common threads are set off. In the section which follows we will trace further some of the intertextuality of the two sets of discourse.

The TLS article suggests the partiality, both in selection and value attached, of Snow's attention to groups. It is not just that they are ones with which his career acquainted him. They have features which coincide both with his moral position and his goals as a novelist. He viewed the world above all as governable, by rational behaviour, and deeply distrusted individual sensibility as a source of order. He is famous for his rejection of literary modernism and the aesthetic novel; he held a similar attitude to wider matters. As he admits, élites give an occasion for generating order. In The Masters and The Affair the stories are concerned above all with the maintenance of order, within the community. If the quarrelling college threatens to become a 'bear-garden', is in danger of having to have the Master's election decided by an outsider, the Visitor, or faces a Fellow's fraud being known beyond the walls, then even the most truculent individuals rally round. Snow dwells with obvious affection on the cosy clubbiness and ritual of college life, which helps to hold unlikely fellows together. In fact these affective, emotionally-laden rewards of group life are more apparent than any advantages accruing from the special abilities which Snow takes to define élites. The College has a sneaking regard for relative mediocrity. Its decision-making processes are scarcely examples of the technocratic rationality which another Snow would claim to admire. But despite the muddles order is preserved, through compromise and consensus.

The desire for order is fundamental to social psychology, in its post-war experimental phase. 'Mixed-up-ness', for example the confounding of variables in an attempted causal explanation, is the reverse of what is required. The control of influences upon the experimental outcome in question is one of the principal objectives in designing a piece of research. And one of the ways in which this has been achieved in group research has been through the creation of 'closed communities' within the laboratory. The experimental subjects' identity is taken as defined exclusively by their present situation within the experiment. They have no social histories, no common presuppositions, no knowledge of one another outside the scenario presented by the experimenter.

Snow's academics are similar. In part this is a result of the novelist's traditional privilege to limit us to details relevant to the story. But it is used extravagantly. We know virtually nothing of most of the characters outside the college; so that it is a shock in several senses when Winslow is taken on an impromptu outing to the cinema by Calvert. The characters seem to know very little of one another, beyond what is immediately happening. (22)

Chapter 7

Even when other parts of the sequence tell us, for example, that Martin Eliot and Francis Getliffe lived together through dramatic circumstances in the war (The New Men), they are strangers to that shared and not wholly irrelevant knowledge in The Affair. If the outside world or a previous existence does impinge, usually it is as a condescension (Pilbrow's extensive European network is nothing to his ineffectual and tardy presence at college meetings; Gay's ninety years are an antediluvian curiosity rather than history); or as a source of embarrassment and trouble to the College - Skeffington's relationship by marriage to a principal in 'the affair', Calvert's giddy cosmopolitanism, Jago's inconvenient loyalty to his 'unsuitable' wife. Even Sir Horace Timberlake's benefaction of six fellowships is not so much a good day for the College, as a source of further ruffling complications in electing the Master.

The exception among the characters in this respect is Lewis Eliot himself, the narrator who also appears as one of the main figures in the novels. But the way in which the exception is handled offers no solution to the problem. As a character he knows much more about his fellow-actors than they do of one another or of him, and sometimes implausibly much. He is sometimes excessively egotistical, in apparently reserving to himself emotions or judgments which others might well, and interestingly, share. And yet he is very reticent as a character; one has a sense of highly controlled impression management. This reticence is in part responsible for some of the most grotesque examples of the fragmentalism in the sequence which has frequently been complained of. Eliot keeps his different lives carefully insulated from one another, so that far from there being, for example, a bond between him and Jago or his brother Martin in respect of their love and marriage relations, as there might well be, there is a fumbling awkwardness and apparent disregard for the most simple emotional truths. The fragmentation is in a number of different ways a structural correlative of the social isolationism which is entailed by the regard given to élites and to a controlled view of the world.

The particular authorial problem in Strangers and Brothers is reflected in the position of the experimenter in social psychology. He both writes the script for the experiment and reserves the leading role for himself. He claims to understand more about his subjects' behaviour, and even of their attitudes, emotions and motivations, than they do themselves. He is reticent, in the sense that he carefully gauges his interaction with his subjects to the minimum; and certainly tells them less than they tell him. At the end of the experiment he has information to test his hypothesis and the basis for a research report to publish. The subjects usually have no more than a curious memory, unrelated to their everyday concern. The reflexive failure of the psychologist to include his own behaviour as a psychologist in his focus of study, and his unwillingness to engage with his subjects on equal terms goes a step further than Eliot's alienation. This is a measure of the difference between the two practices to date. Novelists have confronted the authorial problem and treated its resolution as one of the springboards for writing. Snow's failure is not necessary or even

typical. It derives from his disdain for literary tradition and
his reflex approach to the craft. Psychologists, on the other
hand, have turned their back on the analogous problem 'en masse';
the exception would be the fairly recent realisation that the observer is necessarily implicated in his observations. Very few
psychologists, still, are taking the further step of deliberately
becoming a part of what they examine; of recognising the nature
of the psychologist's role as one of the most interesting issues
to be studied, from within psychological investigations.

We do not need to appeal to the academic psychologists' non-profes-
sional life to find instances of fragmentation. Teaching and research are traditionally justified as mutually reinforcing activities. Yet how often are psychological principles applied when
psychologists teach? (23) The products of psychology are not
usually considered so much the products of individual authors as
has been customary in literary criticism. Fragmentation is more
evident at a different level and is the rule rather than the exception. Traditionally motivation, learning, perception, attitudes and so on have been kept in carefully labelled compartments.
Social, occupational and abnormal psychology are sub-disciplines
with fiercely fought-over territorial markers. It would not be a
natural expectation to find a psychologist examining job interview
behaviour in relation to the social histories and emotional temper-
aments of the parties concerned. Nor does Snow. George Passant's
abortive Civil Service Board is in essence staged (Homecomings)
quite independently of his social background (George Passant) and
his later deviancy (The Sleep of Reason). If psychology needs to
divide itself, so much the worse for the whole person. So much the
worse for George Passant, if Eliot's preoccupation is with his own
identities in the twenties' provinces, the Civil Service, and as
noble Knight in the permissive and decadent sixties. Eliot does
Passant a disservice by denying him a continuous existence, a historical reality; in the same way as he insults his first wife
Sheila by dramatising his agony over her pathology in Homecomings,
and virtually ignoring her existence when The Masters conveniently
cloisters him in Cambridge from Wednesday to Monday each week.

The fragmentation of identity serves to isolate characters from the
web of their social history, as effectively as by placing them
within exclusive social groups. This has been justified (24) as a
valid way of regarding life by calling up Virginia Woolf's distinction: '... life for Snow is no luminous semi-transparent en-
velope but rather a series of gig-lamps symmetrically arranged.'
Each gig-lamp reveals a tightly centred social situation, isolated
in a pool of darkness. The symmetrical ordering is an arbitrary
attempt to impose an order which the lamps are too weak to illuminate. The vogue for field experiments in social psychology which
erupted during the seventies produced a similar image. Highly
naturalistic cameos were enacted of, for example, helping behaviour
on the streets; but the wider social context remained irrelevant.
The elegance or brilliance of individual experiments is analogous
to the sharpness of observation in the social scenes which many
readers admire in Snow. There is a comparable belief that the

units accumulate to teach us what life is like. But life, and
social life, is essentially a system, a network which cannot be
grasped by accumulated detail. One effect of insulating its components from one another is to make doubt and criticism more difficult.

The greatest stumbling-block in Snow's endeavour to integrate the
individual and the social is his oscillating and incomplete preoccupation with each level. With the possible exceptions of <u>The
New Men</u>, <u>Corridors of Power</u> and <u>Last Things</u>, the novels tend to
focus predominantly either on individuals or on social groups and
issues. The latter we have discussed. Snow said that the characters in whom he was most profoundly concerned were those people who
did not 'ride their lives easily'. The prime examples are George
Passant, Roy Calvert and Charles March. Like a more minor character, Martineau, they are essentially world-renouncing types;
though March does eventually, and perhaps uniquely in the sequence,
achieve a harmonious place in society without disillusionment or
disappointment. There is a strong component of pathology in some
of these most vivid individuals; certainly Passant and Calvert
share this with Sheila Eliot. The function of these characters,
and of Martin Eliot (<u>The New Men</u>) and Roger Quaife (<u>Corridors of
Power</u>) seems to be to act as a foil to the good works of Lewis
Eliot, to allow him to observe them, to display his willingness to
be disappointed or hurt by them and remain true. The interest in
the abnormal and the exploitation of individuals' psychology for
quite separate purpose has also characterised much psychological
practice.

The self-destructive inability of such major characters as Passant,
Calvert, Martin Eliot or Quaife to work harmoniously and contentedly
within the social sphere which they have chosen, and within which
they are in many respects highly successful, leaves an impression
that the individual is hopelessly set against society. In the
novels where the group is in the foreground, the individual similarly suffers. A scapegoat or victim appears necessary, though Jago
and Howard provide two very different types of character. Jago's
sensitivity, warmth, and extravagance are characteristics which Snow
appears determined to have fail a person. The grey, sensible compromise at the end of the two academic novels is approved of; the
interests of the group predominate. In this respect Snow can only
reinforce the dichotomy which underlies his art's motivation: the
reaction against style and individual expressiveness in favour of
plain writing and the claims of society. The result is polarisation
rather than integration. In swinging ambivalently between his own
restricted forms of individualism and collectivism, Snow does not
evoke traces of a social psychology which would steer between psychology and sociology.

The primary dichotomies present in Snow's novels, to which we have
referred above, seed a whole series of others: between action and
introspection, reason and sensibility, public and private, office
and idealism, worldly success and self-knowledge. Their repetitive
and parallel usage intensify an image of individual life as iso-

lated, lonely, doubting and precarious. Only living actively in the world, with the exercise of reason, makes life tolerable. Unfortunately the clearest case that could be made for such integration, excepting perhaps Charles March, is the narrator Lewis Eliot. He certainly operates at both poles of all the dichotomies. But the fragmentation ultimately destroys our faith that he might have achieved an integrated life. Furthermore, the authorial conflict between narrator and character is so apparent that we are left with a strong taste of moralising; the story too deliberately provides Eliot with his heroic ease as sensitive, bureaucratic man. It is important to emphasise that we need know nothing of Snow's own career to catch this flavour.

Integration is sinilarly left to the psychologist, and is also pre-empted at times through establishing dichotomies. The psychologist's particular habit has been to dwell at one pole of a dichotomy: to study privacy, as such; moral development, as though a concomitant immoral or amoral development were neither natural nor permissible; reasoning independently of emotion. The conceptualisation of problems, definition of terms and design of experiments seems to be easier that way. Eventually, most dichotomies become realised; though usually in terms of a simple swing to the other pole - leadership to followership, consensus to conflict. It is rare, and difficult with existing methodological values, to study both at once. A trusting layperson might see the psychologist as having extra integrative powers to relate the results of all the profession's separated investigations. But there is no evidence of it in most psychological texts: remorselessly specialised research reports in journals, eponymous monographs, textbooks whose chapter headings ceaselessly reproduce substantive splitting.

STEREOTYPING

The psychological version of this process is categorisation. We are reminded of Snow's 'Whether we like it or not, that is a fact of life.' His most prominent use of categorisation, perhaps, is precisely in respect of his élites. The New Men, for example, is arranged in terms of continual oppositions between administrative, scientific and military groups, which are starkly labelled as such. The 'scientists' in particular are referred to in highly stereotyped ways. Among them in-groups and out-groups are formed of 'American scientists', 'leading scientists', 'engineers and technicians', 'two obscure chemists', in contexts where strongly prejudicial statements are made for or against their activities. The possibility that such processes were an integral, and questionable, part of the politics of atomic fission does not come readily from the text.

By comparison a relatively minor casualty is the stilted and often absurd treatment of personal relationships and emotions in the novel, especially between the two Eliots. Relationships are labelled by roles (brother, sister-in-law, husband and wife) rather than personal names. There are continual contradictions in the Eliots' meetings between their public and private lives, which are difficult to read as other than contingent on the sense-making structure Snow has employed. The Eliots are victims of their author rather than of their bureaucratic positions or the crisis of war. For the latter reading to emerge one would need much more in the way of social analysis and criticism than Snow ever offers.

At the personal level Snow manages to stereotype his characters by his style of creating them; in particular, through descriptions of their external appearance, mannerisms and tricks of speech. This may be intended to place the characters and make them memorable. However the devices are so commonplace and repetitious that the characters become saturated with an attribute which continually refers them to a social category. Roy Calvert's use of the verb 'need' ('I need to give you some fresh air'. 'I need to order you some strawberries for tea'), Arthur Brown's 'Put it another way', or Professor Gay's 'Congratulate the Steward for me' quickly become tokens reminding us that we are in Oxbridge. Similarly, Lord Boscastle and Hector Rose become figures which stand for the aristocracy and the Civil Service mandarinate and suggest that their fellows are essentially the same.

Categorisation and stereotyping have long received attention from social psychologists. More recently, as part of research on groups, they have become a focus of some of the more exciting advances in social psychology. We will use the arguments of one representative review article (25) to illustrate the way in which reading social psychology may illuminate ways of sensemaking in literature. Categorising and stereotyping processes have both cognitive and social functions. At the individual level they are an economical means of dealing with incoming information, simplifying and ordering the environment. For example, what may be a rather hazy, or non-existent, general difference between social categories (dons and laypersons, for example) is accentuated and clarified by exaggerating a few personal attributes of individual members which subjectively can be associated with category membership (speech mannerisms). The significance of something which occurs rather rarely becomes inflated and overrepresented. Snow's stylistic habit of repetition conspires with his love of order.

Most stereotypes are value-laden through their association with valued characteristics. They tend also to be based on rather ambiguous information, when they have to do with people. Disconfirming instances are a threat to the value-system on which the differentiation into categories is based. In most cases, because the evidence will be ambiguous and because differentiation is supported by social consensus, disconfirmation will not occur. The highly selective and exaggerating process whereby categories are formed 'fulfils its function of protecting the value system which underlies the division of the surrounding social world into sheep and goats'. (26)

The groups or categories on which Snow focuses are certainly highly valued, traditionally; they are élites. And they directly represent what have been taken to be his own highest values. The way in

which they are protected is clear. Disconfirmatory evidence is
blurred. The shallowness of characterisation and relationship
which one finds in The New Men should not be treated as evidence
of Snow's lack of psychological insight or writing skills. It can
be interpreted as the means by which very powerful categories -
scientist, administrator, Minister - are established and held.
Rather little information is needed to confirm social stereotypes
of this kind; but considerably more to disconfirm them. (27) The
reader is guarded from acquiring too much detailed knowledge of
their members. That way it is easier to read the making of the
atomic bomb as a matter of science and administration, than of
politics and morals.

The most recent socio-psychological work on stereotypes has attempted to highlight their collective functions. What is achieved
for a group by sharing a derogatory social image? Three functions
have been distinguished: social causality, justification and differentiation. The first refers to 'a search for the understanding
of complex and usually distressful, large-scale social events'; (28)
the example of anti-Semitism is given, of an outgroup which is held
responsible for the world's evil. Secondly, stereotypes may provide
a 'justification of actions, committed or planned, against outgroups' - such as the attitudes of European imperialism. (29)
Thirdly, one may find 'a positive differentiation of the ingroup
from selected outgroups at a time when such differentiation is becoming insecure and eroded'; or when it is not positive, and social
conditions exist which are perceived as providing a possibility for
a change in the situation. 'A simplified illustration is the general syndrome of ethnocentrism.'

During the fifty years of social history covered by Strangers and
Brothers one would expect some attention to such complex, large-
scale and distressful events as the Thirties recession, the Second
World War and nuclear proliferation. 'Search for understanding' may
seem an elaborate and difficult objective; but in the simplifying
and ordering processes assumed by socio-psychological explanations
of stereotyping it is a crude enterprise. We have already suggested
the reductionist role of stereotyping in The New Men. It occurs
also in Corridors of Power, though the more elaborated character
of Roger Quaife diverts us from the excesses of the earlier novel.
The nuclear question is crudely dealt with in the sequence; the
other two cataclysms are present only as gaps.

The stereotypes which psychologists have examined have more usually
involved the negative images of outgroups, because of a super-
ordinate interest in prejudice. Snow's novels can also be read as
being concerned with outgroups; but often in a negative sense.
The concentration on the ingroup, cosy and secure in its clubby
intimacy, isolated from the rest of the world, is continually referred to in commentaries on the novels. The outgroup is correspond-
ingly strongly suggested, but by exclusion. Thus, if unpleasant
occurrences, such as poverty and world warfare, are detected in the
outside world they can be referred to the outgroup. The pre-eminent
ingroup, the Cambridge college, finds the European disturbances an

inconvenience. When one of their number becomes heavily involved – Roy Calvert – he is required to do so at a distance; indeed it becomes a feature of his alienation and separation from the College. (30) More generally, the novels' dichotomising view of the world frequently finds the negative poles resting in the shadowy regions outside academia, the legal profession, science or the Civil Service.

The elaborate attention given to the introspective characteristics of these communities also serves functions of justification and differentiation. In the academic novels the neglect, for example, of women, college servants or students is justified by portraying them in stereotypical and unfavourable terms when they do obtrude. The actions against Donald Howard when he is suspected of scientific fraud in The Affair gain justification from a crude portrayal of his 'red' politics and uncouth manners, neither of which would be suitable in a Fellow. Positive differentiation of the ingroup is, as we have suggested, a continuous feature of the novel. In the context of the socio-psychological scheme being outlined here we can interpret its significance in terms of the élites' insecurity and need for a stronger identity. The value-structure of the aspiring middle class of pre-war Britain, which so thoroughly colours the novel sequence to the end, can be seen to be under attack in most of the writing about the sequence. The values, and especially the way in which they are portrayed, excite quite personal hostility. But whereas much of the criticism refers to Snow's own reactionary portrayal of those values, we are suggesting that the novels may be read, independently of Snow's thoughts and intentions, as being about the fight to preserve a way of life. Because as readers we share in the socio-psychological processes described above, we have the resources to interpret the functions of the stereotyping which runs through the novels. If socio-psychological explanation is to apply at this point – where it refers to collective functions – it is important to reiterate that we are not discussing Snow's individual value-system. The values which are being protected are a collective construction by a community of readers.

The final stage in the argument is to suggest that social psychology now needs to relate the collective functions of explanation, justification and differentiation to the individual functions. Two means are proposed. The first relates the categorisation of a group to which an individual belongs to his self-concept or self-respect. The attributes which positively distinguish his group from other more or less powerful and competitive groups provide a basis for his identity in society. If a positive social identity, in relation to comparison groups, is to be provided, there must be a positive differential in terms of salient and valued attributes.

> The social context of values and of the requirements for adaptation to the environment helps the individual to seek out, to select for special attention, to exaggerate, and, if necessary, to create, those similarities and differences which fit in with the general consensus about what matters and what does not matter in the potentially infinite number of possible structures of social divisions and social equivalence. (31)

The second means of relating the individual and collective levels chiefly concerns the explanatory function of stereotyping, and stems from the socio-psychological study of 'attributions'. These are the perceptions and accounts which people offer of the causes or reasons for events in the world, including human behaviour. They are people's everyday 'scientific' or 'legal' explanations. A social approach to attribution suggests that everyday explanations of behaviour may be based not only on the observer's and actor's individual characteristics, but on the groups or social categories to which they belong, and ultimately on relations between the groups. Hypothetical features of social attribution are that the behaviour of ingroup members would in general be explained in terms of 'reasons' and of outgroup members in terms of 'causes'; and, more specifically, that socially desirable behaviour from ingroup members would be attributed to their own agency, but socially undesirable behaviour would be explained in terms of some external element. The reverse pattern would apply to members of an outgroup.

Both of these means of relating collective and individual functions of categorisation are represented in the structure of Snow's novels. We have already suggested several times that his characters take their identity almost exclusively from institutional or group memberships; and that their self-respect is served by an exclusion of possible rival, comparison groups. Identity problems may also be referred to group membership. Ambiguities or irregularities in, for example, Passant, Sheila, Martineau or Howard are a clear correlative of their failure to form a clear relation with a particular, or just any, positively valued group. Identification with several groups may or may not present problems. In Roy Calvert's case dividing himself between Cambridge, Berlin and the world of the Boscastles is allowed to weaken his identity, causing difficulties for his self-concept and upsetting his position in the College. Lewis Eliot, on the other hand, belongs only to positively valued groups. After perhaps some hesitancy in his self-image while working at law, his self-respect, if not -admiration, is never lost. Those who do seem to lose their identity do so by losing their position in a highly valued group: for example, Jago after his defeat in <u>The Masters</u> or Quaife towards the end of <u>Corridors of Power</u>.

The attribution of reasons as against causes, however, is rather more difficult to illustrate, if only because so little attention is given to outgroups in the novels. Perhaps the best examples are where one finds a collision between two sub-groups within the charmed circle, as in <u>The Masters</u>, <u>The Affair</u> or <u>Corridors of Power</u>. Because Lewis Eliot belongs to one of the two it becomes an ingroup within an ingroup, and his authorial membership gives the reader special access to its highly elaborated and reasoned proceedings. Snow/Eliot's predilection for the world of reason ensures that his plans and actions and those of his associates are presented in those terms - to such an extent that Snow has been criticised for permitting Lewis Eliot an undue omniscience about the inner workings of those who are close to him.

The less-favoured sub-groups in the examples above are composed predominantly of scientists, and their actions are presented more summarily. It is not difficult to read them as being caused by their roles and by associated stereotypical traits. Many of the minor characters also share this feature of having their behaviour apparently determined by monolithic, stereotyping attributes, often themselves of a highly emotional or irrational kind. Because they do not belong or are peripheral to the key ingroups they have no opportunity to reveal their reasons for action through Eliot's sympathetic understanding. By contrast, Eliot himself, in his many guises through the sequence, becomes almost an ingroup of one, representative of all other ingroups, moving with almost total reasoned introspection.

It is this feature in particular which prevents Snow from achieving an integration of the social and individual; and it is at this point that the social psychological discussion of stereotyping fails. It justifies itself as having 'moved from the individual to social functions of stereotypes, and then reversed directions in proposing a sequence of analysis which would *start* from the social functions to reach the individual ones. That is not the usual sequence in social psychological texts'. (32) The procedure is innovative, but ultimately it only serves to perpetuate the very problem to which it appears to be drawing attention. Social identity and attributions remain as individual (psychological) products, brought about by collective (social) processes. An integrative, and radical, socio-psychological approach would take social identity and other hitherto psychological states and processes as constituted essentially in the relation between the individual and the collective.

Lewis Eliot's membership of different groups might have provided Snow with the material for focusing on such relations as a central theme of the novel sequence. But we have already pointed out that widespread polarising tendencies and Snow's particular form of the authorial problem mitigate against it.

CONCLUSION

In this chapter the relation between metatheoretical and theoretical developments in social psychology and the study of literature has been explored in two ways, both of which are intended to illustrate the social context of sense-making. Social psychological reflections on Snow's discussion of élites arise from the social psychologist's relation to his own discipline; that is, a social position of conflict. The <u>Strangers and Brothers</u> novels are an example of how literature can construct and naturalise a stereotyping version of social reality by recourse to structures which are identified in the social psychological study of stereotyping. Social psychology, however, is not presented as a superior means of interpreting the novels. It is itself a form of sense-making and is equally open to criticisms as to its structures. Our assumption is that an academically and scientifically oriented novelist and experimental social psychologist working in the same culture and period are likely to give rise to readings which overlap in a number of ways. This constitutes an essential focus of interaction between two different forms of discourse. In constructing a real or naturalistic account of social life both forms can be found to proceed by similar paths, which open up the basis for a revelatory mutual criticism.

8 THE DISCURSIVE SELF

Anyone familiar with both modern social science and literature will appreciate the extent to which these institutions share in common their understandings of the self. Both duplicate in idiosyncratic ways various transition points in the complicated discursive history of our modes of comprehending ourselves and others. Both draw upon the persistent and pervasive discourse of the alienated and inauthentic, for instance, and also just as frequently retreat to the romantic discourses of self-fulfilment, uniqueness and self-actualisation.

The novel, for its part, has gradually evolved from a plot- and character-centred world where people are their personalities with no remainder, to the acute and disintegrated consciousness of modern Dostoievskian Underground Men. We have seen the Dickensian character who simply manifests his or her disposition and who is best described as a configuration of determining traits rejected as a psychological fraud as the idea of a consistent character, personality or ego dissolves.

Psychology, in a similar fashion, seems to have shifted from the certainties of its narrative characters (the role-player in social psychology, the trait theory approach in personality research) to the divided self of a Laingian existentialist and to a separation of the social selves, the roles and theatrical masks of the me, from the mysterious residual I, the background manager and negotiator of identities who appears to be more than the sum of the roles.

In both social science and literature the traditional humanistic concepts of the solid unfragmented agent are under attack and often, it seems, for much the same reasons. In each case, it can be said that the practitioners and theorists are working out the implications of the transition from a conception of people 'as simply in society as objects are in boxes' (1) to a conception which sees the person in society as 'like a stone in a wall or a drop in a stream through which the energies of the whole pass'. (2)

In this chapter we will trace out and compare some of the conse-

quences of these changes. As in previous chapters the emphasis
will be on sense-making in literature and in psychology; however
a rather more synoptic approach to the subject will be taken. The
intention is to examine some of the generalised representations of
the self found in social psychology or deduced from novels rather
than, for instance, present a fine-grain analysis of a particular
piece of discourse concerning the self. We shall be concerned with
the kinds of codes available for characterising and representing
the self and the presentation of these in social psychology and
literature.

This 'archaeological' exegesis may well also reveal some of the
subtle and complex layers in everyday, nontechnical, self analysis
and description. (3) People wishing to publicly formulate their
'inner' experiences will be able to do so only by drawing upon the
stock of linguistic resources available in contemporary culture.
The meaning accorded to experience in this area, as in other areas,
derives from the fluid and creative combination of conventional and
collectively organised patterns for making sense. The patterns we
identify here are perhaps more salient to the contemplative observer. None the less the general principle holds.

The conclusion this chapter works towards is, therefore, that the
best analytic strategy for studying the self is not necessarily the
attempt to specify its phenomenology or supposed essential nature,
contents and structure but involves examining the language of self-
reference whether it be of the highly formalised type presented
here or the references contained in everyday parlance. Thus in the
following discussion we will not be concerned with evaluating the
best model of the self or trying to demonstrate that either psychology or literature has produced the most satisfactory explanations in this area. It is the structure rather than the quality
of the models which is at stake. Our aim is to explicate the
organisation of certain forms of self-accounting shared by both
psychology and literature.

The analysis begins with the most basic of self-portraits - the
solid narrative character - familiar to any fan of the realist tradition, and its psychological analogue - trait theory.

'HONEST SCULS': THE NARRATIVE CHARACTER AND TRAIT THEORY

> Mr. Podsnap was well to do, and stood very high in Mr. Podsnap's
> opinion. Beginning with a good inheritance, he had married a
> good inheritance, and had thriven exceedingly in the Marine
> Insurance way, and was quite satisfied. He could never make out
> why everybody was not quite satisfied, and he felt conscious that
> he set a brilliant social example in being particularly well
> satisfied with most things, and, above all other things, with
> himself.
>   Thus happily acquainted with his own merit and importance,
> Mr. Podsnap settled that whatever he put behind him he put out
> of existence. There was a dignified conclusiveness - not to add

a grand convenience – in this way of getting rid of disagreeables
which had done much towards establishing Mr. Podsnap in his lofty
place in Mr. Podsnap's satisfaction. 'I don't want to know about
it; I don't choose to discuss it; I don't admit it!' Mr. Podsnap had even acquired a peculiar flourish of the right arm in
often clearing the world of its most difficult problems, by
sweeping them behind him (and consequently sheer away) with
those words and a flushed face. For they affronted him.
  Mr. Podsnap's world was not a very large world, morally; no,
nor even geographically: seeing that although his business was
sustained upon commerce with other countries, he considered other
countries, with that important reservation, a mistake, and of
their manners and customs would conclusively observe, 'Not
English!' when, PRESTO! with a flourish of the arm, and a flush
of the face, they were swept away [...]

  These may be said to have been the articles of a faith and
  school which the present chapter takes the liberty of calling,
  after its representative man, Podsnappery. They were confined
  within close bounds, as Mr. Podsnap's own head was confined by
  his shirt-collar; and they were enunciated with a sounding
  pomp which smacked of the creaking of Mr. Podsnap's own boots. (4)

In these few brief paragraphs, Dickens has introduced the reader to
a complete character, Mr Podsnap, a particularly unpleasant example
of the Victorian commercial classes. Despite the brevity of the
characterisation, it presents itself as unquestionably complete:
for Mr Podsnap conforms precisely to a familiar theory of personality which verifies and sustains his reality. He is an honest
soul; his embodiment suggests that people simply are their actions
and qualities and can be read purely in terms of these dispositions.

The term honest soul is an invention of the critic Lionel Trilling.
(5) It includes all the stock and stereotypical characters and
many of the main characters in bourgeois realist novels: the
squires, the husseys, the governesses, the rich benefactors, the
miserable poor, the ever so humble, the martyred mothers and so on.
Honest is used here not in its literal sense but because it conveys,
what Trilling calls, the 'sentiment of being': the appropriate aura
of solidity, unreflectiveness and identification with the contemporary ethos.

What are the features imputed to this type of consciousness? As we
can see in the extract from Our Mutual Friend, the actions of a
traditional type of narrative character like Mr Podsnap are depicted
as following naturally and inevitably from their personality rather
than from the demands of a particular situation. Mr Podsnap's personality also provides, in itself, sufficient cause and motive for
his actions. The character in question may be represented as a
complex mixture of traits or in terms of one or two dominant characteristics. But, whether simple or heterogeneous, he or she is completely summed up by the amalgam of usual habits and temperament.

Take Mr Podsnap's comic pomposity, chauvinism and self-righteousness, for instance. These traits are identified as enduring and consistent, belonging to him as surely as any material possession. They are most definitely not passing reactions occasioned by specific scenes and events of Victorian business life. In this sense, it is a highly decontextualised portrait reliant on an abstract notion of, for example, the 'Marine Insurance way' or of the likely reference of his 'I don't want to know about it' phrase. The appearance of coherence and harmony this characterisation suggests to the reader depends upon the impression that Mr Podsnap's traits are internalised and are the sum, the all, of Mr Podsnap.

Honest souls like the one before us are essential to plot development. Their personalities provide the narrative linkage and predictability which will bind a story together. The two-dimensionality required for this function is achieved through the reader's sense that the text makes Mr Podsnap transparent, laying him bare before our eyes. Indeed, an interesting opposition emerges as the contrast develops between the honest Podsnap soul and the narrator who exposes the objects of the Podsnap self for our amusement and scrutiny. Dickens's text is organised to give the impression that we are being confided in by one who, unlike the Podsnaps, is capable of irony, conscious self-evaluation and criticism. The linguistically created tension which results only serves to sharpen and flatten the reader's image of the honest soul character.

Honest souls are the type of personalities which are regularly described in traditional (and not so traditional) psychological terms. (6) The parallels between this version of personhood and even relatively current psychological models are indeed unmistakable. Without too much difficulty, we can see that the honest soul has featured throughout the history of psychology as well as the novel. However, among the psychologists who have organised their thinking on these lines, it is the trait theorists in particular who have most conspicuously assumed that other people are best viewed as solid narrative characters embedded in a plot.

Trait theorists maintain that human behaviour is lawful and in the main part caused by the structure and dynamics of personality. (7) Like the text of Our Mutual Friend, they assert that people not events cause the regularity in human affairs. People are constituted from bundles of traits and attitudes: so much intelligence, gregariousness, introversion, self-esteem etc. The particular combination of traits will determine a person's behaviour just as Mr Podsnap's pride and snobbery seem to determine his place in the plot of Dickens's novel.

The study of personality must start, therefore, with taxonomy. The psychologist must be able to describe the basic structures which make up an individual's nature, identify the interaction of various traits and comment on the normality of particular trait profiles, the spread of traits through sample populations and so on. Inspired by the chemist, the trait theorist draws up the periodic table of the elements of personality. (8)

Fortunately, according to one of the most eminent trait theorists, R.B. Cattell, the central source traits which constitute a personality appear to fall into three neat categories (ability, temperament and dynamics). Part of a person's psychological makeup will be defined by his or her cognitive style (ability traits), another part by persistent emotional or affective reactions (stylistic or temperament traits) and the remainder will consist of habitual reactions to incentive situations (the motivational or dynamic traits). Each constitutive source trait may result in several surface traits, emotional lability, for instance, may manifest itself in many different individual forms and this complexity of source and surface interaction accounts for the variety of individual personalities.

Measurement techniques, psychometrics, are thus indispensable to the trait theorist. Many people's interaction with psychologists will in fact most likely take place through a questionnaire or personality inventory designed on trait theory lines. Someone filling in Eysenck's famous personality inventory, for example, may be asked 'Do you suddenly feel shy when you want to talk to an attractive stranger?' or 'Do you daydream a lot?' or 'Do you often do things on the spur of the moment?'. (9)

The results produced by these psychometric tests are a bit like a respectable version of the astrological horoscope. A person completing the more extensive 16 P.F. inventory might discover, for example, that they have a sten (score out of ten) of 2 on a submissiveness-dominance personality factor where 2 is close to the pole described as humble, mild, obedient, conforming and might note that only 4.4 per cent of adults obtain this score (the average scores are in the 5-6 range). (10) The profile they build up over all the sixteen personality factors will reveal to them their self in all its constituent parts with the predominant traits highlighted and the moderate, normal, amounts of other traits also noted.

Both the trait theorist and the excerpt from Dickens thus assume that people are their dispositions and the unity inherent in these dispositions with no core outside this personality. The novelist sets these characters in motion to work out the consequences of their particular configurations of traits but it is the psychologist who can freeze them and dissect the predictable structuring of these characteristics. As Amelie Rorty has pointed out, it is difficult to imagine either a literary honest soul type or for that matter the people studied by trait theory having an identity crisis. (11) The conception is simply not included in this type of discourse about what selves are like. One can imagine a tragic flaw caused by a disharmony of traits but not, she says, an innervating collapse into fragmentation.

The main criticisms directed against trait theory parallel the points made by modern novelists, such as Virginia Woolf, concerning traditional novelistic modes of characterisation. (12) People are simply not that consistent and solid. Their behaviour is more fragmented, more responsive to the momentary demands of the situation and more dynamic. The psychologist would note that trait theory fails the empirical test, it cannot reliably predict behaviour in actual situations. (13) Given enough test data, trait theorists can comment extensively on the traits individuals possess and to a high level of sophistication in spite of disputes over the statistical techniques used. However, in their own terms, this effort is wasted if these traits bear little relation to how people perform in non-test situations.

In addition, as Mischel has noted, the type of traits identified for a particular individual undoubtedly tell us more about the organisation of the trait theorist's own interpretative schemas than the individual's actual behaviour. In fact the real value of trait theory may lie in the thoroughness with which it has investigated the structure of everyday descriptive concepts for personality. (14) It has a familiar aura, it captures a common-sense model of what people are like and thus provides yet another example to add to those in Chapters 4 and 5 of how a psychological researcher may mistake people's own proto-psychologies and occasioned descriptions of themselves and others for literal accounts.

Both trait theory and the honest soul models of the self are extremely asocial: paying little attention to the situations in which self-presentation occurs. According to Trilling, the novelistic honest soul is engaged in the 'heroism of dumb service' since self-realisation is achieved in harmony with the definitions provided by the external power of society. (15) The service the honest soul renders is necessarily 'dumb' because there is no framework for perceiving the relationship between self and society as in any way problematic. Mr Podsnap, for instance, can be said to be unaware of social forces as they have not yet been articulated for him as an external presence. As we have seen, there is no textual concept of a true or real self behind the facade to give sense to the notion of playing a part in society. Thus, throughout the novel, Mr Podsnap will be depicted as more or less identifying with his performance without ever appreciating that it is a performance. Indeed such flashes of insight would start to undermine the function of this character in the text.

To a social psychologist it seems self-evident that people's activities are moulded by the norms and conventions present in any social situation and also by the roles they are playing within that situation. It is this dimension - the capacity for flexible reaction to social demands - which trait theory and traditional characterisation neglect, although Cattell, at least, does include the concept of role in his category of transient situational states or 'conditions of the moment' which he sees as affecting behaviour. These social variables are viewed, however, as only an adjunct to the expression of traits. Thus Cattell does not concede the possibility that the particular mixture of traits a person demonstrates may be determined by the playing out of a temporary social role. As the roles change the internal traits might as well, belying their supposed consistency and enduring nature. People may be able to assume various different personae or personality profiles as the situational demands force the playing out of different parts.

Literary honest souls and trait theory people differ in subtle ways and it would take a sophisticated analysis to pinpoint the core incongruities between these models of the self. None the less on superficial examination, at least, these potential conceptualisations of oneself and others share certain central features. To summarise, the frame of reference demands one thinks in terms of characteristics and dispositions consistently manifested across different situations and throughout a lifetime. These traits are seen as whole and unified and expressive of one's true nature. Society, if thought about at all, appears as separate from the self, as an external environment rather than as a contaminating force which could determine the form of personality.

In the next section we will turn to a model of the self, based on the notion of role-playing, which tries to supersede the old-fashioned individualism of the honest soul or trait theory person by seeking to incorporate society within the self. This recognition of social pressures allows some new elements to enter the discourse of self-experience. However, as we shall see, there is a tension, particularly in the practical application of role theory, between the innovative elements and the still compelling image of the honest soul. To some extent, traits are merely replaced in this model with internalised roles.

THE PERFORMING SELF

The concept of human life as a play where individuals learn to act out several roles in the span allotted to them is an old and yet still radical notion. To indicate its venerable history, we can take an example that Trilling discusses and quotes in some detail - Diderot's Rameau's Nephew written some time between 1761 and 1774. In the following passage Trilling and then Diderot describe the revolutionary self-image vouchsafed by the Nephew.

> The social being, he tells us, is a mere histrionic representation - every man takes one or another 'position' as the choreography of society directs. With the mimetic skill which is the essence of his being, the Nephew demonstrates how he performs the dance upon which his survival depends. 'Thereupon he begins to smile, to ape a man admiring, a man imploring, a man complying. His right foot forward, the left foot behind, his back arched, head erect, his glance riveted as if on someone's face, open-mouthed, his arms are stretched out towards some object. He waits for a command, receives it, flies like an arrow, returns. The order has been carried out; he is giving his report. He is all attention, nothing escapes him. He picks up what is dropped, places pillow or stool under feet, holds a salver, brings a chair, opens a door, shuts a window, draws curtains, keeps his eye on master and mistress. He is motionless, arms at his sides, legs parallel; he listens and tries to read faces. Then he

says, "there you have my pantomime; it's about the same as the flatterer's, the courtier's, the footman's and the beggar's".' (16)

This extract can be read as proclaiming a self-evident fact - that people can 'perform' in social interaction, 'managing' the impressions they give of themselves to others. The Nephew's mimesis is depicted as a creative social skill even though, through participating in society, he must become deceptive and insincere as he scripts and puts on the facades and shows which his livelihood demands. This route is not only open to the sycophant nephew either. For others as well, the possibility of 'acting out' the usual activities of social intercourse, politeness, demonstrating competence, interest, and control, can equally well become self-conscious.

In contrast to the honest soul mode of self, acts in this extract no longer appear to flow naturally from the character or traits, indeed the essentially sincere, honest man can be made temporarily insincere without necessarily changing his basic character traits. The social situation not the character is seen as channelling behaviour. A person's actions are, as a result, no longer truly expressive of his or her particular unique personality since most individuals are interchangeable when it comes to playing roles. Roles can be readily assumed on the surface, so to speak, irrespective of the 'real' personality underneath; clearly, an image which differs sharply from the one which emanates from a traditional narrative character such as Mr Podsnap.

The modern role theories of sociology and social psychology which attempt to give some substance to these notions of a performing self can be seen as the scientific and analytically precise development of a way of interpreting personality already implicit in literature and ordinary discourse. Social psychology has taken over the concept of role as a means of accommodating what appear as two basic facts: the fact of individual personality and the fact of society. (17) It is argued that the reconciliation of these two constancies can be achieved through the elaboration of a set of analytic categories such as social roles which describe the site of the interaction between self and society and fix the person in entirety. (18)

To achieve this integration of the individual into the social the analyst obviously needs to go further than the mere recognition evident in Diderot's text of our performing abilities. The nature and content of the performance needs to be specified. The description of social roles serves this function and if one assumes that the roles are internalised or learnt, becoming 'second nature' to the individual, then we can explain why the individual's behaviour seems to be patterned and determined by social forces, while remaining also, apparently, a series of personal, freely engaged in, acts.

Roles are generally defined as sets of activities, qualities and styles of behaviour that are associated with social positions. (19) Social positions are constructed and exist independently of any particular individual; they include occupational, national, religious, recreational, kin categories: husbands, wives, truck drivers, dental nurses, football hooligans, Hindus, etc. People in one of these positions are expected to act out the behaviours, the roles, that go with being a dental nurse or a husband, for example. Only if they do so will they be credited with that occupation or position and be able to reap its rights and rewards.

According to role theorists, people conform to these social expectations not merely because of obvious sanctions and rewards (prison sentences and decorations are Dahrendorf's examples) but because of the more subtle mechanisms of the socialisation and interactive process. The society which directs the play, exerts the pressures and assigns the roles is not an idealist construction or a faceless, conspiring authority, but a set of social groups and classes with particular vested interests. The individual learns to 'refer' to these groups and through the process of gaining an identity and participating in the duties and benefits of membership, the codes of behaviour associated with particular roles are learnt, enforced and maintained.

With the development of this theoretical perspective the social scientist can make sense of the notion of self-consciously playing a part or managing an impression. The substance, the performance being acted out is a set of social expectations which can be investigated and described. Furthermore, if we take the theory to its logical conclusion most elements of an individual's public behaviour can be accounted for, not just the self-conscious machiavellian aspects Diderot describes in the Nephew. People become seen as the sum of their roles. Most life events and unthinking habitual reactions can be classified in this way, the most pervasive being the masculine and feminine roles. Individuality, the differences between people, arise because everybody has a different mixture of present characters and precipitates of past roles as well as possessing idiosyncratic biological characteristics and psychological reactions to role conflict. (20)

The new elements this talk of roles and acting performances introduces are clearcut. The possibility of individual fragmentation is suggested, a crisis of identity, and division and conflict between the various assumed characters. In contrast to the honest soul, the role-player has a set of possibly discordant identities relevant to different situations rather than one unvarying identity. More interestingly, the capacity for symbolisation proposed by role theorists working in the symbolic interactionist tradition, paves the way for an internal concept of society as a sort of theatrical agent and director of the play, scheduling the performance of the roles, supplying and cueing the scripts. Both these new self concepts are beyond the ken of the trait theory person or the conception of self based on the traditional narrative character.

With the development of an internal notion of social process or the belief that one is consciously filling the requirements set by an external agency, a double self begins to emerge. On the one hand there is the social self, the role-player, the Nephew's courtier personality, and separate from this there is a mysterious 'real' self or personality which chooses to act out the roles, and which can also survey the success or failure of the performance. It is this possibility of self-division which has generated the most intractable problems for role theory.

Two solutions are possible to this dilemma. One denies any doubling of consciousness and harks back to the honest soul, the other accepts the implications of a divided self. Practical, empirical, investigative role theorists have mainly favoured the first solution. (21) Their formulations generally seem to work simply as socialised versions of trait theory with roles replacing the dispositions or traits studied by Cattell or Eysenck.

Empirical investigations tend to centre on the specification of roles or role combinations and, as in trait theory, the individual is considered to be these role combinations with no remainder. The role-playing honest soul may verge on awareness of society and the potential fragmentation of self but tends, in practice, to continue just the same to fulfil and unify, in semi-automatic mode, his or her disparate characteristics. Role theorists of this persuasion desire the omniscience of the narrator, detached and all-seeing; their portraits claim to offer a complete explanation of the individuals studied.

The other solution, which deliberately builds on the possibilities inherent in a divided and doubled self, and which rejects the maxim that man is the sum of his roles will be considered in the next section. To the social scientist struggling against the over-socialised model of self apparent in the role-playing honest soul, the answer seems to lie in the distinction found in certain kinds of ordinary discourse between a real self and a social or inauthentic self. This distinction is, again, a familiar one in literary self-conceptualisation as we shall demonstrate with the work of the novelist Robert Musil.

SELF-ALIENATION, ESTRANGEMENT AND THE I VERSUS THE ME

So far we have considered two central representations of the self. Trait theory has it that people are simply like the narrative characters one can read about in books. They react to situations on the basis of their enduring character traits. As we have seen, this way of representing the self comes into conflict with the notion that people, chameleon-like, can play act out any number of characters on demand. It comes into conflict with socio-psychological role theory which makes sense of human behaviour by referring to the internalisation of the structured expectations of society as roles. But this self-representation has itself become a victim of its own innovation.

In introducing self and society as part, to some unspecified extent, of the same dimension, role theory opens up the possibility of two selves, a social self and a background real self which controls the role-player. The existence of another, real self, however, undermines role theory's claim to be a complete explanation. One solution is to deny any division: the real self is the social self and nothing more. In this case the role theory person comes to resemble the solid narrative character of trait theory. The other alternative is to postulate self-division as an active self principle; working out the implications of a real, private, authentic self behind the roles.

For the social scientist, this alternative has been most authoritatively defined by William James using the famous stream of consciousness metaphor. (22) James, elaborating on the Kantian philosophical tradition, distinguished between two kinds of self which can be discriminated in the stream of consciousness. On the one hand, there is the I, on the other, there is the me. The total self is, he says, 'duplex, partly known and partly knower, partly object and partly subject'. (23) The I is the knower, the thinker, the unifying principle of the stream of consciousness and the me is the known, the empirical ego and the contents of the stream of consciousness.

When introspecting one becomes aware, according to James, of a flood or successive series of thoughts, images and feelings. This content is intimately recognisable as the substance of oneself. However, there is also a being which is aware of this series of images and thoughts and can independently survey its nature. If the me is the flow of the stream of consciousness, then, continuing the metaphor, the I, or watching self, is the banks of the stream, the container for the flow.

Within the me aspect of the self we can include the social aspects of the individual: roles, professional identities and so on. In fact, the me can be fragmented into any number of compartments which could be studied separately. James, for instance, partitions the social self or the role-playing facets from the material me which involves, among other things, the body image, the individual's sense of his or her possessions etc., and from the spiritual me which might include the person's feelings and emotions about themselves.

The I aspect is more difficult to classify. James argued that it should not be regarded as a transcendental soul or in mystical terms as pure agency but seen merely as the functional, connective, unifying identity of the stream of consciousness. Little progress has been made since on its definition for the social sciences. James's I/me formulation, however, has proved to be extremely convenient for the role theorist.

The main criticism directed against traditional role theory is that it turns the person into a social dope, into a puppet or victim of social circumstances. (24) How, says Dahrendorf, can we recognise in man the role-player the person we know ourselves and our friends to be? The role-player is but a pale imitation. Admittedly we often do perform as though social life were a stage and we were actors playing out parts. However, even if all these roles could be satisfactorily classified and described, there would still be more to the person. How can social science account for the rest?

The answer is simply that it need not account for it. By dividing the self into two realms, it is possible to carve up the theoretical and explanatory responsibility. Social science is responsible for the me aspect, its tools are well-suited to the analysis of this part of the self. The I, however, is the province of philosophy or religion. All the social scientist needs to do is note its unifying, executive function and leave its delineation to those better qualified to speculate on such matters. Man is both a free moral agent and a determinate being. These two facets of the self need not contradict one another because, according to Dahrendorf, they relate to fundamentally different spheres of knowledge. Role theory is thus rescued as a viable approach to the self without necessarily committing social psychology to a social dope, anti-humanistic model of the person. (25)

This concept of a divided and many-faceted self has also, of course, appealed to the novelist, consistently recurring as a theme throughout the modern novel. The equanimity of the old solid narrative character seems inappropriate in a modern context and also, it is claimed, no longer true to experience. The honest soul continues to feature but as a stereotype reserved for the minor characters, frequently providing an example of an inauthentic self to contrast with the hero or heroine's struggles with self-estrangement and alienation.

Among the novelists who have attempted to present what they see to be a new phenomenal experience of the self using the concepts of discourses of alienation, disintegration and self-estrangement, Robert Musil's novel series A Man Without Qualities is pre-eminent. (26) It is interesting to note that Musil had a short-lived career as an experimental psychologist before turning wholeheartedly to literature. He was a pupil of Stumpf's in Berlin, completing his dissertation on Ernst Mach in 1908, and inventing a chromatometer for the study of perception. According to his biographers, Musil continued to take an interest in human experimental work throughout his life much preferring it to the depth psychologies of the psychoanalytic writers. (27)

Despite his early interests Musil argued that both philosophy and psychology were ultimately unsatisfactory means for conveying the machinations of the human mind. And he characterised his short stories, novels and essays as a more successful means of embodying his theories and psychological investigations. The rational understanding of the self would, in his view, be achieved through the subtle spinning of metaphor and simile which constitute reflective analysis of conscious experience.

As befits a devotee of Mach's, Musil strongly endorsed scientific positivism. Opposed to the romantic reaction against science he desired a science or mathematics of the psyche, a similarly precise

and complete account of feelings and emotions. Yet this would be
an artistic rather than a laboratory-based account. This goal is
also attributed to the hero of his <u>Man Without Qualities</u>, Ulrich,
who develops the new prototype of the cerebral man, 'monsieur le
vivisecteur', systematically and objectively analysing human activity and attempting to act only on the basis of this rational analysis. (28)

Early in the novel, the following account of the general principles
of selfhood is presented in the form of one of Ulrich's insights.

> the inhabitant of a country has at least nine characters: a
> professional one, a national one, a civic one, a class one, a
> geographical one, a sex one, a conscious, an unconscious and perhaps even too a private one; he combines them all in himself,
> but they dissolve him, and he is really nothing but a little
> channel washed out by all these trickling streams, which flow
> into it and drain out of it again in order to join other little
> streams filling another channel. Hence every dweller on earth
> also has a tenth character, which is nothing more or less than
> the passive illusion of spaces unfilled; it permits a man everything, with one exception: he may not take seriously what his at
> least nine other characters do and what happens to them, in other
> words, the very thing that ought to be the filling of him. This
> interior space - which is, it must be admitted, difficult to describe - is of a different shade and shape in Italy from what it
> is in England, because everything that stands out in relief
> against it is of a different shade and shape; and yet both here
> and there it is the same, merely an empty invisible space with
> reality standing in the middle of it like a little toy brick
> town, abandoned by the imagination. (29)

In this often quoted extract, the concept of self is organised
around two basic metaphors: stream and structure. The contents of
conscious experience and hence the contents of the person are, just
as for William James, seen as the substance of the stream or the
objects which partially fill the space. These characteristics again
could correspond to the roles of role theory and the traits of trait
theory; they include entities which are both social and personological. However the metaphor also demands a container for the
stream, a space around the objects and thus as well as the impersonal self which belongs to society there is a hidden, other, self.
Two kinds of phenomenal entities are therefore proposed. There is
the I, the subject, of little substance which contemplates the me,
the object, of solid brick-like proportions.

The hero, Ulrich, is in fact the Man Without Qualities of the title.
The following extract explains this nomenclature.

> he could with little exaggeration say of his life that everything
> in it had fulfilled itself as if it all belonged together more
> than it belonged to him. He had always been 'in for a penny, in
> for a pound', whether in contest or in love. And so he more or
> less had to believe that the personal qualities he had gained in

152   Chapter 8

> this way belonged more to each other than to him, indeed that
> every one of them, when he examined it closely, was no more
> intimately bound up with him than with other people who might
> also happen to possess it.
>
>   But undoubtedly one was nevertheless conditioned by them and
> consisted of them, even if one was not identical with them, and
> so sometimes when at rest one seemed to oneself precisely as much
> a stranger as when in motion. (30)
>
> the belief that the most important thing about experience is the
> experiencing of it, and about deeds the doing of them, is begin-
> ning to strike most people as naive. Doubtless there are still
> people who experience things quite personally, saying 'we were
> at So-and-So's yesterday' or 'we'll do this or that today' and
> enjoying it without its needing to have any further content or
> significance [...] Perhaps they are very happy; but this kind
> of people now usually appears absurd to the others, although it
> is as yet by no means established why. (31)

Ulrich thus earns his title not because he is unskilled or feature-
less but because his qualities, like the characters which make up
the inhabitant of a country in the previous extract, are divorced
from his sense of real self. Any unity in these qualities which
might prevent them from being a mere random collection occurs independently and probabilistically. A man in such and such a profession is likely over time to develop such and such attributes as the
roles and habits of the profession are taken over. Qualities developed in this way, the only way possible, appear to Ulrich as
fraudulent and impersonal, not to be taken seriously as a basis
for the self.

He is presented as being unable to unify his character traits as he
would if they were naturally expressive of his being, their unity
is correlational, statistical or social rather than organic and
vital. They have nothing to do with him; rather they are contingent, supra-personal and accidental. In another context he notes
that people are of different inner sizes. However, they can wear
the most various clothes in that size if they are laid out for them,
just as there are different categories of roles and within those
categories many diverse options. (32)

It is not that Ulrich is depicted as pathological in his self-
experience, a particularly estranged member of an otherwise coherent
species. On the contrary, Ulrich is portrayed as an especially
acute member who perceives the general human condition when others
close their eyes to it.

> For all this Klementine and Leo, like everyone in the world who
> is talked into it by prevailing morality and literature, laboured
> under the delusion that they were dependent on each other through
> their passions, characters, destinies and actions. In fact, of
> course, life is more than half made up not of actions but of
> harangues, the gist of which one absorbs, and of opinions and
> corresponding counter-opinions, and of the accumulated non-

personality of all one has heard and knows. The destiny of these
two spouses to a great extent depended on a dreary, tough, un-
ordered stratification of thoughts that were not even their own
but were part of public opinion and had changed with it, without
their being able to protect themselves against the process. (33)

The division in experience between the part of the self constructed
out of common socio-cultural elements and the sense of an active
perceiving agent which is in some way beyond conventional pressures
applies not only to accustomed habits and character traits but to
the actual process of thought as well. According to Musil, one can
make a phenomenological distinction between the shape of a thought
as it is experienced and the shape of the thing thought. There is,
he says, a fleeting moment between the two. But, the experience of
the thought immediately becomes cloaked in language; at which point
it adopts a public, non-personal, collective appearance, and becomes
an object.

Similarly, in this way of making sense of subjectivity, intuition,
inspiration or insight are not seen as transcendent moments or
events of high personal, creative, and subjective significance;
they are 'only something non-personal, namely the affinity and kin-
ship of things themselves that meet inside one's head'. (34)

Inevitably, a different concept of society emerges in association
with this representation of self. Society becomes a material, complex mechanism with its own laws, grinding on slowly in directions
which are opaque to the inhabitants. Emotions and reactions become
collectively experienced, hatred and hostility or love flow through
the air penetrating people in turn as they act as unwitting radio
receivers tuning into the Zeitgeist. (35) The generation, the ebbs
and surges of these collective emotions, illustrated in the novel
by the public feeling spawned by the trial of a mass murderer or
the genesis of a patriotic sentiment, remain mysterious and supra-
personal. The hidden laws of a larger mechanism are at work.

One obvious consequence of this perceived alienation and over-
socialisation is that the basis for personal decision-making or
moral evaluation, in Musil's text, is cut from under the hero's
feet. Without an authentic self there is no foundation, no first
causes, no reasons for particular commitments or moral stances.
What does it mean, asks Ulrich, to choose a career, to become a
man of importance, to participate in a movement? Certainly the
motives and justifications suggested by the determinate being, the
non-personal, social, part of consciousness will not suffice, and
what other motives and qualities are there? The result is inertia,
failure to become committed and a sense of individual impotence.
All that is possible is to participate in some collective 'ant-like
heroism' working unconsciously with millions of others in the production of a new social formation or, alternatively, there is the
non-committal detached analysis, the science or true record of the
self, which Ulrich engages in as his first attempt at self-salva-
tion.

One can, therefore, document in Musil's novels a systematic way of making sense of the self which explores some of the possibilities evident in formulations of role theory. The self-aware individual attentive to his or her experience of self learns to perceive the substance of the stream of consciousness as a collectively constructed, trans-individual, social product. Ulrich discovers that 'there is no longer a whole man confronting a whole world but a human something floating about in a universal culture-medium'. (36) Individual uniqueness, as a consequence, appears to lie only in the new combination of characters which are also part of other individuals. Even intellectual activity, the forms of thought, are determined and limited by the cultural possibilities and the conventions of language.

But, in spite of this indoctrination, Musil's text seems to maintain that careful phenomenological investigation also reveals another self experience best conveyed, as we have seen, metaphorically as the container around the social self, the consciousness of being conscious, 'the passive illusion of spaces unfilled', the being which can reflexively focus on the social self. The nature of this 'human something' is shown to elude Ulrich, at times it appears as merely the sense of agency at other times as a more substantial private core to consciousness. The tension within the double consciousness forms the basis for the particular experiences of alienation and estrangement since the elusive I, the real self, cannot be expressed through the acts, social gestures and rhetorics of the social self which must appear foreign to it.

In seeming to embody this model of self-experience Musil's text follows, of course, a well-established philosophical tradition. Neither his perspective nor that developed by William James is a new one. Both Kant and Hegel based their systems around the possible compartmentalisation of the self. Hegel, for instance, postulated this kind of divided or disintegrated self as a specific stage - skepticism - in the movement of what he understood as geist, spirit or universal truth, while Kant used the division of self as a device to protect human agency. (37) Existential phenomenology has since claimed that there is some experiential substance to this logical argument.

The divided self remains, however, only one possible discourse among many other discourses. It is a carefully manufactured linguistic construct. We shall argue that it is much more profitable to study the organisation and development of this interpretative framework and the contexts in which it appears as the most appropriate self-characterisation than dispute its logical or empirical validity. We shall turn to this argument in the concluding section. First, however, one last central and pervasive self portrait will be very briefly considered - the romantic images of actualisation and authenticity.

Chapter 8

ROMANTIC SELF-FULFILMENT

Without any difficulty one can easily identify a representation of the self which circumvents, while partly agreeing with, the negative picture painted by the discourses of self-division. It gives the impression that there is a route to a whole, unified, authentic self which by-passes alienation and disintegration. It is a set of discourse which gives a particular meaning to phrases such as 'I want to be me' and 'to thine own self be true'.

There appear to be at least two main, intertwined, versions of this romantic vision: first, one can identify a natural, authentic, impulsive self and, second, there is the willed self that one deliberately creates out of the wreckage of the cultural debris which clutters up the psyche. The natural authentic self depends upon a mystic, harmonious union with nature or, alternatively, emphasises the letting go of culturally fostered inhibitions and the full experiencing of instinctual and unconscious urges.

The essential difference between the natural self and the willed self lies in the degree of work and control deemed necessary. The natural, romantic self stresses spontaneity and simply being. Authenticity, here, vitally depends upon the courage to let civilised control lapse. The other self, in contrast, demands hard work and creative concentration on the new psychical elements which will combine to form the promised self-actualised future. In the majority of literary and psychological guides to self-fulfilment these two apparently contradictory notions are to some extent fused together but, generally, the emphasis is more on one than the other.

The natural self model assumes that the conventions of social and public life form a veneer over an older, deeper, more basic self which we all share in common. Socialisation, the assumption of a civilised style, alienates the person from their true human nature. In Freudian models this alienation, supported and encouraged by the super-ego, is seen as beneficial and even benevolent; none the less the feeling remains that the truly authentic integrated human being should be aware of these other impulses from the hidden parts of the psyche. The therapist's task is to present this other self in a palatable form so that the new insights gained can be assimilated into ordinary everyday experience thereby strengthening the individual.

More radical psychological therapies recommend total, though perhaps temporary, absorption in the unconscious or the non-social primeval aspects of the self. Through Janov's primal scream techniques, Gestalt acting out or Laingian dwelling in psychotic regression, health, wholeness and a more authentic self are guaranteed to emerge. (38) As in psychoanalytic therapy, the trick is to permit the self to be sufficiently open to these experiences to allow their full power to become evident.

Literary analogues of this psychological perspective abound. The example Trilling uses to make a similar point concerns Conrad's novel <u>Heart of Darkness</u> recently played out in a new form in the film <u>Apocalypse Now</u>. In this novel an archetypal civilised Englishman, Marlow, encounters and learns to respect, albeit ambivalently, Kurtz, a man who has renounced society in favour of giving free rein to the bestial side of his personality. Marlow respects Kurtz because through acting out the horror of power, sadism and cruelty to others Kurtz has the courage to explore a side of human nature common to all. He attains a kind of authenticity through dwelling in the darkness underlying the civilised veneer.

Other versions of the natural self conceptualise the casting off of social constraints in much more positive, less instinctual terms. Mystical models, for instance, base their route to authenticity on peak experiences which overwhelm the individual under special conditions of heightened awareness brought about by fatigue, drugs or meditative contemplation. (39) The experience is usually beyond words; indescribable, it connects the individual with a 'cosmic pulse' or harmony running through all things while, paradoxically, reaffirming the particularity, uniqueness and wholeness of the individual endowed with these experiences. The unfortunate prosaic individual who is unable to get in touch with these deeper facets of experience is, unfortunately, condemned to the mundane world of everyday non-events and trivialities. It is the authentic individual's duty, almost a moral imperative, to get 'in touch' with his or her impulses.

In the novels of Virginia Woolf and D.H. Lawrence the grandiose cosmic harmony experience also tinges the more ordinary experience of the natural world. Particularly in Lawrence's work, the union felt is organic as well as spiritual or mystical. A rustic picture develops involving the simple, sensual man or woman at home in their environment, and whose activities cohere with that environment. This ideal can clearly be read into the following comments by one of Musil's characters. (Incidentally, Musil's text scorns this romantic ideology while at the same time endorsing other of the mystic 'islands of consciousness'.)

> Look, Clarisse, there is nothing that everybody needs so urgently today as simplicity, nearness to the earth, health - and, yes, definitely, you can say whatever you like - a child too, because a child is what ties one firmly to the ground. All the things Ulo tells you are inhuman. I assure you, I *have* got the courage, when I come home, simply to have my cup of coffee with you, and listen to the birds, go for a bit of a walk, have a little chat with the neighbours, and let the day fade out quietly. That is human life! (40)

In these natural self models the appreciation of sunsets, country lanes or the spontaneous thrashing about in the throes of subterranean forces suffice to let the individual's true, real, self arise and develop. Volitional romantic self-discourses, on the other hand, require a much more controlled process of patient self-investigation and self-assertion. The psychological classics here are found among neo-Freudian texts, Karen Horney's work for in-

stance, or among humanist psychologists such as Carl Rogers. (41)
While the literary presentation generally involves, say, the story
of an English lad from a Northern town or a young subdued housewife,
working through the garbage of parental pressures and cultural
stereotypes to discover finally, after many painful experiences,
their own unique identity.

Common to all these different frameworks is the notion that each
individual possesses a distinctive real self: a set of qualities,
traits and aspirations which are 'right' for them. (42) Normally
people express this self freely in their daily lives; however, if
the growing child is subjected to distorting inter-personal
pressures, or to too many of the wrong kind of cultural constraints,
the real self becomes hidden behind a neurotic, inauthentic self.
(43) The person must learn to discard the imperfect self and discover through therapy, politics, social movements or just through
the 'hard school of life' itself, the real 'me'. This process is
not depicted as an easy one; moreover, there are many snares and
delusions along the way. It is a life-long struggle; the real self
is encountered, only to be lost again and perhaps individuals never
discover their real selves but only a series of closer and closer
approximations.

It must have occurred to the reader that the romantic selves which
are aspired to closely resemble the original honest soul or traditional narrative character. They have the same solidity, aura of
'rightness', and sense of harmony with the natural and social world.
As Trilling points out, the modern alienated self model of self includes the desire to be an honest soul and envies the solid narrative character type of self perceived in the oppressed, the poor,
the primitive, and the violent. There is, however, an essential
difference. The romantic self is not only a glossier version of
the honest soul with any potentially negative traits removed but
also both the volitional and natural selves possess the concept of
authenticity, a goal which would never occur to the narrative
character or the trait theory person. The latter type of self can
be sincere, without effort they can obey the maxim 'to thine own
self be true', they will appear authentic to the modern observer,
but, crucially, they cannot strive for authenticity. This quest
seems to require the prior elucidation of the discourse of self-
division.

THE SELFISH TEXT

In a recent paper, a social psychologist well known for his research
on the self concept, proposed yet another version of selfhood: one
which could easily be added to the collection gathered here. Again
he is not proposing an especially original notion. Gergen suggests,
basing his arguments on several different lines of empirical evidence, that the contents of the self are so much 'undifferentiated
murk'. 'When people reflect on their experience during most interaction sequences, they would appear', he says, to be 'faced with
what might be described as undifferentiated rousing. That is, they

are aware of changes in momentary intensity - qualitative shifts across time - but states without clear boundary lines'. (44) The self is, in other words, a site for chaos. Its substance lies in a jumble of passing states rather than in a coherent flow. The individual who pays close attention to internal experience and who thus penetrates the self will confirm, according to Gergen, its contradictory and nebulous nature.

By implication, a person's description of the feelings, hopes and fears of the moment, or of the thought processes required to solve a problem can scarcely derive from the actual inner experiences. Invariably, these inner experiences are too ambiguous, fleeting and formless to allow definitive categorisation in terms of the labels we conventionally use to express emotion, intellectual activity and so on. Inner experience is not sufficiently differentiated or reliable to guide self-analysis.

But, if our commentaries on the self are not anchored by an actual experience to which they correspond, what determines their form? Gergen considers the behaviourist hypothesis that we find out about our natures and learn to describe ourselves by observing our own behaviour much as any observer might find out about a person; but rejects it as inadequate. He is left with the vague conclusion that 'in effect, one's identifying characteristics are not a given but a mythological creation' (45) without being able to precisely specify the process behind this mythological construction except that it is in some way social.

What is interesting about Gergen's thesis is not the model itself, which is simply another attempt at pre-emptive phenomenology but the fact it should not occur to him that the forms of language might determine and give meaning to self commentary. Evidently the expressive-realist model of language as a neutral, blank transmitter of experience is so predominant in social psychology that the role of discourse is effectively obscured. Behaviour and internal experience occur to Gerçen, but not socio-linguistics.

We would suggest that in all areas, when accounting for subjective experience, we are dependent on the available linguistic resources. The individual's ability, for example, to divide himself into several different characters arises because of linguistic concepts such as the I and the me and the way these are marked in the rules of syntax and used in everyday accounting for action. The meaning attributed to the self in the case of the I vs the me or romantic authenticity or trait theory reflect our system for making sense of the world not a basic inner experience or an observation of physical action. Moreover, accounts of the self are given in the course of social interactions in which certain goals and norms are deemed appropriate and we must therefore attempt to explore the ways in which they are constructed to fit the specifications.

In a famous extract from S/Z, Barthes comments that ultimately our subjectivity has the generality of stereotypes; it is merely the 'wash of all the codes which make up the I'. (46) These codes are linguistic ones, infinitely more subtle, varied and fragmented than the static roles of role theory, they can be seen to form the basis for intersubjectivity and open the possibility for any kind of self-analysis.

In this chapter we have considered a number of, admittedly rarified, representations of the nature of self. Each version, the romantic model, the honest soul, the alienated self, etc. claims to be the only valid portrait (hence the title of this concluding section); either because it supposedly encapsulates some phenomenological or experiential truth, is supported by psychometric research, or appears to be the most appropriate analytic tool. Each representation also shares in common the assumption that people are indeed defined by substantial entities, their selves, which sit within and, queen bee like, direct or unify operations. The meaning of actions and experiences derives from the person. It is taken for granted that through patient investigation whether it be the phenomenological stripping away of layers or the observation of large numbers of people in action, the true nature and substance of the self will be made manifest.

By lining up together some of these potential codes for self-analysis and treating them as shifting and interchangeable discourses rather than as competing claims to the truth, we were asserting our opposition to this kind of picture. It is not necessary to attribute a determinate, perhaps ultimately private, self to the individual in order to study subjectivity. (47) What we have, readily available, is socio-linguistic discourse of all kinds - ordinary speech, literature, the media, scientific accounts, conversations, participant observer's accounts, etc. This quick trip through several academic and literary models alone has illustrated some of the dominant cultural possibilities for constructing the contemplative observation of the self. A more general, less holistic, analysis is thus called for, examining the contexts and accounts (attributions, justifications and explanations) where certain pieces of self-talk are deemed most appropriate and enumerating through careful fine-grain analysis, the many different methods of situational self-characterisation.

A specific example might make this point clearer. As we have seen, the I and the me or the subject and object of consciousness have been put forward as definitive aspects of the self. They are said to have a concrete ontological existence as part of the flow of consciousness. Our alternative would be to see this kind of philosophical approach to the self as 'nothing but fanciful expressions of the rules of grammar of personal pronouns as used in the giving and constructing of accounts'. (48) It is a distinction which emerges through the conventions for explaining and justifying one's actions, a conceptual possibility which is then extended until it becomes a complete self-diagram. It is also, on a more global level, a literary convention best suited to and found in a certain kind of literary genre. What is a purely textual tradition becomes, in an author such as Musil, and as we have seen in Doris Lessing, attributed to an experiential reality. (49)

According to Harré, an interesting everyday case of the establishment of the I versus the me, one of its many linguistic manifestations, is that of self-deception. Following Finagrette's analysis, Harré takes the fundamental accounting statement '*You* are deceiving *your*self' and notes that the competent decoding of this very common utterance depends upon splitting the person into two components: an I, the first you, and an out of control me, the second yourself. (50) There are good interactional reasons why at times we may want to portray a friend as both the integrated centre and originator of their actions and as a character who is unwittingly contradicting the real self; for instance, to justify a friend's negatively viewed actions, while not taking them to be typical of behaviour. It is a linguistic distinction, however, a mode of speech. We do not need to make any reference to an essential experience of a split ego which determines this contradiction. In Harré's words,

> In this way the problem that loomed so threateningly as a problem in the ontology of persons is resolved by referring it to a mode of speech whose social role is readily available to commonsense understanding. It is primarily an imposed scenario, a 'you' - 'yourself' separation in the speech of another, leading to the adoption of an 'I' - 'me' separation in the speech of the one concerned. (51)

The identification of some of the possible modes of self-characterisation carried out in this chapter can be seen as an essential first stage in a much longer process of empirical investigation. We not only need to describe the interpretative models and social representations which are available and explicate their structure in 'abstract'; we also must be able to offer a more functional analysis delineating the contexts in which these accounts are used. Character descriptions are often third person in style. They are told to others and therefore open to considerable flexibility. One would expect them to be contingent upon the interpersonal and group interests of the moment and these connections need to be made explicit. And so, although literature is an interesting place to start, eventually the social psychologist's attention must shift to everyday uses.

The self is indeed a complex area. The reader of novels and the social scientist alike are seemingly faced with a bewildering variety of potential descriptions. In this chapter, the aim was to demonstrate the cultural overlap and the connections, normally repressed, between literary and socio-psychological modes of understanding. In the end, the number of self descriptions turns out to be remarkably finite with a few common themes predominating to be repeated over and over again as each new observer of the self twists and turns the available categories hoping to hit upon a definitive version which will capture the elusive nature of self-experience. Our conclusion was that this search for the ultimate definition is a sterile one, and, finally, we argued that it is much more interesting to study the construction and organisation of self discourses, perhaps discovering in this manner, all there 'is' to the self.

NOTES

CHAPTER 1   WRITING GENDER

1   R. Coward, 'Are women's novels feminist novels?', p.53.
2   A.C. Elms, 'The crisis of confidence in social psychology'.
3   D. Lessing, Ripple From The Storm, pp.46-7.
4   The following literary critical essays describe these aspects of Lessing's work in detail: E.W. Brooks, 'The image of woman in Lessing's The Golden Notebook', and A.B. Markow, 'The pathology of feminine failure in the fiction of Doris Lessing'. For more general critical discussions of Lessing's work see A. Pratt and L.S. Dembo (eds), Doris Lessing: Critical Studies and R. Rubenstein, The Novelistic Vision of Doris Lessing: Breaking the Forms of Consciousness.
5   The following discussion of the value of literature for the woman reader relies on Burr-Evans's analysis, N. Burr-Evans, 'The value and peril for women of reading women writers'.
6   Ibid., p.310.
7   F. Katz-Stoker, 'The other criticism: Feminism or Formalism', p.315.
8   A.V. Pratt, 'The new feminist criticisms: Exploring the history of the new space', p.175.
9   For a general anthology of this type of feminist criticism see S.K. Cornillon (ed.), Images of Women in Fiction: Feminist Perspectives.
10 I. Murdoch, cited in C. Belsey, Critical Practice, p.13. Belsey offers a more comprehensive description of this model of literature, which she calls expressive-realism, in Chapter 1 of her book.
11 M. Zeraffa, 'The novel as literary form and as social institution', p.36.
12 N. Armistead, 'Experience in everyday life', p.118.
13 This proposal has been put forward by Armistead, ibid. and M.S. Wetherell, 'Socio-psychological and literary accounts of femininity', see also the references for Chapter 3.
14 Cf. A. Oakley, Sex, Gender and Society.
15 Cf. K. Deaux, The Behavior of Women and Men; F. Fransella and K. Frost, On Being a Woman; C. Tavris and C. Offir, The Longest

War: Sex Differences in Perspective and R.C. Wylie, The Self-Concept: Theory and Research on Selected Topics, vol.2, chapter 5.
16 Cf. I.K. Broverman, S.R. Vogel, D.M. Broverman, F.E. Clarkson and P.S. Rosenkrantz, 'Sex-role stereotypes: A current appraisal'.
17 Tavris and Offir, op.cit., Chapter 6.
18 E. Maccoby and C. Jacklin, The Psychology of Sex Differences.
19 New areas of research include, among other things, work on attributions for success and failure, cf. K. Deaux and T. Emswiller, 'Explanations of successful performance on sex-linked tasks: What is skill for the male is luck for the female', and on sex differences in achievement motivation, cf. M. Horner, 'Toward an understanding of achievement-related conflicts in women'.
20 A. Oakley, Subject Women, Chapter 4.
21 J. Cooper, Emily, pp.19-20,21.
22 D. Lessing, Martha Quest, p.202.
23 B. Cartland, Moments of Love, p.298.
24 W. Allen, Tradition and Dream, p.298.
25 A more detailed rationale for her work which outlines basic humanist-realist tenets can be found in D. Lessing, 'A small personal voice'.
26 D. Lessing, A Ripple From The Storm, p.126.
27 D. Lessing, The Golden Notebook, p.314.
28 Ibid., pp.595-6.
29 R. Harré, 'The self in monodrama'.
30 For a detailed critique of this model and expansion on the critical points which follow see Belsey, op.cit.; a similar critique orientated towards the same kind of doctrines in socio-linguistics can be found in M. Black and R. Coward, 'Linguistic, social and sexual relations: A review of Dale Spender's Man-Made Language'.
31 Cf. R. Barthes' discussion of similar fragments of discourse in his book A Lover's Discourse.
32 T. Eagleton, 'How the critical revolution started rolling', p.9.
33 Ibid.
34 The argument for this enterprise is laid out in Coward, op.cit. N. Furman, 'Textual feminism' contains a general manifesto for this type of literary criticism as do the following special issues of Critical Inquiry, vol.8 and Yale French Studies, vol.62 while S. Heath, The Sexual Fix gives examples of the kind of deconstruction which is possible in the general area of sexual talk.
35 For another attempt to specify the assumptions behind the notion of sexual identity from quite a different frame of reference see M. Eichler, The Double Standard, Chapter 3.
36 Cf. Eichler, op.cit., pp.62-9.
37 A man never begins by presenting himself as an individual of a certain sex: it goes without saying that he is a man. The terms *masculine* and *feminine* are used symmetrically only as a matter of form, as on legal papers. In actuality the relation of the two sexes is not quite like that of two electrical poles, for man represents both the positive and

the neutral, as indicated by the common use of *man* to designate human beings in general; whereas woman represents only the negative, defined by limiting criteria, without reciprocity. (S. de Beauvoir, The Second Sex, p.15)
38 Black and Coward, op.cit.
39 Fransella and Frost, op.cit., p.9.
40 J. Shotter, 'Men the magicians: The duality of social being and the structure of moral worlds'.
41 Note in this context Parsons and Bales's classic discussion of the instrumental and socio-emotional division of labour between men and women in the family which assumes this kind of 'knowledge' - T. Parsons and R. Bales (eds), Family, Socialization and Interaction Process. Eichler, op.cit., uses the following anecdote to illustrate a similar point. It concerns the group of successful business women at a conference who, nodding their heads sagely, note that the problem with women generally is that they fear success, don't know how to assert themselves, are not sufficiently articulate and so on. The irony being that all of these women were articulate, highly successful and assertive ...
42 S. Moscovici, 'Society and theory in social psychology'.

CHAPTER 2   CHARACTER AND ENVIRONMENT

1 Introductions to environmental psychology may be found in, for example, C. Mercer, Living in Cities, or T.R. Lee, Psychology and the Environment.
2 Cited in D. Bucsescu, 'Concept of "place" - a tool for investigating environmental cognitions'.
3 D.V. Canter, The Psychology of Place.
4 Thomas Hardy, The Mayor of Casterbridge. All references are to the New Wessex Edition of 1974.
5 P. Stringer, 'A politico-psychological perspective on crowding'.
6 An introductory and a recent treatment of such models can be found respectively in J. Shotter, Images of Man in Psychological Research and A.J. Chapman and D.M. Jones, Models of Man.
7 See J. Israel, 'Stipulations and constructions in the social sciences'. Well-known examples of these models can be found in, respectively, the work of B.F. Skinner, E. Goffman and G.H. Mead.
8 Ibid., p.140.
9 Hardy, op.cit., pp.90-1.
10 Ibid., p.168.
11 Ibid., pp.179-81.
12 Ibid., p.192.
13 Ibid., pp.195-6.
14 Ibid., p.185.
15 Ibid., pp.187-8.
16 Ibid., p.189.
17 D.C.D. Pocock, Humanistic Geography and Literature.
18 Ibid., pp.14-15.
19 Which is drawn from, but does not exactly parallel, Israel, op.cit.
20 A. Enstice, Thomas Hardy: Landscapes of the Mind.

21 The themes of these three paragraphs are dealt with in a work in preparation: P. Stringer, Place and Displacement: Thomas Hardy and the Deconstruction of Social Psychology.
22 Hardy, op.cit., p.289.
23 There is not the space to exemplify these points about the nature of social psychological experiments. They are certainly over-generalised in form. But they are part of a critique of social psychological practice which constituted an important part of the discipline during the 1970s. They are dealt with more fully in Stringer, op.cit.
24 Cf. Israel, op.cit., pp.138-40.
25 This fragmentation also occurs in previous social science readings of Hardy's novels, which have been either sociological or psychological, rather than socio-psychological. On the one hand, L. Lerner, Thomas Hardy's The Mayor of Casterbridge and J.C. Maxwell, 'The "sociological" approach to the Mayor of Casterbridge'; on the other, R. Sumner, Thomas Hardy: Psychological Novelist and G. Thurley, The Psychology of Hardy's Novels.
26 P. Stringer, 'A politico-psychological perspective on crowding'.
27 Bucsescu, op.cit.

CHAPTER 3 SOME UNSATISFACTORY TRADITIONS

1 J.R. Townsend, Written for Children.
2 An almost Manichean stress on influence for good and evil is clearly visible in the huge quantity of mass media research conducted by social psychologists. Compare, for example, J.P. Murray and S. Kippax, 'From the early window to the late show: international trends in the study of television's impact on children and adults' and J.P. Rushton, 'Effects of prosocial television and film material on the behaviour of viewers'.
3 D.C. McLelland, The Achieving Society.
4 D.C. McLelland, 'Values in popular literature for children'.
5 A number of these studies are reviewed in detail in D.W. Chambers, Children's Literature in the Curriculum.
6 Loban's work is discussed in Chambers, op.cit.
7 A.M.E. Goldschmidt, 'Alice in Wonderland Psychoanalysed'.
8 F.A. Favat, 'Child and tale: an hypothesis on the origins of interest'.
9 D.G. Singer, 'Piglet, Pooh and Piaget'.
10 There is an enormous quantity of secondary literature on Lukacs and Goldmann's classic work. Useful introductions are provided by J. Routh and J. Wolff, The Sociology of Literature: Theoretical Approaches and J. Wolff, The Social Production of Art.
11 R. Fernandez, Social Psychology Through Literature. Other studies concerned with the use of literature in teaching are reviewed in D. Rose and J. Radford, 'The use of literature in teaching psychology'.
12 F.E. Merrill, 'The sociology of literature', p.656, emphasis added.
13 J. Finkelstein, 'Novels as data for phenomenological research', pp.14-15.

14 There are many references to literature in Freud's work. In particular *The Interpretation of Dreams* discusses *Hamlet*, *Oedipus Rex*, *Julius Caesar*, *Midsummer Night's Dream*, *Othello*, and *Romeo and Juliet*; while *The Psychopathology of Everyday Life* discusses *Julius Caesar*, *Richard III* and the *Merchant of Venice*.
15 E. Jones, *Hamlet and Oedipus*.
16 N. Holland, *The Dynamics of Literary Response*, p.26.
17 E. Dalton, *Unconscious Structure in The Idiot*.
18 The significance of Lacan's very difficult work is discussed in detail in R. Coward and J. Ellis, *Language and Materialism: Developments in Semiology and the Theory of the Subject*, Chapter 6.
19 S. Moscovici, *La Psychoanalyse: son image et son public*.
20 D.W. Harding, 'Practice at liking: a study of experimental aesthetics'.
21 Although there is a lack of utilisation at the social psychological level, other critics have drawn upon broader, sociological theory. M. Bradbury, *The Social Context of Modern English Literature* is an example of work which tries to illuminate the nature of modernist literary texts in the light of broader social processes and changes in society's intellectual world views. Bradbury draws upon a variety of sources - sociological, historical and literary - to support his claim that there was an emergence of a new style of writing, new themes and new conceptions of the nature of literary creation in the late nineteenth century.
22 S. Moscovici, 'Society and theory in social psychology'.
23 D.L. Hamilton and R.K. Gifford, 'Illusory correlations in interpersonal perception: a cognitive basis of stereotypic judgements'.
24 H. Tajfel, 'Social stereotypes and social groups'.
25 Interesting and important discussions of this issue are found in, for example: R.S. Peters, *The Concept of Motivation*, M. Hollis, *Models of Man: Philosophical thoughts on social action*, and D. Papineau, *For Science in the Social Sciences*, Chapter 4.
26 R. Harré and P.F. Secord, *The Explanation of Social Behaviour*.
27 See, for instance, R. Barthes, *Writing Degree Zero*, and *Image-Music-Text*, J. Kristeva, *Desire in Language: A semiotic approach to literature and art*. Useful introductions to this work are provided by J. Culler, *Structuralist Poetics*, and *The Pursuit of Signs*, and C. Belsey, *Critical Practice*.
28 Belsey, op.cit., p.7, author's emphasis. This expressive realist position is not a straw man. It appears even in some of the most sophisticated of recent literary theory. For instance, W. Iser, *The Act of Reading*, replicates, in a fascinating examination of the phenomenology of reading, the central features of the expressive realist approach. The text is the author's vision: 'We may assume that every literary text in one way or another represents a perspective view of the world put together by (though not necessarily typical of) the author', (p.35) and this vision is transmitted to the reader: 'the structure of the text sets off a sequence of mental images which lead to the text translating itself into the reader's consciousness' (p.38).

29 Fernandez, op.cit., p.xvi.
30 A discussion of Festinger's theory of cognitive dissonance is an essential part of any introductory textbook to social psychology.
31 The classic study is Roland Barthes, S/Z. This is described in detail in Coward and Ellis, op.cit., Chapter 4. Some studies of non-literary texts which arrive at essentially the same conclusion are discussed in Chapter 5.

CHAPTER 4   FROM ACTION TO DISCOURSE

1   R. Harré, Social Being.
2   N. Chomsky, Aspects of a Theory of Syntax.
3   R. Harré, 'Rules in the explanation of social behaviour' and 'Some remarks on "rule" as a scientific concept'.
4   P. Marsh, E. Rosser and R. Harré, Rules of Disorder, pp.16-18. Further explication of this distinction is provided in J. Searle, Speech Acts, pp.33-42, and P. Collett, 'Rule as a scientific concept'.
5   Marsh et al., op.cit., Chapter 4. See also P. Marsh, 'Rules in the organisation of action: empirical studies'.
6   Marsh et al., op.cit., p.83.
7   P. Willis, Learning to Labour.
8   Willis was not concerned with the processes which lead some pupils to join the oppositional culture and others not to.
9   Willis, op.cit., p.13.
10 This issue is discussed in detail in S. Hall and T. Jefferson (eds), Resistance Through Rituals, and D. Hebdige, Subculture: The Meaning of Style.
11 R. Harré and P.F. Secord, The Explanation of Social Behaviour, and D. Wrong, 'On the oversocialised conception of man in modern sociology'. Some of the complexities of this issue are discussed in A. Giddens, Central Problems in Social Theory, Chapter 2.
12 R. Harré, 'The ethogenic approach: theory and practice', pp. 298-302. See also M.B. Scott and S.M. Lyman, 'Accounts'.
13 Marsh et al., op.cit., p.97.
14 Ibid.
15 R. Harré, Social Being, pp.89-91, and 'Psychological variety'.
16 F. Yates, cited in R. Harré, 'Psychological variety'.
17 R. Harré, 'Psychological variety', p.95.
18 Ibid., p.92.
19 R. Middleton, 'Fertility values in American magazine fiction'. This and similar studies are discussed in E.J. Webb, D.T. Cambell, R.D. Schwartz and L. Sechrest, Unobtrusive Measures.
20 R. Barthes, S/Z.
21 Ibid., p.21.
22 J. Culler, The Pursuit of Signs, Chapter 1.
23 See, for example, references in Chapter 3, note 27, and J.V. Harari (ed.), Textual Strategies, and S.R. Suleiman and I. Crosman (eds), The Reader in the Text.
24 On this issue see I. Crosman, 'Do readers make meaning', in Suleiman and Crosman, op.cit.

25 The approach to textual analysis known as 'deconstruction' goes furthest in exploiting the internal tensions and ruptures which are a pervasive feature of literary and other kinds of discourse. This work is lucidly discussed in C. Norris, Deconstruction: Theory and Practice.
26 R. Barthes, 'From work to text', p.161.
27 J. Culler, op.cit. and Structuralist Poetics.
28 See references in Chapter 5, note 25.
29 J. Culler, Structuralist Poetics, pp.113-21.
30 Barthes constantly stresses the interpenetration of literary and other signifying systems such as clothing (Système de la Mode), food and household goods (Mythologies), forms of prayer and sexual deviation (Sade, Fourier, Loyola). Other criticisms of this feature of Culler's approach are found in R. Fowler, Literature as Social Discourse, and D. Silverman and B. Torode, The Material Word.
31 See, for instance, M. Mulkay, J. Potter and S. Yearley, 'Why an analysis of scientific discourse is needed'.
32 J. Potter and M. Mulkay, 'Scientists' interview talk: interviews as a technique for revealing participants' interpretative practices'.
33 Useful discussions of the notion of intertextuality are found in Barthes, S/Z, R. Coward and J. Ellis, Language and Materialism, Chapter 4, J. Culler, The Pursuit of Signs, Chapter 5.
34 One important exception has been the theory of speech acts, developed by Searle from the work of Austin, which has been used by a number of literary theorists, e.g. W. Iser, The Act of Reading. An interesting and at times amusing debate has taken place between Searle and the deconstructionist philosopher Derrida over the applicability of speech act theory to written language: see J. Derrida, 'Signature Event Context', J. Searle, 'Reiterating the Differences' and J. Derrida, 'Limited Inc. abc'.

CHAPTER 5   DISSECTING FACTUAL TEXTS

1 J. Culler, The Pursuit of Signs, p.217.
2 T. Eagleton, 'How the critical revolution started rolling' and 'The end of criticism', R. Fowler, Literature as Social Discourse.
3 D.R. Holsti, 'Content analysis'; E.J. Webb, D.T. Cambell, R.D. Schwartz and L. Sechrest, Unobtrusive Measures.
4 D. Smith, 'K is mentally ill: the anatomy of a factual account'.
5 Ibid., p.28, lines 6-9. The entire account of K's illness is reproduced in the paper.
6 Ibid., p.29, lines 33-45.
7 Ibid., p.31, lines 119-24.
8 Ibid., p.37.
9 Ibid., p.39, lines 34-46.
10 Smith here makes the important distinction between rules which must be extracted from the particular occasion. There is no previously known rule which suggests that working intensively

in a garden is anomalous, yet the linguistic context, by implying that this work should properly be casual, creates the sense of anomaly.
11 Smith, op.cit., p.43, lines 21-3.
12 Ibid., line 81.
13 Ibid.
14 The problems with Smith's attempt to extrapolate from the text to what is really happening to K are discussed in E.C. Cuff, 'Some issues in studying the problem of versions in everyday situations'.
15 T. Trew, '"What the papers say"; linguistic variation and ideological difference'.
16 Ibid., pp.120-1.
17 G. Kress, Halliday: System and Function in Language, Chapter 2.
18 It appears to be a ubiquitous feature of descriptive terminology that it conveys more than 'mere' description. It may, for example, give a tacit indication of motive (J. Coulter, The Social Construction of Mind, Chapter 2) or even do the work of an accusation (P. Drew, 'Accusations: the occasioned use of religious geography in describing events').
19 Trew, op.cit., p.135.
20 H.H. Kelley, 'The process of causal attribution', and E.E. Jones and R.E. Nisbett, 'The actor and the observer: divergent perceptions of the causes of behaviour'.
21 S. Moscovici, 'Society and theory in social psychology', and I. Lubek, 'Aggression research'.
22 Studies such as Trew's show the practical significance of issues of agency and causation for people in numerous everyday situations. See also J.M. Atkinson, Discovering Suicide, and S. Yearley, 'Vocabularies of freedom and resentment'.
23 See, for example, G.N. Gilbert and M. Mulkay, Opening Pandora's Box: An analysis of scientists' discourse, J. O'Niell (ed.), Science Texts, S. Woolgar, 'Discovery: logic and sequence in a scientific text' and S. Yearley, 'Textual persuasion: the role of social accounting in the construction of scientific arguments'.
24 R. Harré, 'The ethogenic approach: theory and practice' and P. Marsh, E. Rosser and R. Harré, The Rules of Disorder, p.84.
25 D.L. Wieder, 'On meaning by rule' and J. Heritage, 'Aspects of the flexibilities of natural language use'.
26 K.R. Popper, Conjectures and Refutations, W.V.O. Quine and J.S. Ullian, The Web of Belief, Chapter 5, and T.S. Kuhn, The Essential Tension, Chapter 13.
27 J. Potter, 'Testability, flexibility: Kuhnian values in psychologists' discourse concerning theory choice'.
28 G.N. Gilbert and M. Mulkay, Opening Pandora's Box: A sociological analysis of scientists' discourse, Chapter 5.
29 This is a pseudonym.
30 A useful review of earlier work is found in M. Coulthart, An Introduction to Discourse Analysis.
31 This problem is not limited to qualitatively based research. See M. Mulkay, J. Potter and S. Yearley, 'Why an analysis of scientific discourse is needed'.

Notes to chapter 6

CHAPTER 6 VICTIM OF REALREAD

1 J.H. Goldstein, Social Psychology, pp.334-5. Such textbook accounts, incidentally, are interesting in themselves, as accounts. A majority of today's social psychology textbooks refer to this work of Janis, sometimes at unusual length. Its reference to real-world events is clearly welcome in the task of engaging student interest. But invariably the authors render it as an unproblematic achievement, and thereby take one stage further the naturalising process which we criticise in this chapter.
2 The interested reader is referred to the second edition of I.L. Janis, Victims of Groupthink, due to be published in 1982.
3 I.L. Janis, Victims of Groupthink, p.iii.
4 Ibid.
5 Ibid., p.v.
6 Ibid., p.vi. Whether these hopes are realised can be gauged from W.H. Blanchard, Aggression American Style; A. George, Presidential Decision-making in Foreign Policy: the Effective Use of Information and Advice; R. Wyden, Bay of Pigs: the Untold Story.
7 See, for example, D. Rose and J. Radford, 'The use of literature in teaching psychology'.
8 Janis, op.cit., p.13.
9 T.C. Sorensen, Kennedy, p.7.
10 Janis, op.cit., p.16.
11 Sorensen, op.cit., p.295.
12 Ibid.
13 A.M. Schlesinger Jr, A Thousand Days, pp.262-3.
14 Though Sorensen did spend a night writing Kennedy's post-Bay of Pigs speech; and after the incident became an inseparable member of the President's immediate entourage.
15 Schlesinger, op.cit., pp.227-8.
16 Ibid., p.231. In a note to his main text Janis (op.cit., p.227) recognises this 'somewhat self-abasing confession', but interprets it as an attempt by Schlesinger to protect his dead leader and the team. While accepting that this is an objective of Schlesinger, we prefer to take the passage as being more particularly a part of a complex, self-centred rhetoric.
17 Schlesinger, op.cit., p.262.
18 Ibid., p.232.
19 Ibid., p.217.
20 Ibid., p.231.
21 Ibid., pp.252-8.
22 This expectation is referred to frequently, but appears to be discounted by Janis, as deluded rather than reasonable, in the interests of 'purifying' Kennedy's stance. The President certainly insisted throughout that there would be no US military intervention in any form. But it is clear that the CIA and the Joint Chiefs, as well as the Cubans, did not believe that this position would be upheld before a prospect of defeat. Indeed, Kennedy did eventually authorise the use, albeit ineffectual, of unmarked Navy planes. It is arguable that his most serious mistake was consistently to misunderstand that an expectation

of military support would form a basis for the invasion plan; and that his implicit trust in the experts and in the Cuban force's morale precluded his adopting their perspective in this matter.
23 Nor these chapters in relation to the rest of Schlesinger's book.
24 We make no reference to straightforward errors on Janis's part – for example, his attribution (Janis, op.cit., pp.37-8) of the stereotyped perception of Castro and Cuba. We are concerned with alternative, not definitive, interpretations.
25 Though if we read the mood naturalistically, why are no other blunders referred to on the part of an inexperienced and over-confident administration?
26 Ibid., p.41.
27 Again we do not wish to be read as ascribing motives to Schlesinger. We are pointing to an interpretation of the structuring of the text.
28 Ibid., pp.43-6.
29 Ibid., p.196.
30 Ibid., p.227.
31 Ibid., p.249.
32 Ibid., pp.196-7.
33 Ibid., p.v.

CHAPTER 7 ELITES AND STEREOTYPES

1 S. Ramanathan, The Novels of C.P. Snow, p.65.
2 B. Raven and J. Rubin, Social Psychology: People in Groups.
3 See, for example: H. Tajfel, Human Groups and Social Categories; and Differentiation between Social Groups; J.C. Turner and H. Giles, Intergroup Behaviour.
4 It was in the case of the present writer! Most of the observations which follow are very well illustrated by the novels which fall in these two settings.
5 Ramanathan, op.cit., p.18.
6 'Interview with C.P. Snow', p.105.
7 Cf. H. Tajfel, 'Experiments in a vacuum' for an early statement of the criticism.
8 'In the communities of the elite'.
9 Public Affairs.
10 Later in the article the fight is escalated. We are told both that egalitarianism will always win and that élites are likely to become more prominent. Was Snow anticipating revolution, or merely having it both ways?
11 C.P. Snow, 'In the communities of the elite', p.1249: 'The Victorians could write naturally about class ... The Victorians had class naturally in the background'.
12 In The Situation of the Novel, p.137.
13 Earlier in the article Snow goes to somewhat comical extremes to discount the problem by citing as one of the most dramatic élites of contemporary society, that of 'professional soccer players [who] come overwhelmingly from the working class, even [sic] in countries like Sweden and West Germany'. And even East

German players are drawn in as evidence of footballers being a tight-knit and classless élite!
14 Other essays, such as the well-known writings on the two cultures, fare no better under close examination than 'In the communities of the elite'.
15 Cf. his The Realists: Portraits of Eight Novelists.
16 Sequential habits of writing make us distort the reading process. As social psychologists, we read Snow and social psychology simultaneously; both sets of text, and many others, are produced together in reading.
17 The critical remarks made about social psychology in this chapter, as in Chapter 2, are necessarily general in nature. They should not be read as all-embracing. A self-critical debate began in the early seventies. Some social psychologists would claim now that their practice had altered. But if we persist with the criticisms it is in part because they still apply to much of what is done; and in part because the body of social psychology is a diachronic achievement - we cannot simply expunge everything done before 1970.
18 This ethnocentrism takes three forms. One is to ignore the psychological literature of other countries - a particularly American habit. The second is to assume that one's culture is no different from any other - in the sense of implying that there is no specifically cultural component in, say, North American social psychology. The third form has infected most cross-cultural psychology until recently and assumes the universality of Western structures.
19 Though similar arguments have variously been proposed from within the discipline.
20 In parenthesis, Snow's The Affair and his earlier The Search would make an intriguing study for sociologists of science - cf. Chapter 5. Written by a scientist they might be read by many people as depicting what scientists 'really do', in distinction from the picture given through formal scientific presentations. We would argue that neither type of discourse should be treated as a privileged account of what scientists do. In both cases the objectives and techniques of their rhetoric is of central interest.
21 Analyses of psychologists' talk can be found in J. Potter, 'Speaking and writing science'.
22 We may have such a feeling in any university group! But Snow is not commenting on that interesting social fact.
23 Two recent social psychology textbooks produce interesting examples which go further than psychologists' reluctance to apply the psychology of learning. Throughout the 1970s Kenneth Gergen produced a series of often-cited articles in criticism of traditional and experimental social psychology. In 1981 he published a textbook (K.J. Gergen and M.M. Gergen, Social Psychology) in which these criticisms are thrust into the background as one more instance of the products of social psychology. They are not allowed to inform the representation of social psychology which he offers to 'innocent' students.

In the same period David Stang produced a number of articles on the employment of social psychologists. In his 1981 textbook

(B.J. Stang, Introduction to Social Psychology) this all-important issue for students is relegated to a two-page epilogue. It is not allowed, for example, to structure and direct their assimilation of the subject throughout the book. Employment is a separate and subsequent issue from the university course.
24 Ramanathan, op.cit., p.16.
25 H. Tajfel, 'Social stereotypes and social groups'.
26 Ibid., p.156.
27 Ibid.
28 Ibid., pp.160-1.
29 Tajfel refers to V.G. Kiernan, The Lords of Human Kind.
30 On the other hand the decadence of the 1960s, in the shape of the Moors Murders and sexual permissiveness among students (The Sleep of Reason) is allowed to come close to home. The responsible parties are specifically identified and characterised. Perhaps they come too close to home. Lewis Eliot's eye disorder takes on a distinctly psychosomatic aspect.
31 Tajfel, op.cit., p.165.
32 Ibid., p.167.

CHAPTER 8   THE DISCURSIVE SELF

1 D. Morley, The Nationwide Audience, p.16.
2 R. Musil, cited in D. Luft, Robert Musil and the Crisis of European Culture.
3   concepts of identity ... remain as undercurrents in our lives, (they) provide the norms by which we judge ourselves and others. Implicitly, they form our conceptions of the principles that ought to guide our choices. Our philosophical intuitions - the intuitions that guide our analyses of the criteria for personal identity - they have been formed by these notions: they are the archaeological layers on which our practices rest. (A. Rorty, 'A literary postscript: Characters, persons, selves, individuals', p.319.)
4 C. Dickens, Our Mutual Friend, pp.174-5.
5 L. Trilling, Sincerity and Authenticity.
6 Cf. Guiguet's description of the honest soul minor characters in Virginia Woolf's works.
    The primary quality of all these characters, the one which ensures for them a convincing presence in the novels and the power of surviving in our memories, is their very limitedness. They are fixed, static, in every respect. They have a history, a profession, a passion or a mania, a gesture, an attitude or a turn of phrase that defines them; and their fidelity to themselves is unfailing; thus they are, and thus they remain. Around them the author has, like St. John Hirst, traced the chalk circle which gives them their being but which also confines them. They correspond exactly to the traditional notion of personality, made of a bundle of more or less complex tendencies and manifested by constant reactions. (J. Guiguet, Virginia Woolf and her Works, pp. 353-4.)

Notes to chapter 8

7   Cf. the following works: G.W. Allport, Personality: A Psychological Interpretation; R.B. Cattell, The Scientific Analysis of Personality; H.J. Eysenck, The Structure of Human Personality.
8   L.A. Pervin, Personality: Theory, Assessment and Research, p.387.
9   H.J. Eysenck and S.B. Eysenck, The Eysenck Personality Inventory, University of London Press, c. 1964.
10 16 P. F., c. 1956, Institute for Personality and Ability Testing, 1602-04 Colorado Drive, Champaign, Illinois, USA.
11 Rorty, op.cit.
12 V. Woolf, 'The character in fiction'.
13 W. Mischel, Personality and Assessment.
14 G.R. Semin, E. Rosch and J. Chassein, 'A comparison of the common-sense and "scientific" conceptions of extroversion-introversion'.
15 Trilling, op.cit., p.35.
16 Ibid., p.31.
17 P. Berger and T. Luckmann, The Social Construction of Reality.
18 This argument has been presented in its most complete form by the structuralist-functionalist school, cf. T. Parsons, 'The position of identity in the general theory of action'.
19 A classic description of roles and role theory can be found in R. Dahrendorf, Homo Sociologicus.
20 For the presentation and defence of this perspective on individuality see Heading's arguments in his debate with Bradbury and Hollis: M. Bradbury, B. Heading and M. Hollis, 'The man and the mask: A discussion of role theory'.
21 Again note Heading's perspective in Bradbury et al., ibid.
22 W. James, 'The self'.
23 Ibid., p.41.
24 Cf. Bradbury et al., op.cit., and D.W. Hamlyn, 'Person perception and our understanding of others'.
25 See J. Coulter, The Social Construction of Mind, Chapter 6, for a detailed account of George Herbert Mead's development of this solution for role theory (later adopted by Dahrendorf). Coulter also analyses the problems inherent in this model.
26 R. Musil, A Man Without Qualities.
27 For literary critical and biographical accounts of Musil's work see Luft, op.cit.; F.G. Peters, Robert Musil: Master of the Hovering Life; B. Pike, Robert Musil; W. Sypher, Loss of the Self in Modern Literature and Art.
28 Luft, op.cit., p.42.
29 Musil, op.cit., Vol. One, p.34.
30 Ibid., p.173.
31 Ibid., p.175.
32 Ibid., p.134.
33 Ibid., p.244.
34 Ibid., p.129.
35 'He flowed on like a wave among his wave-brothers, if it may be put so.' Musil, op.cit., p.149. 'The subterranean river of untapped, ferocious, lonely, romantic desires, that concentration of ecstasy and violence which is the dream-life of the nation.' Norman Mailer, cited in E. Goodheart, The Cult of the Ego.

36 Musil, op.cit., p.257.
37 R. Solomon, From Rationalism to Existentialism, Chapters 1 and 2. Literary critics, of course, frequently draw upon these philosophical works as a resource for explicating the models of self they detect in various novels. Trilling, for instance, takes Hegel as one of his principal examples for the disintegrated or fragmented self while E. Engleberg, The Unknown Distance, also makes the same points based on a Hegelian analysis of Dostoievsky's Notes From the Underground.
38 A. Janov, The Primal Scream; R.D. Laing, The Politics of Experience and the Bird of Paradise; F.S. Perls, Gestalt Therapy Verbatim.
39 For a psychological version of this see A.H. Maslow, Toward a Psychology of Being. Other sources include Carlos Castaneda and John Lilly's writings. C. Castaneda, A Separate Reality and J. Lilly, The Centre of the Cyclone.
40 Musil, op.cit., p.73.
41 K. Horney, Neurosis and Human Growth; C. Rogers, On Becoming a Person.
42 The sociologists Cohen and Taylor have noted a curious irony here. Each person must assemble their own distinctive, unique identity kit out of what are, after all, culturally shared resources: musical styles, clothes, ironic modes of self-presentation, material goods, leisure activities, etc. They chart the struggles that result as each individual attempts to escape the collective mythology only to seize upon other elements which will themselves shortly become cultural cliches. The search for a distinctive identity is thus a never-ending vicious circle. S. Cohen and L. Taylor, Escape Attempts.
43 Note that as well as endorsing natural impulsive models of the self, Laing also, at times, suggests versions of this volitional model, tracing the origins of schizophrenia, for example, back to disordered family relationships. R.D. Laing, The Divided Self.
44 K.J. Gergen, 'The functions and foibles of negotiating self conception', p.59.
45 Ibid., p.66.
46 R. Barthes, S/Z, p.17.
47 This argument is developed in detail in Coulter, op.cit.
48 R. Harré, 'The self in monodrama', p.325.
49 For a more extensive discussion of the I and the me as textual conventions see C. Belsey, Critical Practice, Chapter 4.
50 Harré, op.cit.; H. Finagrette, Self-Deception.
51 Harré, op.cit., p.332.

BIBLIOGRAPHY

ALLEN, W. (1964), Tradition and Dream, London, Phoenix House.
ALLPORT, G.W. (1937), Personality: A Psychological Interpretation, New York, Holt.
ARMISTEAD, N. (1974), 'Experience in everyday life', in N. Armistead (ed.), Reconstructing Social Psychology, Harmondsworth, Middlesex, Penguin.
ATKINSON, J.M. (1978), Discovering Suicide: Studies in the Social Organisation of Sudden Death, London, Macmillan.
BARTHES, R. (1967), Système de la Mode, Paris, Seuil.
BARTHES, R. (1972), Mythologies, London, Jonathan Cape.
BARTHES, R. (1975), S/Z, London, Jonathan Cape.
BARTHES, R. (1976), Sade/Fourier/Loyola, New York, Hill & Wang.
BARTHES, R. (1977), Image-Music-Text, London, Fontana.
BARTHES, R. (1977), 'From work to text', in R. Barthes, Image-Music-Text, London, Fontana.
BARTHES, R. (1979), A Lover's Discourse: Fragments, London, Jonathan Cape.
BELSEY, C. (1980), Critical Practice, London, Methuen.
BERGER, P.L. and LUCKMANN, T. (1966), The Social Construction of Reality, Harmondsworth, Middlesex, Penguin.
BERGONZI, B. (1970), The Situation of the Novel, Pittsburgh, University of Pittsburgh Press.
BLACK, M. and COWARD, R. (1981), 'Linguistic, social and sexual relations: a review of Dale Spender's Man-Made Language', Screen Education, vol.39, pp.69-86.
BLANCHARD, W.H. (1979), Aggression American Style, Santa Monica, California, Goodyear.
BRADBURY, M. (1971), The Social Context of Modern English Literature, Oxford, Blackwell.
BRADBURY, M., HEADING, B. and HOLLIS, M. (1972), 'The man and the mask: a discussion of role theory', in J.A. Jackson (ed.), Role, Cambridge, Cambridge University Press.
BROOKS, E.W. (1973), 'The image of woman in Lessing's The Golden Notebook', Critique, vol.15, pp.101-9.
BROVERMAN, I.K., VOGEL, S.R., BROVERMAN, D.M., CLARKSON, F.E. and ROSENKRANTZ, P.S. (1972), 'Sex role stereotypes: a current appraisal', Journal of Social Issues, vol.28, pp.59-78.

BUCSESCU, D. (1977), 'Concept of "place" - a tool for investigating environmental cognitions', unpublished thesis, University of Surrey, UK.
BURR-EVANS, N. (1972), 'The value and peril for women of reading women writers', in S.K. Cornillon (ed.), Images of Women in Fiction: Feminist Perspectives, Bowling Green, Ohio, Bowling Green University Press.
CANTER, D. (1977), The Psychology of Place, London, Architectural Press.
CARTLAND, B. (1982), Moments of Love, London, Pan Books.
CASTANEDA, C. (1973), A Separate Reality, Harmondsworth, Middlesex, Penguin.
CATTELL, R.B. (1966), The Scientific Analysis of Personality, Chicago, Aldine.
CHAMBERS, D.W. (1971), Children's Literature in the Curriculum, New York, Rand McNally.
CHAPMAN, A.J. and JONES, D.M. (eds) (1980), Models of Man, Leicester, British Psychological Society.
CHOMSKY, N. (1965), Aspects of a Theory of Syntax, The Hague, Mouton.
COLLETT, P. (1977), 'Rule as a scientific concept', in P. Collett (ed.), Social Rules and Social Behaviour, Oxford, Blackwell.
COHEN, S. and TAYLOR, L. (1978), Escape Attempts: The Theory and Practice of Resistance to Everyday Life, Harmondsworth, Middlesex, Penguin.
COOPER, J. (1980), Emily, London, Corgi.
CORNILLON, S.K. (ed.) (1972), Images of Women in Fiction: Feminist Perspectives, Bowling Green, Ohio, Bowling Green University Press.
COULTHARD, M. (1977), An Introduction to Discourse Analysis, London, Longman.
COULTER, J. (1979), The Social Construction of Mind, London, Macmillan.
COWARD, R. (1980), 'Are women's novels feminist novels?', Feminist Review, vol.5, pp.53-65.
COWARD, R. and ELLIS, J. (1977), Language and Materialism: Developments in Semiology and the Theory of the Subject, London, Routledge & Kegan Paul.
CROSMAN, R. (1980), 'Do readers make meaning?', in Suleiman, S.R. and Crosman, I. (eds), The Reader in the Text: Essays on Audience and Interpretation, Princeton, N.J., Princeton University Press.
CUFF, E.C. (1980), 'Some issues in studying the problem of versions in everyday situations', Occasional Paper No.3, Department of Sociology, University of Manchester.
CULLER, J. (1975), Structuralist Poetics: Structuralism, Linguistics and the Study of Literature, London, Routledge & Kegan Paul.
CULLER, J. (1981), The Pursuit of Signs: Semiotics, Literature, Deconstruction, London, Routledge & Kegan Paul.
DAHRENDORF, R. (1973), Homo Sociologicus, London, Routledge & Kegan Paul.
DALTON, E. (1979), Unconscious Structure in The Idiot: A Study in Literature and Psychoanalysis, Princeton, N.J., Princeton University Press.
de BEAUVOIR, S. (1972), The Second Sex, Harmondsworth, Middlesex, Penguin.

DEAUX, K. (1976), The Behavior of Women and Men, Monterey, California, Brooks/Cole.
DEAUX, K. and EMSWILLER, T. (1974), 'Explanations of successful performance on sex-linked tasks: what is skill for the male is luck for the female', Journal of Personality and Social Psychology, vol.29, pp.80-5.
DERRIDA, J. (1977a), 'Signature Event Context', Glyph, vol.1, 172-97.
DERRIDA, J. (1977b), 'Limited Inc. abc', Glyph, vol.2, 162-254.
DICKENS, C. (1971), Our Mutual Friend, Harmondsworth, Middlesex, Penguin.
DREW, P. (1978), 'Accusations: the occasioned use of religious geography in describing events', Sociology, vol.12, 1-22.
EAGLETON, T. (1980), 'How the critical revolution started rolling', Times Higher Education Supplement, 19 September, 9.
EAGLETON, T. (1981), 'The end of criticism', Southern Review: Literary and Interdisciplinary Essays, vol.14, 99-107.
EICHLER, M. (1980), The Double Standard, London, Croom Helm.
ELMS, A.C. (1975), 'The crisis of confidence in social psychology', American Psychologist, vol.30, 967-76.
ENGLEBERG, E. (1972), The Unknown Distance: From Consciousness to Conscience: Goethe to Camus, Cambridge, Mass., Harvard University Press.
ENSTICE, A. (1979), Thomas Hardy: Landscapes of the Mind, London, Macmillan.
EYSENCK, H.J. (1953), The Structure of Human Personality, New York, Wiley.
FAVAT, F.A. (1971), 'Child and tale: an hypothesis on the origins of interest', Dissertation Abstracts, June.
FERNANDEZ, R. (1972), Social Psychology Through Literature, New York, Wiley.
FINAGRETTE, H. (1969), Self-deception, London, Routledge & Kegan Paul.
FINKELSTEIN, J. (1978), 'Novels as data for phenomenological research', paper given at Illinois Sociological Association Meeting, Chicago, October.
FOWLER, R. (1981), Literature as Social Discourse: The Practice of Linguistic Criticism, Batsford Academic, London.
FRANSELLA, F. and FROST, K. (1977), On Being a Woman, London, Tavistock.
FRENCH, M. (1978), The Woman's Room, London, Sphere Books.
FREUD, S. (1953), 'The interpretation of dreams', in J. Strachey (ed.), The Standard Edition of the Complete Psychological Works, London, Hogarth Press.
FREUD, S. (1960), 'The psychopathology of everyday life', in J. Strachey (ed.), The Standard Edition of the Complete Psychological Works, London, Hogarth Press.
FURMAN, N. (1980), 'Textual feminism', in S. McConnell-Ginet, R. Borcker and N. Furman (eds), Women and Language in Literature and Society, New York, Praeger.
GEORGE, A. (1980), Presidential Decision-Making in Foreign Policy: The Effective Use of Information and Advice, Boulder, Col., Westview.
GERGEN, K.J. and GERGEN, M.M. (1981), Social Psychology, New York, Harcourt Brace Jovanovich.

GERGEN, K.J. (1981), 'The functions and foibles of negotiating self-conception', in M.D. Lynch, A.A. Norem-Hebessen and K.J. Gergen (eds), Self Concept: Advances in Theory and Research, Cambridge, Mass., Ballinger.
GIDDENS, A. (1979), Central Problems in Social Theory: Action, Structure and Contradiction in Social Analysis, London, Macmillan.
GILBERT, G.N. and MULKAY, M. (1983), Opening Pandora's Box: A Sociological Analysis of Scientists' Discourse, Cambridge, Cambridge University Press.
GOLDSCHMIDT, A.M.E. (1971), 'Alice in Wonderland psychoanalysed', in R. Phillips (ed.), Aspects of Alice: Lewis Carroll's Dreamland as Seen Through the Critical Looking-Glasses 1865-1971, Harmondsworth, Middlesex, Penguin.
GOLDSTEIN, J.H. (1980), Social Psychology, London, Academic Press.
GOODHEART, E. (1968), The Cult of the Ego: The Self in Modern Literature, London, Chicago University Press.
GUIGET, J. (1965), Virginia Woolf and her Works, London, Hogarth Press.
HALL, S. and JEFFERSON, T. (eds) (1976), Resistance Through Rituals: Youth Subcultures in Post-war Britain, London, Hutchinson.
HAMILTON, D.L. and GIFFORD, R.K. (1976), 'Illusory correlations in interpersonal perception: a cognitive basis of stereotypic judgments', Journal of Experimental Social Psychology, vol.12, 392-407.
HAMLYN, D.W. (1974), 'Person perception and our understanding of others', in T. Mischel (ed.), Understanding Other Persons, Oxford, Blackwell.
HARARI, J.V. (ed.) (1979), Textual Strategies: Perspectives in Post-Structuralist Criticism, London, Methuen.
HARDING, D.W. (1968), 'Practice at liking: a study of experimental aesthetics', Bulletin of the British Psychological Society, vol.21, 3-10.
HARDY, T. (1974), The Mayor of Casterbridge, London, Macmillan.
HARRE, R. (1974), 'Some remarks on "rule" as a scientific concept', in T. Mischel (ed.), Understanding Other Persons, Oxford, Blackwell.
HARRE, R. (1977), 'Rules in the explanation of social behaviour', in P. Collett (ed.), Social Rules and Social Behaviour, Oxford, Blackwell.
HARRE, R. (1977a), 'The self in monodrama', in T. Mischel (ed.), The Self: Psychological and Philosophical Issues, Oxford, Blackwell.
HARRE, R. (1978), 'The ethogenic approach: theory and practice', in L. Berkowitz (ed.), Advances in Experimental Social Psychology, London, Academic Press.
HARRE, R. (1979), Social Being: A Theory for Social Psychology, Oxford, Blackwell.
HARRE, R. (1982), 'Psychological variety', in P. Heelas and A. Lock (eds), Indigenous Psychologies: The Anthropology of the Self, London, Academic Press.
HARRE, R. and SECORD, P.F. (1972), The Explanation of Social Behaviour, Oxford, Blackwell.
HEATH, S. (1982), The Sexual Fix, London, Macmillan.
HEBDIGE, D. (1979), Subculture: The Meaning of Style, London, Methuen.

HERITAGE, J. (1978), 'Aspects of the flexibilities of natural language use', Sociology, vol.12, 79-105.
HOLLAND, N.N. (1968), The Dynamics of Literary Response, New York, Oxford University Press.
HOLLIS, M. (1977), Models of Man, Cambridge, Cambridge University Press.
HOLSTI, O.R. (1968), 'Content analysis', in G. Lindzey and E. Aronson (eds), Handbook of Social Psychology, vol.2, Reading, Mass., Addison-Wesley.
HORNER, M. (1972), 'Toward an understanding of achievement-related conflicts in women', Journal of Social Issues, vol.28, 157-76.
HORNEY, K. (1950), Neurosis and Human Growth, New York, Norton.
ISER, W. (1978), The Act of Reading: A Theory of Aesthetic Response, London, Routledge & Kegan Paul.
ISRAEL, J. (1972), 'Stipulations and constructions in the social sciences', in J. Israel and H. Tajfel (eds), The Context of Social Psychology, London, Academic Press.
JAMES, W. (1968), 'The self', in C. Gordon and K.J. Gergen (eds), The Self in Social Interaction. Vol.1: Classic and Contemporary Perspectives, New York, Wiley.
JANIS, I.L. (1972), Victims of Groupthink, Boston, Houghton Mifflin.
JANOV, A. (1973), The Primal Scream, London, Abacus.
JONES, E.E. and NISBETT, R.E. (1972), 'The actor and the observer, divergent perceptions of the causes of behaviour', in E.E. Jones, D.E. Kanouse, H.H. Kelley, R.E. Nisbett, S. Valins and B. Weiner (eds), Attribution: Perceiving the Causes of Behaviour, Morristown, N.J., General Learning Press.
JONES, E. (1945), Hamlet and Oedipus, London, Tavistock.
JONG, E. (1974), Fear of Flying, New York, Holt, Rinehart & Winston.
KATZ-STOKER, F. (1972), 'The other criticisms: feminism vs. formalism', in S.K. Cornillon (ed.), Images of Women in Fiction: Feminist Perspectives, Bowling Green, Ohio, Bowling Green University Press.
KELLEY, H.H. (1973), 'The process of causal attribution', American Psychologist, vol.28, 107-28.
KIERNAN, V.G. (1972), The Lords of Human Kind: European Attitudes to the Outside World in the Imperial Age, Harmondsworth, Middlesex, Penguin.
KUHN, T.S. (1977), The Essential Tension: Selected Studies in Scientific Tradition and Change, London, University of Chicago Press.
KRESS, G. (ed.) (1976), Halliday: System and Function in Language, London, Oxford University Press.
KRISTEVA, J. (1980), Desire in Language: A semiotic Approach to Literature and Art, Oxford, Blackwell.
LAING, R.D. (1967), The Politics of Experience and the Bird of Paradise, Harmondsworth, Middlesex, Penguin.
LAING, R.D. (1973), The Divided Self, Harmondsworth, Middlesex, Penguin.
LEE, T.R. (1976), Psychology and the Environment, London, Methuen.
LERNER, L. (1975), Thomas Hardy's The Mayor of Casterbridge, London, Sussex University Press.
LESSING, D. (1966a), Martha Quest, London, Granada.
LESSING, D. (1966b), Ripple from the Storm, London, Granada.

LESSING, D. (1972), 'A small personal voice', in T. Maschler (ed.), Declarations, Port Washington, New York, Kennikat Press.
LESSING, D. (1973), The Golden Notebook, New York, Bantam.
LILLY, J.C. (1973), The Centre of the Cyclone, London, Paladin.
LUBEK, I. (1979), 'Aggression research', in A.R. Buss (ed.), Psychology in Social Context, New York, Irvington.
LUFT, D. (1980), Robert Musil and the Crisis of European Culture 1880-1942, Berkeley, University of California Press.
MACCOBY, E. and JACKLIN, C.N. (1974), The Psychology of Sex Differences, Stanford, California, Stanford University Press.
MARKOW, A.B. (1974), 'The pathology of feminine failure in the fiction of Doris Lessing', Critique, vol.16, 88-99.
MARSH, P. (1982), 'Rules in the organisation of action: empirical studies', in M. Von Cranach and R. Harré (eds), The Analysis of Action: Recent Theoretical and Empirical Advances, Cambridge, Cambridge University Press/Paris, Maison des Sciences de l'Homme.
MARSH, P., ROSSER, E. and HARRE, R. (1978), The Rules of Disorder, London, Routledge & Kegan Paul.
MASLOW, A.H. (1968), Toward a Psychology of Being, 2nd edn, Princeton, N.J., Van Nostrand.
MAXWELL, J.C. (1968), 'The "sociological" approach to The Mayor of Casterbridge', in M. Mack and I. Gregor (eds), Imagined Worlds, London, Methuen.
McLELLAND, D.C. (1961), The Achieving Society, Princeton, N.J., Van Nostrand.
McLELLAND, D.C. (1963), 'Values in popular literature for children', Childhood Education, November.
MERCER, D. (1975), Living in Cities, Harmondsworth, Middlesex, Penguin.
MERRILL, F.E. (1967), 'The sociology of literature', Social Research, vol.34, 648-59.
MIDDLETON, R. (1960), 'Fertility values in American magazine fiction', Public Opinion Quarterly, vol.24, 139-43.
MISCHEL, W. (1968), Personality and Assessment, New York, Wiley.
MORLEY, D. (1980), The Nationwide Audience, London, B.F.I Television Monographs.
MOSCOVICI, S. (1972), 'Society and theory in social psychology', in J. Israel and H. Tajfel (eds), The Context of Social Psychology: A Critical Assessment, London, Academic Press.
MOSCOVICI, S. (1976), La Psychoanalyse: Son Image Et Son Public, rev. edn, Paris, Presses Universitaires de France.
MULKAY, M., POTTER, J. and YEARLEY, S. (1983), 'Why an analysis of scientific discourse is needed', in K. Knorr-Cetina and M. Mulkay (eds), Science Observed: Perspectives on the Social Study of Science, London and Beverley Hills, Sage.
MURRAY, J.P. and KIPPAX, S. (1979), 'From the early window to the late show: international trends in the study of television's impact on children and adults', in L. Berkowitz (ed.), Advances in Experimental Social Psychology, vol.12, London, Academic Press.
MUSIL, R. (1979), A Man Without Qualities, vols 1-3, London, Picador.
NORRIS, C. (1982), Deconstruction: Theory and Practice, London, Methuen.
OAKLEY, A. (1972), Sex, Gender and Society, London, Temple Smith.

OAKLEY, A. (1981), Subject Women, New York, Pantheon.
O'NIELL, J. (ed.) (forthcoming), Science Texts, London, Routledge & Kegan Paul.
PAPINEAU, D. (1978), For Science in the Social Sciences, London, Macmillan.
PARSONS, T. (1968), 'The position of identity in the general theory of action', in C. Gordon and K.J. Gergen (eds), The Self in Social Interaction, vol.1: Classic and Contemporary Perspectives, New York, Wiley.
PARSONS, T. and BALES, R. (eds) (1955), Family, Socialization and Interaction Process, Chicago, Free Press.
PERLS, F. (1971), Gestalt Therapy Verbatim, New York, Bantam.
PERVIN, L.A. (1970), Personality: Theory, Assessment and Research, New York, Wiley.
PETERS, F.G. (1978), Robert Musil: Master of the Hovering Life, New York, Columbia University Press.
PETERS, R.S. (1958), The Concept of Motivation, London, Routledge & Kegan Paul.
PIKE, B. (1961), Robert Musil, Ithaca, New York, Cornell University Press.
POCOCK, D.C.D. (ed.) (1981), Humanistic Geography and Literature, London, Croom Helm.
POPPER, K.R. (1963), Conjectures and Refutations, London, Routledge & Kegan Paul.
POTTER, J. (1983), 'Speaking and writing science: issues in the analysis of psychologists' discourse', unpublished D.Phil. thesis, University of York, UK.
POTTER, J. (forthcoming), 'Flexibility, testability: Kuhnian values in psychologists' discourse concerning theory choice', Philosophy of the Social Sciences.
POTTER, J. and MULKAY, M. (1982), 'Scientists' interview talk: interviews as a technique for revealing participants' interpretative practices', in M. Brenner, J. Brown and D. Canter (eds), The Research Interview: Uses and Approaches, London, Academic Press.
PRATT, A.V. (1976), 'The new feminist criticisms: exploring the history of the new space', in J.I. Roberts (ed.), Beyond Intellectual Sexism: A New Woman, A New Reality, New York, D. McKay Co.
PRATT, A. and DEMBO, L.S. (eds) (1974), Doris Lessing: Critical Studies, Wisconsin, University of Wisconsin Press.
QUINE, W.V.O. and ULLIAN, J.S. (1970), The Web of Belief, New York, Random House.
RAMANATHAN, S. (1978), The Novels of C.P. Snow: a Critical Introduction, London, Macmillan.
RAVEN, B. and RUBIN, J. (1976), Social Psychology: People in Groups, New York, Wiley.
ROGERS, C. (1961), On Becoming a Person, Boston, Houghton Mifflin.
ROSE, D. and RADFORD, J. (1981), 'The use of literature in teaching psychology', Bulletin of the British Psychological Society, vol.34, pp.453-5.
RORTY, A.O. (1976), 'A literary postscript: characters, persons, selves, individuals', in A.O. Rorty (ed.), The Identities of Persons, Berkeley, University of California Press.
ROUTH, J. and WOLFF, J. (eds) (1977), The Sociology of Literature: Theoretical Approaches, Keele, Sociological Review Monograph 25.

RUBENSTEIN, R. (1979), The Novelistic Vision of Doris Lessing: Breaking the Forms of Consciousness, Urbana, Chicago, University of Illinois Press.
RUSHTON, J.P. (1979), 'Effects of prosocial television and film material on the behavior of viewers', in L. Berkowitz (ed.), Advances in Experimental Social Psychology, vol.12, London, Academic Press.
SCHLESINGER, A.M. Jr (1965), A Thousand Days: John F. Kennedy in the White House, London, Deutsch.
SCOTT, M.B. and LYMAN, S.M. (1968), 'Accounts', American Sociological Review, vol.33, 46-62.
SEARLE, J.R. (1977), 'Reiterating the differences', Glyph, vol.1, 198-208.
SEARLE, J. (1969), Speech Acts: An Essay in the Philosophy of Language, Cambridge, Cambridge University Press.
SEMIN, G.R., ROSCH, E. and CHASSEIN, J. (1981), 'A comparison of the commonsense and "scientific" conceptions of extroversion-introversion', European Journal of Social Psychology, vol.11, 77-86.
SHERIDAN, A. (1980), Michel Foucault: The Will to Truth, London, Tavistock.
SHOTTER, J. (1975), Images of Man in Psychological Research, London, Methuen.
SHOTTER, J. (1980), 'Men the magicians: the duality of social being and the structure of moral worlds', in T. Chapman and D. Jones (eds), Models of Man, Leicester, The British Psychological Society.
SILVERMAN, D. and TORODE, B. (1980), The Material Word: Some Theories of Language and its Limits, London, Routledge & Kegan Paul.
SINGER, D.G. (1972), 'Piglet, Pooh and Piaget', Psychology Today, vol.6, June, 70-4.
SMITH, D. (1978), 'K is mentally ill: the anatomy of a factual account', Sociology, vol.12, pp.23-53.
SNOW, C.P. (1934), The Search, London, Gollancz.
SNOW, C.P. (1940), George Passant, London, Faber & Faber (originally entitled Strangers and Brothers).
SNOW, C.P. (1947), The Light and the Dark, London, Faber & Faber.
SNOW, C.P. (1951), The Masters, London, Macmillan.
SNOW, C.P. (1954), The New Men, London, Macmillan.
SNOW, C.P. (1956), Homecomings, London, Macmillan.
SNOW, C.P. (1958), The Conscience of the Rich, London, Macmillan.
SNOW, C.P. (1960), The Affair, London, Macmillan.
'Interview with C.P. Snow' (1962), Review of English Literature, vol.3.
SNOW, C.P. (1964), Corridors of Power, London, Macmillan.
SNOW, C.P. (1968), The Sleep of Reason, London, Macmillan.
SNOW, C.P. (1970), Last Things, London, Macmillan.
SNOW, C.P. (1971), 'In the communities of the elite', Times Literary Supplement, 15 October, 1249-50.
SNOW, C.P. (1971), Public Affairs, London, Macmillan.
SNOW, C.P. (1978), The Realists: Portraits of Eight Novelists, London, Macmillan.
SOLOMON, R. (1972), From Rationalism to Existentialism, New York, Harper & Row.
SORENSEN, T.C. (1965), Kennedy, London, Hodder & Stoughton.

STANG, D.J. (1981), *Introduction to Social Psychology*, Monterey, Brooks/Cole.
STRINGER, P. (1979), 'A politico-psychological perspective on crowding', in M.R. Gurkaynak and W.A. Lecompte (eds), *Human Consequences of Crowding*, New York, Plenum.
SULEIMAN, S.R. and CROSMAN, I. (eds) (1980), *The Reader in the Text: Essays on Audience and Interpretation*, Princeton, Princeton University Press.
SUMNER, R. (1981), *Thomas Hardy: Psychological Novelist*, London, Macmillan.
SYPHER, W. (1962), *Loss of the Self in Modern Literature and Art*, New York, Vintage Books.
TAJFEL, H. (1972), 'Experiments in a vacuum', in J. Israel and H. Tajfel (eds), *The Context of Social Psychology: a Critical Assessment*, London, Academic Press.
TAJFEL, H. (ed.) (1978), *Differentiation Between Social Groups: Studies in the Social Psychology of Intergroup Relations*, London, Academic Press.
TAJFEL, H. (1981), *Human Groups and Social Categories: Studies in Social Psychology*, Cambridge, Cambridge University Press.
TAJFEL, H. (1981), 'Social stereotypes and social groups', in J. Turner and H. Giles (eds), *Intergroup Behaviour*, Oxford, Blackwell.
TAVRIS, C. and OFFIR, C. (1977), *The Longest War: Sex Differences in Perspective*, New York, Harcourt Brace and Jovanovich.
THURLEY, G. (1975), *The Psychology of Hardy's Novels*, St Lucia, University of Queensland Press.
TOWNSEND, J.R. (1974), *Written for Children*, Harmondsworth, Middlesex, Penguin.
TREW, T. (1979), '"What the papers say": linguistic variation and ideological difference', in R. Fowler, R. Hodge, G. Kress and T. Trew (eds), *Language and Control*, London, Routledge & Kegan Paul.
TRILLING, L. (1974), *Sincerity and Authenticity*, London, Oxford University Press.
TURNER, J. and GILES, H. (eds) (1981), *Intergroup Behaviour*, Oxford, Blackwell.
WEBB, E.J., CAMBELL, D.T., SCHWARTZ, R.D. and SECHREST, L. (1966), *Unobtrusive Measures: Nonreactive Measures in the Social Sciences*, Chicago, Rand McNally.
WETHERELL, M.S. (1982), 'Socio-psychological and literary accounts of femininity', in P. Stringer (ed.), *Confronting Social Issues: Applications of Social Psychology*, vol.2, London, Academic Press.
WIEDER, D.L. (1970), 'On meaning by rule', in J.D. Douglas (ed.), *Understanding Everyday Life*, London, Routledge & Kegan Paul.
WILLIS, P. (1977), *Learning to Labour: How Working Class Kids Get Working Class Jobs*, Farnborough, Saxon House.
WOLFF, J. (1981), *The Social Production of Art*, London, Macmillan.
WOOLF, V. (1950), 'The character in fiction', in V. Woolf, *The Captain's Death-Bed and Other Essays*, New York, Harcourt Brace and World.
WOOLGAR, S. (1980), 'Discovery: logic and sequence in a scientific text', in K. Knorr, R. Krohn and D. Whitley (eds), *The Social Process of Scientific Investigation*, Dordrecht, Reidel.

WRONG, D. (1961), 'On the oversocialised conception of man in modern sociology', American Sociological Review, vol.26, 183-93.
WYDEN, P. (1979), Bay of Pigs: The Untold Story, New York, Simon & Schuster.
WYLIE, R.C. (1979), The Self Concept: Theory and Research on Selected Topics, rev. edn, vol.2, Lincoln, University of Nebraska Press.
YEARLEY, S. (1981), 'Textual persuasion: the role of social accounting in the construction of scientific arguments', Philosophy of the Social Sciences, vol.11, 409-35.
YEARLEY, S. (forthcoming), 'Vocabularies of freedom and resentment: a Strawsonian perspective on the nature of argumentation in science and the law', Philosophy of the Social Sciences.
ZERAFFA, M. (1973), 'The novel as literary form and as social institution', in E. Burns and T. Burns (eds), Sociology of Literature and Drama, Harmondsworth, Middlesex, Penguin.

AUTHOR INDEX

Allen, W., 162
Allport, S.W., 173
Amis, K., 125
Armistead, N., 13,15,161
Atkinson, J.M., 168
Austen, J., 124,127

Bales, R., 163
Balzac, H., 76
Barthes, R., 62,76,78-9,158,
 162,165-7,174
Beauvoir, S. de, 11,15,163
Belsey, C., 62,161,165,174
Bem, S., 26-8
Berger, P., 173
Bergonzi, B., 124
Black, M., 27,162-3
Blanchard, W.H., 169
Bradbury, M., 165,173
Brooks, E.W., 161
Broverman, D.M., 162
Broverman, I.K., 162
Bucsescu, D., 163-4
Burr-Evans, N., 161

Cambell, D.T., 166-7
Canter, D.V., 163
Carroll, L., 54,61-2
Cartland, B., 16-19,22,29,82,
 162
Chambers, D.M., 164
Chapman, A.J., 163
Chomsky, N., 66-7,166
Chassein, J., 173
Clarkson, F.E., 162

Cohen, S., 174
Collett, P., 166
Conrad, J., 155
Cooper, J., 16-18,22,29,82,162
Cornillon, S.K., 161
Coward, R., 9,27,161-3,165-7
Coulter, J., 168,173,175
Crosman, I., 166
Cuff, E.C., 168
Culler, J., 77-9,84,165-7

Dahrendorf, R., 147,149-50,173
Dalton, E., 165
Deaux, K., 161-2
Dembo, L.S., 161
Derrida, J., 167
Dickens, C., 139,141-2,172
Diderot, D., 145-7
Dodgson, C., 54
Dostoievsky, F., 139,174
Drabble, M., 11,24
Drew, P., 168

Eagleton, T., 24,84,162
Eichler, M., 162-3
Ellis, J., 165-7
Elms, A.C., 161
Emswiller, T., 162
Engleberg, E., 174
Enstice, A., 163
Eysenck, H.J., 143,148,173
Eysenck, S.B., 173

Favat, F.A., 55,164

Fernandez, R., 56,62-3,164,166
Festinger, L., 63,166
Finagrette, H., 160,174
Finkelstein, J., 56-7,63,164
Fowler, R., 84,167
Fransella, F., 161,163
French, M., 9,24
Freud, S., 28,54,57,155,165
Frost, K., 161,163
Furman, N., 162

Gard, F. du, 63
George, A., 169
Gergen, K.J., 157-8,171,174
Gergen, M.M., 171
Giddens, A., 166
Gifford, R.K., 165
Gilbert, G.N., 76,168
Giles, H., 170
Goffman, E., 163
Goldmann, L., 55,164
Goldschmidt, A.M.E., 54,61-2, 164
Goldstein, J.H., 169
Goodheart, E., 173
Guiget, J., 172

Hall, S., 166
Halliday, M.A.K., 91
Hamilton, D.L., 165
Hamlyn, D.W., 175
Harari, J.V., 166
Harding, D.W., 58-9,165
Hardy, T., 4,30,32-5,38,42-5, 48,82,163-5
Harré, R., 3,61,65-8,71-80,94, 98,101,108,160,162,165-6, 168,174
Heading, B., 173
Heath, S., 162
Hebdige, D., 166
Hegel, F., 154,174
Heritage, J., 168
Holland, N., 165
Hollis, M., 165,173
Holsti, D.R., 167
Horner, M., 162

Iser, W., 165,167
Israel, J., 46,48,163-4

Jacklin, C., 15,162

James, W., 149,151,154,173
Janis, I., 4,100-13,118-19, 169-70
Janov, A., 155,174
Jefferson, T., 166
Jensen, W., 57
Jones, E., 57,165
Jones, E.E., 168
Jung, E., 9

Kant, I., 154
Katz-Stoker, F., 161
Kelley, H.H., 168
Kiernan, V.C., 172
Kippax, S., 164
Kress, G., 168
Kristeva, J., 62,165
Kuhn, T.S., 168

Lacan, J., 24,58,165
Laing, R.D., 139,155,174
Lawrence, D.H., 156
Lee, T.R., 163
Lerner, L., 164
Lessing, D., 2,9,11-13,15-24, 27,29,82,121,159,162
Lilly, J., 174
Loban, W., 53
Lubek, I., 168
Luckmann, T., 173
Luft, D., 172-3
Lukács, G., 55,164
Lyman, S.M., 166

McLelland, D., 52-4.60-2,164
Maccoby, E., 15,162
Mach, E., 150
Mailer, N., 173
Markow, A.B., 161
Marsh, P., 67-8,72-4,80,96,166, 168
Marx, K., 46
Maslow, A.H., 156,174
Maxwell, J.C., 164
Mead, G.H., 46,163,173
Mercer, C., 163
Merrill, F.E., 56,63,164
Middleton, R., 75,166
Mischel, W., 144,173
Morley, D., 172
Moscovici, S., 28,58-9,163,165, 168

Author index

Mulkay, M., 96,167-8
Murdoch, I., 12,161
Musil, R., 148,150,153-4,156, 159,172-4

Nisbett, R.E., 168
Norris, C., 167

Oakley, A., 15,161-2
Offir, C., 161-2
O'Niell, J., 168

Papineau, D., 165
Parsons, T., 163,173
Perls, F.S., 174
Pervin, L.A., 173
Peters, F.G., 173
Peters, R.S., 165
Piaget, J., 54-5
Pike, B., 173
Plath, S., 11
Popper, K.R., 168
Potter, J., 167-8,171
Pratt, A., 161

Quine, W.V.O., 168

Radford, J., 164,168
Ramanathan, S., 170-1
Raven, B., 170
Rogers, C., 157,174
Rorty, A., 143,172
Rosch, E., 173
Rose, D., 164,169
Rosenkrantz, P.S., 162
Rosser, E., 67-8,72-4,80,166, 168
Routh, J., 164
Rubenstein, R., 161
Rubin, J., 170
Rushton, J.P., 164

Schlesinger, A., 100-2,104-12, 114-15,169-70
Schwartz, R.D., 166-7
Scott, M.B., 166
Searle, J., 166-7
Sechrest, L., 166-7
Secord, P.F., 61,165-6
Semin, G.R., 173
Shakespeare, W., 57,74-5
Shotter, J., 28,163
Silverman, D., 167

Singer, D.G., 55,164
Skinner, B.F., 163
Smith, D., 86-91,97,167-8
Snow, C.P., 4,119-37,170-1
Solomon, R., 174
Sontag, S., 57
Sorensen, T.C., 101,104-6,110-12, 114,169
Stang, B.J., 172
Stringer, P., 163-4
Stumpf, C., 150
Suleiman, S.R., 166
Sumner, R., 164
Sypher, W., 173

Tajfel, H., 59,165,170,172
Tavris, C., 161-2
Taylor, L., 174
Thurley, G., 164
Tolstoy, L., 74-5
Torode, B., 167
Townsend, J.R., 164
Trew, T., 90-3,97,168
Trilling, L., 141,144-5,155,157, 172-4
Trollope, A., 124,127
Turner, J.C., 170

Ullian, J.S., 168

Vogel, S.R., 162

Webb, E.J., 166-7
Weber, M., 53
Wetherell, M., 161
Wieder, D.L., 168
Willis, P., 65,68-73,77,79-80,96, 98,101,108,166
Wolff, J., 164
Woolf, V., 130,143,156,172-3
Woolgar, S., 168
Wrong, D., 166
Wyden, R., 169
Wylie, R.C., 162

Yates, F., 75,166
Yearley, S., 167-8

Zeraffa, M., 161
Zola, E., 3,56

SUBJECT INDEX

Academic novels, 125
Accounting, 1
Accounting devices, 18-19,21-3, 87-90,96-7,109-11
Accounting systems, 2,18-19,23, 61,68,81,85,93
Account of K's illness, 86-90
Accounts, 13,29,66-9,72-5, 79-80,85-94,96,101,105-8; analysis of, see analysis of discourse; contradictions in, 74-5,80; depicting order and disorder, 73,80; documentary, 4; factual, 73-4,79-81,83-94,97,108; functional, 68,73-4,79; naturalised, 120; status of, 18
Achievement motivation, 52-3,60
Achievement themes in school-books, 53
Actions, 66-8,71-3,80,94-5
Active model, 61-2,64,72
Actualisation, 154-5,157
Adolph, 16,18-19,21
The Affair, 120,128-9,135-6
Agency, 61
Aggression, 52,67
Alice in Wonderland, 54,61-2
Altruism, 52
Analysis of discourse, 24,28, 30-1,47-8,66,72,75,77,79-81, 82,84,90,97-8,154,159-60
Androgeny, 26
Anna, 13,19-20,22
Apocalypse Now, 156
Art, 3,12,18,63

Attribution theory, 93,136-7
Authors, 2,5,23,45,51,54-7,77-8, 80; pre-eminent role of, 62, 75,77-8; beliefs and intentions of, 2,4,23,75,78, 102-3,114
Authorial: abuses, 45; contra-dictions, 44-5; devices, 43-5; problem, 119,129-30, 137; problem in social psychology, 129-30,137
Authenticity, 154-7

Battle of Borodino, 75
Behaviourism, 32,158
Biochemists, 96-7
Boscastle, Lord, 133,136

Career choice, 69-71
Carrie Jones, 18-21
Categorisation: in literature, 132; presupposed in research, 96; in social psychology, 132,133,136
Casterbridge, 32,34,41,43-4,48
Causal power of text, 52,54,61
Censorship, 52
Characters, 3,12,20-2,34,41-5, 56-8,63,129-32,136,139,143-4, 152-4: beliefs and motives of, 4; contradictions in, 43-5; in environment, 42; reality of, 4,63
Children of Violence, 11,18
Children's literature, 52-5

Children's and Young Persons (Harmful Publications) Act, 52
Choice, 153; of authors, 5; of topics, 4
Christopher Robin, 55
Code, 18,30,34,44-8,76,140, 158-9; see also accounting systems
Cognitive dissonance, 63; processes, 59-60,63; psychology, 60
Collectivism, 121,131
Commerce, 37-8,40
Competence, 66-7
Connotation, 76
Consciousness-raising role of literature, 12
Consensus as an accounting device, 96-7
Constraints on interpretation, 2,79
Construction: of discourse, 13,18,22,45,48,79,81,85, 93-4,97-8,101,106,126,142; of femininity, 18,22,28,82; of objectivity, 87-8; of personality, 61; of self, 22; of social worlds, 94,98
The Conscience of the Rich, 121
Consciousness as social product, 154
Contemporary culture, 30
Contingency of accounts, 90,97
Context dependence, 29,79-81, 95,97,159
Contraposition as accounting device, 109
Contrast structures, 88-9
Control group, 53
Conversational analysis, 82,85, 97
Competence, 66-7
Correlational studies, 53
Corridors of Power, 120,131, 134,136
Creativity, 80
Criteria for theory selection, 94-5,97
Crowding, 30-3,35,46
Culture: local, 69,71; oppositional, 69-71; of school, 70; of shop floor, 70

Cultural: forms, 69, meaning systems, 70

Death Kit, 57
Deconstruction, 28,43
Decontextualisation: of experimental subjects, 128; of gender, 28; of literary characters, 128-9,142,145; of reading, 109
Denotation, 76
Dependent variable, 54,61
Depiction of agents and processes, 91-3
Detective stories, 124
Discourse, 2,30,72; analysis, see analysis of discourse; of common sense, 19; of self, 139,143,148-9,154-60; varieties of, 32,47,85
Disciplines, 1,3-5,33,65,130
Discursive structures, 21,34,48
Disintegrated consciousness, 139
Displacement, 42
Divided self, 21-2,148-55,157, 159-60

Ear'oles, 69-70,98
Economics, 52-3,60,69
Education, 52
Egalitarianism, 122-3,126
Elites, 119,121-9,132-3,135; academic, 122-3,125; artistic, 123,125; administrative, 122-5,132; class origins, 125-6; membership, 124; military, 132; as natural phenomenon, 124; power of, 125; scientific, 122-3,125-6,132; as source of order, 128; writers, 127
Elitism, 123; in social psychology, 126
Elizabeth-Jane, 34-8,41,43-5,47
Emergent motives, 111-12
Emily, 16,162
Environment, 2,31-3,41-2,44; as character, 41-2
Environmental: movement, 30; perception, 41; psychology, 4,30-1,42
Ethogenics, 3,65-8

Subject index

Existential phenomenology, 154
Experience, 9-11,13,18,21,25, 140,153; feminine, 11, 16-17,19-23,31
Experimental: aesthetics, 58-60; subjects, 3,45,126-8
Experiments, 35,42,45,54,61-3, 80,114,120,128-9,132; as constructions, 45; on literary influence, 53,61
Expressive v. practical realm, 67
Epistemological status of literature and social psychology, 4
Everyday talk, see ordinary talk

Facts, as accomplishment, 108; as accounting resources, 87; as opposed to myth, 101,113
Factual: accounts, see accounts; discourse, 84, 98-9
Farfrae, 34,36-41,43-4
Fear of Flying, 9
Femininity, 2,4,15,22,26-7,30, 82
Feminist: discourse, 19; literary criticism, 11-13, 23-4; novels, 11
Field experiments, 130
Fighting, 67-8
Football fans, 65-8,71-3,75,80, 97
Formalism, 12
The Four-Gated City, 20
Frivolous literature, 17
Fragmentation, 45-7; consequences of, 131; in social psychology, 56-7,111, 119,121,130-2,136-7; in literature, 45,47,119,121-2, 129-30,132,135,137; of literary characters, 43-5, 130-2,136,139; of self, 147
Function: of accounts, 28-9, 85,94-8,101,103,106; of stereotypes, 133-6

Gay, 129,133

Gender, 9,14-15,24-6,28; as natural assumption, 15
Genderisation, 22,25
Genre, 17,51
Geography, 40-1
George Passant, 120,130
George Passant, 124,131,136
Gestalt therapy, 155; The Golden Notebook, 9,18,20-2
Gradiva, 57
Greeting ceremonies, 66
Groups, 1-2,4,57,59-60,71-2,101, 120-1,123-4,128,131-6; decision-making, 100,108-9, 120; dynamics, 4,59,103-4; see also elites
Groupthink, 4,100,103,105, 108-10,112,114-15; as accounting device, 110-11

Hamlet, 58
Heart of Darkness, 156
Henchard, 34-9,41,43-5
High Place Hall, 34-5,38,44
History, 75,103-5,109,111, 113-14,120,134
Homecomings, 130
Homologies: text and author, 54; text and reader, 54-5; text and social structure, 55
Howard, 131,135-6
Humanistic: critics, 15; novelists, 13; psychologists, 3,15,55,157
Hypodermic model of influence, see literary influence

I (opposed to me), 21,148-51,154, 158-60
Identification, 63
Identity from group membership, 136
Ideology, 14,19,23-5,28,60-1,72, 93,101,111,114,127; of educational opportunity, 71; of psychology, 32; of science, 127; of writing, 124
Independent variable, 54
Individualism, 32,46,51,59-61, 65,71,93,121,131,145

Interpretation: of norms, 79; variability in, 62-3,77-8,80
Interpretative: practices, 79-82,85,111; resources, 60,78; sociology, 82; systems, see accounting systems
Interpenetration of character and environment, 42
Inter-reading, 119,128
Intersubjectivity, 159
Intervening variables, 62
Interviews, 72
Istanbul, 32

Jago, 129,131,136
Justification of action, 66
Justificatory accounts, 119,123

King Lear, 57

The Lads, 69-72,98
Language, 2,66; knowledge of, 66; organising thought, 154; of self-reference, 140,158
Last Things, 121,131
Laws of social behaviour, 126
Lay: causal explanations, 90-3; social psychologies, 90,98
Lewis Eliot, 120,122,129-33, 136-7
The Light and the Dark, 121
Linguistics, 66-7,97
Literary: conventions, 17-18, 22,79; criticism (modern), 58,77-8,80-2; criticism (traditional), 10,30,59,62, 71,75,77-9,82; influence, 51-3,57-8,61; production, 12,62,64,80-1; theorists, 1,84
Literature: as data, 13,55,63; embodying descriptions, 55, 62-3,75-7,80,120; embodying social theory, 13,57,63,75, 150-1; as experimentation, 56; as institution, 24; realism, 76,81; as resource for social psychology, 3, 10-11,15,23,25,40,48,51,55, 62-3,76,119-20; as social commentary, 122; as storehouse of knowledge, 13-16, 55-6,57; as teaching aid, 56
Love's Labour's Lost, 75
Lucetta, 34-41,43-4

Manual work, 70-1
A Man Without Qualities, 150-1
Martha, 11,13,16-22
Martha Quest, 16,20,162
Martineau, 124,131,136
Martin Eliot, 129,131
Marxist theory, 55
Masculinity, 15,17,22,26-7
The Masters, 120,128,130,136
The Mayor of Casterbridge, 31-41,43,45-6,82
Me (opposed to I), 148-51,157-60
Meaning: of actions, 66-7; of literary texts, 77-8
Mechanism, 32,59,61-2,65
Mechanisms of sense-making, 87-9; see also accounting devices
Mental illness, 86-9
Meta-language, 18-22
Metaphors for self, 151
Mimesis, 12,17-18
Minority groups, 59-60
Models-of-Man, 32-41,43-8; transitions between, 32-40, 43,46-7
Models of self, 145,148
Moments of Love, 17,162
Mystical models of self, 156

Narrator, 122,129; conflict with character, 132
Narrative, 33,38,42,44,48,142; voice, 19,21
Natural authentic self, 155-7
Naturalising process, 2,81-2,93, 126,137; see also realism
Naturalistic reading, 108-9
The New Men, 120,129,131-2,134
Newspaper accounts, 90-3
New Town of Milton Keynes, 31,46
Norms, 14,33,59,78-9,88-9,144; see also rules

Objectivity, 4,80;
   construction of, 87-8
Observation, 66-7,74
Oedipus Rex, 57
Official discourse, 70
Operationalisation of themes, 122
Order: in group decision-making, 128; in social psychology, 128; in science, 127
Ordinary explanations, 136
Ordinary talk, 2,5,28-31,46-7, 58,65,75,82,97,160
Organismic model, 32-5,38,40, 121
Origin of research topics, 127
Our Mutual Friend, 141-2
Outgroups, 132,134,136

Participant observation, 69
Penetration of official discourse, 70-2
Performance, 66-7
Personal identity, 43-5,48
Personality, 14,52-3,60-1,63, 141-6,148; of children, 53; dynamics, 54; inventory, 143
Phallic criticism, 12
Phenomenology, 140
Philosophy of action, 61
Place, 4,30-1,32-3,35-6,38, 40-2; sense of, 30-1,42,48; specificity of behaviour, 30
Mr Podsnap, 140-2,144,146
Polarisation: psychological and functional modes, 123
Positivism, 150
Power, 127
Prejudice, 59-60,134; see also stereotyping
Psychological: origins of texts, 51,54-5; theory in criticism, 51,57-9,62

Radical therapies, 155
Rameau's Nephew, 145
Rational influence, 52
Readers, 1-4,9,17,23-4,44-5, 51-2,54-5,58,77,88-9,135, 142

Reading, 2,46,48,53,57-9,62-5, 72,74,77-8,81,98,101-2,104; practices, 77-9,106,108,114; simple view, 65; as topic, 79; see also interpretations
Realism, 12,17-18,22-3,27,73-4, 101,108,112-14,119-20,126, 140-1; as accounting device, 18-19,21-3
Regulation of action, 67
Reflexive reading, 126; see also inter-reading
Reification: of femininity, 30; of literature, 79; of literary characters, 63; of participants' versions, 98-9; of self-discourse, 159-60; of sexual categories, 25,27, 82
Relation: analysts' and participants' discourse, 85,90, 93-4,97-9,110-12,144; description and evaluation, 90-3; intellect and passions, 75; individual and social, 131,136-7,146-7,153; literature and life, 3,12; social psychology and life, 3
Relational model, 32-5,38,40, 46-7
Representation of self, 140
The Return of the Native, 42
Roger Quaife, 131,134,136
Role: conflict, 147; model, 32-5,38,40,46-8,121; theory, 3,32,146-51,154,159
Roles, 144-5,147-8,151-2,159
Romantic fiction, 17,24
Roy Calvert, 123-4,128-9
Rules, 14,67-9,71-2,78,88,94-5; breakdown, 72; interpretative and regulative, 67-8; in sense-making, 94; as templates, 94

Scientific discourse, 81,94-7
The Second Sex, 11
Self, 139-40,143-60; accounting, 158-60; alienation, 148-54; deception, 160; discovery, 9, 10,12,13; justification, 106-8,112,115; revelation, 23; social, 148-9,154; as

undifferentiated murk, 157-8
Sense of betrayal, 20-1
Sense-making, 1-2,22-3,30,60, 76,81-2,111,119,137,140
Semiology, 58,66,76-8
Sex, 70; differences, 15,25; role, 11,14,30,147
Sex Role Inventory, 26,27
Sexual: essence, 13; identity, 10,14-15,25-8, see also gender; self-concept, 14; stereotype, 14,17-18, 24,26-7
Sheila Eliot, 130-3,136
Signifying systems, 76; see also accounting systems, code
The Sleep of Reason, 121,130
Social: anthropology, 14; change, 53; class, 65,68-9, 127; competence, 66-7,71-2, 78; context, 1,4,24,41-2, 60-1,65,69,93,97,130; conventions, 66-7,69,71,79; differentiation, 69-70; identity, 135; knowledge, 66,71; mobility, 70-1; positions, 146-7; processes, 59,61; representations, 24,120; situations, 146; studies of science, 127; vacuum, 42,121
Socialisation, 15,53,147,155
Social psychology: assumptions of, 33,42; crisis in, 10, 121; as discourse, 30,48, 79,126; explanations, 61, 72,135; methodology, 6-7, 72; privileged relation to literature, 1-5,55-6; qualitative, 94; as sense-making, 1,137; theory, 2, 14,56-8,62,75,82,93-4,97,99, 101; traditional, 80
Sociolinguistics, 91,158,159
Sociology, 14,17-19,41,46,56, 72,82,125,127,131,146; of literature, 4,55; of sex role, 28
Solid narrative character, 140-2,146,149-50,157
Source accounts, 101-6,114
Stereotyping, 15,17-18,24,26-7, 59-60,119,132-4,137; collective function, 133-7; in evaluation, 133; individual function, 133, 135-7; of literary characters, 133; of texts, 23
Structure of book, 4; of experience, 153-4,158
Style, 37,70
Symbolism, 54,64
Symbolic interactionism, 147

Taxonomy, 142
Teaching, 51,55-6
Technical discourse, 58
Tess of the d'Urbervilles, 13
Testability, 94-5
Texts: in psychology, 113-14; social consequences, 52; structure, 51
The Thibaults, 63
Textual devices, see accounting devices
Time, 109,120
Theory construction, 51
Traits, 141-6,152; as form of sense-making, 144; as predictors of behaviour, 144
Trait theory, 140-5,149,151,157
Truth and insight model of literature, 12-13,15-17,22-3, 25; see also expressive realist model

Ulrich, 151-2,154
Unconscious, 54,62
Unemployment, 127
Unitary meaning of text, 75,77-8
Universalisation, 22,25

Values, 53,71
Variables, 54,128
Verbatim records, 114
Versions, 86,90,93,95,105,108-9, 113; of author's intentions, 78; of fans' behaviour, 68; of female experience, 16-18, 28-9; problem of, 17-18,23; of social life, 85; of texts' meaning, 78
Vocabulary of justification, 114

Voices, 18-21, 23-4

War and Peace, 75
Winnie the Pooh, 55
Willed self, 155-7
Woman as marginal category, 27-8

Women: readers, 9,13; writers, 13
Women's: discourse, 9,21; novels, 9-11,14,24; role, 15
The Woman's Room, 9
Writing, 124; see also literary production